FOUNDATIONS
AND PRINCIPLES
OF MUSIC EDUCATION

FOUNDATIONS AND PRINCIPLES OF MUSIC EDUCATION
SECOND EDITION

CHARLES LEONHARD

Professor of Music
University of Illinois, Champaign-Urbana

ROBERT W. HOUSE

Director
School of Music
Southern Illinois University, Carbondale

McGraw-Hill Book Company

*New York, St. Louis, San Francisco, Düsseldorf, Johannesburg,
Kuala Lumpur, London, Mexico, Montreal, New Delhi,
Panama, Rio de Janeiro, Singapore, Sydney, Toronto*

Foundations and Principles of Music Education

Library of Congress Catalog Card Number   72-160711

07-037199-7

67890BPBP7987

This book was set in Century by Creative Book Services, division of McGregor & Werner, Incorporated, and printed and bound by The Book Press, Inc. The designer was Creative Book Services, division of McGregor & Werner, Incorporated. The editor was Robert P. Rainier. Sally Ellyson supervised production.

Contents

Preface

The intent of this book is to give a systematic treatment to the total music education program. In addition to examining the historical, philosophical, and psychological foundations of music education, the book develops principles for all aspects of the operation of the music education program including program development, methods of teaching, administration, supervision, and evaluation. The book is both general and specific; general in that it treats not one level or phase of the music education program but the total program, specific because the concepts developed are applied to every aspect of music education by the use of numerous examples. This approach has been uniquely valuable since its applications to music education are based on a comprehensive conceptual framework.

The book is divided into three parts. Part One, Orientation, *presents an overview of the work of the school, describes the processes involved in education, and delineates the nature and function of principles in music education. Part Two,* Foundations of Music Education, *explores the historical, philosophical, and psychological factors relevant to the establishment of a theoretical foundation for the music education program. Part Three,* Principles of Music Education, *presents the principles of objectives, program building, method, administration, supervision, and evaluation, and applies them to the theoretical and practical problems of music education.*

The book is intended as a basic text for undergraduate and graduate courses in music teacher preparation programs such as Orientation to Music Teaching, Introduction to Music Education, Principles of Music Education, History and Philosophy of Music Education, *and the general methods courses that frequently precede special methods courses in the music teacher preparation sequence. It may also be used in courses offered in the senior year of music teacher preparation, to synthesize and amalgamate what has been learned in previous courses in education and music education.*

In the preface to the first edition we expressed the hope that the book would make a significant contribution to the preparation of intellectually competent and educationally perceptive music educators. There is convincing evidence that this hope has been realized.

The book has been widely adopted throughout the United States and the world as a standard text in music teacher education programs. It has had a marked influence on music teacher education curricula and on publications in the field of music education. Since the publication of the first edition in 1959, colleges and universities in the United States have almost universally developed courses organized around the content of Foundations and Principles of Music Education.

The second edition maintains the basic pattern of the first edition, but the content has been revised to reflect recent developments not only in music education but also in music, aesthetics, education, and psychology. It is our hope that the second edition will provide an influential conceptual framework for music education in the next decade just as did the first edition in the past decade.

Charles Leonhard
Robert W. House

P A R T 1 ORIENTATION

Part One consists of two chapters, "The Objectives and Processes of Education" and "The Role of Principles in Music Education." The first chapter establishes the basic purpose of music education and appraises several current types of music education programs in relation to that purpose. Objectives are defined and the distinction among levels of objectives is clarified. The work of the school is analyzed, resulting in the definition of five interrelated processes: curriculum, instruction, administration, supervision, and evaluation.

Chapter Two presents a definition of principles and identifies the sources of and bases for principles of music education. The reader gains information about the process of formulating principles, levels of principles, and the use of principles in increasing his professional competence as a music educator.

The Objectives and Processes of Education

1 it is the viewpoint of this book that music education has a highly important function in the education program and that music education must be shaped logically and realistically within the framework of the total program of the school. The primary purpose of the music education program is to develop the aesthetic potential, possessed by every human being, to its highest possible level.

Music education has a unique mandate in contemporary American education—to provide a varied, significant, and cumulative musical experience for every American child. If this mandate is to be fulfilled, school music experiences must be of such quality as to enable every child to:

1. establish working standards in his valuation of music
2. bring imaginative vision to all his experience with music
3. develop the resources for the heightened quality of symbolic experience available through music
4. attain the highest level of musical understanding of which he is capable
5. gain sufficient proficiency in singing and in playing an instrument to make it possible for him to be an active participant in music throughout his life

Music has intrinsic value: it requires no external justification. Dewey provided a clear-cut focus for music education in saying:

> They [the arts] reveal a depth and range of meaning in experiences which otherwise might be mediocre and trivial. They supply, that is, the organs of vision. Moreover, in their fullness they represent the concentration and consummation of elements of good which are otherwise scattered and incomplete. They select and focus the elements of enjoyable worth which can make any experience directly enjoyable. They are not luxuries of education but emphatic expressions of that which makes any education worthwhile.[1]

Clearly, music merits full rights in the curriculum; it can and should be taught as music, and for its own sake.

The point of view presented in this book is that the music program should be dedicated to the development of musical responsiveness and musical understanding on the part of all pupils in the school. The task of the school music program is to create a favorable musical environment, one in which every pupil can undergo the maximum musical growth consistent with his ability and his interests. The school must be especially concerned that it provide musical experiences which have significance in the daily living of the pupils both in and away from school.

These experiences fall into two broad categories, general music and musical specializations. The first consists of a planned sequence of musical experiences selected for their usefulness in promoting musical responsiveness, broad musical understanding, and overall musical competence. These experiences should be available to all pupils throughout their period of schooling. The musical specializations properly represent a natural and desirable outgrowth of significant and successful general music experiences. All aspects of the program should

---

[1] John Dewey, *Democracy and Education*, The Macmillan Company, New York, 1916, p. 279. Reprinted by permission of the publisher.

be considered as means to musical development of the pupils and never as ends in themselves.

This view of the purpose of music education differs markedly from views exemplified in many current programs of music education. The music education scene includes several diverse kinds of programs which fail to take into account the nature of the aesthetic experience and its importance in the life of the human being. These faulty programs include the following:

1. Programs with undue emphasis on performance. In these programs every effort is made to discover as early as possible the students with superior performance facility. They are started early on some specialized aspect of music with a consequent neglect of their broad musical development. Students who cannot or will not conform to the rigidly prescribed pattern are gradually eliminated with little attention given to meeting their musical needs.

2. Programs aimed principally at the musical entertainment of students. Here, standards in literature and performance have little importance, and no one cares whether musical learning takes place or not as long as everybody is happy. Students make little progress from year to year, and contact with music is superficial, with only momentary rewards, and no goals.

3. Programs emphasizing music as an instrument for achieving unmusical ends such as health, citizenship, and so on. Such programs ignore the unique values inherent in the musical experience and attempt to justify music by preposterous and unconvincing claims concerning the utility values of music.

4. Programs in which music loses its identity through specious integration with other subject areas of the school. This condition is especially prevalent in elementary schools having a fused, core, or other type of integrated curriculum and an inadequate staff of specialized music

personnel. Although it is true that music can illuminate some other subject matter, the music program which fails to stand on its own feet and provide for cumulative musical learning denies the importance of musical experience itself, musical learning, and musical independence.

5. Programs aimed largely at securing public approbation. Here the music program is viewed as a public relations arm of the school. Principal attention is given to the preparation of performing groups likely to gain popular approval. No request for a performing group is denied even though the excessive number of appearances interferes seriously with the education of the students not only in music but in other phases of their schoolwork. Excesses in this direction occur in schools at all levels but reach most damaging proportions in some college music schools where students may be absent for weeks on extended tours. Viewed objectively, such practices constitute unjustified exploitation of students.

Because of the vitality of the musical art and the devotion of thousands of music educators to their profession, music education has undergone startling development and has made outstanding accomplishments in the United States. Looking at the situation dispassionately, however, one cannot be complacent about the position of music education in American schools. In the eyes of many school administrators and many laymen, music remains an educational frill, an adjunct rather than an integral part of the general education program. As a result, when the educational program must be cut, music seems to them to be a logical place in which to begin.

Furthermore, objective evaluation of the products of music education indicates that the program has many shortcomings and is in urgent need of improvement. Some of the more obvious indications of the need for reappraisal of the program are the following: the small percentage of student participation in secondary school music programs; the low level of musical competence and interest shown by many elementary classroom teachers and prospective teachers who are products of music education programs; the low level of accomplishment outside of performance shown by freshman music majors in colleges and universities; the small impact of the music program on adolescents compared with the impact of the latest popular music trend; and the small demand for good music programs on radio and television.

This situation is due, at least in part, to the failure of music education to develop a sound theoretical and philosophical orientation for the music program. Most music education professional literature gives assent to the importance of music in education and attempts to justify it by showing a more or less tenuous connection between music and the general objectives of education. While music can make contributions of varying importance to the achievement of such objectives as health, citizenship, command of fundamental processes, and so on, the weakness of attempts to justify music in this way lies in the fact that none of these objectives is unique to music and that many other areas of study point more directly and convincingly to their attainment than does music.

The practicing music educator, confronted with this hazy and unconvincing theoretical justification for music in general education, almost inevitably either favors unmusical ends at the expense of musical ones or emphasizes performance for the few and neglects the general musical education of the many. This, in turn, reinforces the impression of the administrator and the public that music has little or no value outside of performance.

To consolidate the position of music education in American schools and to ensure further progress, music educators on all levels need to develop these fundamental qualifications:

1. They must understand the total work of the school and the interrelatedness of all aspects of the school program.
2. They must be well informed about the general objectives of the school.

3. They must understand the unique place of music in the total curriculum of the school.
4. They must be able to work and communicate with administrators in other areas of the school.

The primary purpose of this book is to assist music educators and prospective music educators in developing these essential understandings. The present chapter presents a short summary treatment of the objectives of education and a discussion of the processes involved in education. All phases of the music education program are treated in subsequent chapters.

THE OBJECTIVES OF EDUCATION

Objectives are defined as precise, clear statements of values, goals, or directions of education. Definite statements of objectives are essential in the educational process for, in their absence, educational experiences lack focus, meaning, and motivation and are likely to be chosen at random on the basis of tradition or at the whim of teachers or students.

Since objectives clarify the purposes of education and indicate the nature of desired outcomes, they provide the only sound basis for organizing and conducting educational activity; for determining content, materials of instruction, methods of teaching and administrative policies; and for guiding the evaluation of outcomes.

To illustrate the influence of objectives on all these processes let us assume that an important objective of the music education program is to develop the potential for the use of music in out-of-school life. The implication of this objective for the selection of experiences is that the experiences should point toward the development of musical independence on the part of the student. Thus, the program must be organized to enable the student to participate in a variety of musical activities including individual as well as small- and large-group participation. The student whose only musical experience is derived from playing an instrument in the band or orchestra would be unlikely to attain this objective. Unless his instrument is one having substantial solo possibilities and unless he has attained extraordinary facility on it, he is almost certain to store or sell it after leaving school and participate in music in a limited way from then on. In order to achieve this objective the music program must include, in addition to band and orchestra experience, small-ensemble playing, singing in large and small groups, voice classes, meaningful listening experiences, fretted instrument classes, piano classes, and other musical activities which are potent forces in developing musical independence and the ability and desire to use music in out-of-school life.

The influence of this objective on determining the content of the experiences and the materials of instruction is likewise apparent. If a pupil's experiences are to have the greatest appeal and are to develop the desire to participate on his own in music, the instruction must be centered in music of high quality and expressive value. Undue emphasis on exercise material or the selection of music of pedestrian quality or music with a utilitarian function is not likely to attain this objective. Furthermore, the level of difficulty of the music must be such that it challenges the student but does not discourage him or make him needlessly dependent on the instructor.

The implications of this objective for methods of instruction are equally clear. Constant emphasis on the expressive value of the music is essential. The provision of opportunities for student selection of music, student suggestions for the interpretation of music, free discussion of student preferences for different pieces of music and styles of interpretation, and individual and group practice without restriction from the instructor are all indicated. Likewise, the instruction should seek to provide a link between school music experience and the music participation of the students outside the school. Community, radio, and television programs of music can provide the basis for discussion of music in the classroom and serve as points of departure in the pursuit of musical learning. The inclusion of music indigenous to and accepted by the community is also suggested.

Democratic teaching procedures which consider student musical interests, involve student choice, and point toward the development of discrimination and independence on the part of students are recommended in attaining this objective. Autocratic teaching in which the instructor dominates all facets of the musical experience, on the other hand, is unlikely to contribute to this end since it almost inevitably results in undue dependence on the instructor.

Administrative policies must also be directed toward this objective. For example, scheduling needs to be sufficiently flexible to enable students to gain a variety of musical experience. High school class schedules are often so rigid that a student can choose only one musical activity, and administrative or teacher pressure often precludes participation in an activity other than the large groups. Facilities and equipment for individual listening, individual practice, and small-group practice are also essential. The mere provision of one large music room for group rehearsals inevitably proves inadequate for attaining this objective. A library of easily available recordings and music, listening rooms or listening tables in the library, practice rooms of varying size, and instruments available to students without charge are essential to the administration of a program that purports to attain this objective.

This goal must also be taken into account in any realistic evaluation of the music program. The success of musical organizations in contests, the number of students participating in the program, and the number of a group's public performances do not represent valid criteria for the evaluation of the success of a music program in relation to this goal. Much more valid evaluation would be secured by determining the extent to which students participate in community and church music activities, the number of students having record collections, the kind and extent of students' radio and television listening, the patronage by students of concerts and recitals, the ability of students to make sound musical judgments and choices, and so on.

The previous discussion has illustrated the influence of one objective on the entire music program. It also supports the contention that the statement of valid objectives represents the only reasonable basis for organizing a program of instruction, for selecting experiences, for selecting methods of teaching, for establishing administrative procedures, and for evaluating the program. The necessity for a clear understanding of objectives on the part of all music educators is apparent.

THE LEVELS OF OBJECTIVES

It is important to recognize that several levels of objectives exist. Much of the confusion surrounding teachers' efforts to develop objectives and a great deal of the lack of success attending efforts to organize objectives-oriented educational programs arise because of the failure to comprehend the various levels of objectives and their relationship to actual classroom instruction. As a result, statements of objectives for classroom instruction are often so vague and abstract as to have little worth in giving focus to the efforts of teacher and students. For example, "worthy use of leisure" and "good citizenship" are abstract concepts of great complexity and remoteness, but they are nevertheless typical of objectives that teachers proclaim for day-to-day instruction in music. The connection between a music lesson and these objectives is so obscure and tenuous as to provide little or no direction for the teacher or students in planning and conducting their musical experiences.

In this chapter objectives are considered on four levels: (1) broad social objectives, (2) concrete social objectives, (3) program objectives, and (4) instructional objectives. Each of these levels will be explained and illustrated in the following discussion.

BROAD SOCIAL OBJECTIVES OF EDUCATION

From the beginning, American education has been guided by two ideas which are basic to the concept of a democratic society: (1) the need for a literate and well-informed citizenry and (2) equality of opportunity for each individual. Implied in the Constitution of the United States, these ideas have provided a consistent focus for American education. Educational philosophy and practice, legislation, custom, and public thinking have long recognized the necessity for education for all citizens and have been increasingly dedicated to this ideal.

The Educational Policies Commission, in *The Unique Function of Education in American Democracy*, reaffirms the philosophy underlying American education in these words:

> The primary business of education, in effecting the promise of American democracy, is to guard, cherish, advance and make available in the life of the coming generations the funded and growing wisdom, knowledge and aspirations of the race. This involves the dissemination of knowledge, the liberation of minds, the development of skills, the promotion of free inquiries, the encouragement of the creative or inventive spirit, and the establishment of wholesome attitudes toward order and change—all useful in the good life for each person, in the practical arts and in the maintenance and improvement of American society, as our society, in the world of nations.[2]

Broad social objectives are stated on the highest level of generalization and serve to provide the basic philosophical orientation for each successively more concrete and specific level of objectives.

---

[2] Educational Policies Commission, *The Unique Function of Education in American Democracy*, National Education Association, Washington 1937. Reprinted by permission of the publisher.

CONCRETE SOCIAL OBJECTIVES OF EDUCATION

The progress of education has been marked by the formulation of statements of objectives by various individuals and groups. Following the lead of Herbert Spencer, who in 1860 proposed that education should be directed toward the preparation of the individual for productive participation in the activities basic to society, most recent statements have sought to interpret the concrete social objectives of education through an analysis of life activities. According to Spencer, "to prepare us for complete living is the function which education has to discharge." His objectives included (1) self-preservation, (2) securing the necessities of life, (3) rearing and caring for offspring, (4) maintaining proper social and political relations, and (5) gratifying tastes and feelings and pursuing other leisure-time activities.

In 1918 the Commission on the Reorganization of Secondary Education proposed seven objectives for education based on a similar analysis of life activities. These appeared in a publication entitled *Cardinal Principles of Education* and, for that reason, are frequently referred to as The Seven Cardinal Principles of Education. They enumerate and describe in detail the functions of education and have exerted a tremendous influence. Although subsequent statements of objectives have appeared, these remain a pertinent and useful synthesis of thought concerning the functions of education. The broad objectives are:

1. health
2. command of fundamental processes
3. worthy home membership
4. vocation
5. civic education
6. worthy use of leisure
7. ethical character

An important departure in the statement of the concrete social objectives of education occurred in *The Purposes*

of Education in American Democracy, a publication origi-
nating with the Educational Policies Commission and published by the National Education Association. These objectives are unique in being stated in terms of the desired
behavior of an educated person. This characteristic makes
them a great deal more specific and more directly applicable
to actual teaching situations than most statements of objectives on this level. They describe behavior under four categories: (1) the objectives of self-realization (the person as an
individual), (2) the objectives of human relationships (the
person as a family member and social being), (3) the objectives of economic efficiency (the person as a producer), and
(4) the objectives of civic responsibility (the person as a citizen). Because these objectives have remained influential to
the present day, the complete statement is given here:[3]
     The objectives of self-realization are:

The inquiring mind. The educated person has an appetite for
learning.

Speech. The educated person can speak the mother tongue.

Reading. The educated person reads the mother tongue efficiently.

Writing. The educated person writes the mother tongue effectively.

Number. The educated person solves his problems of counting and calculating.

Sight and hearing. The educated person is skilled in listening
and observing.

Health knowledge. The educated person understands the
basic facts concerning health and disease.

Public health. The educated person works to improve the
health of the community.

[3] Educational Policies Commission, "The Purposes of Education in
American Democracy," *Policies for Education in American Democracy*,
National Education Association, Washington, 1946, Book III, pp. 192,
212, 226, and 240. Reprinted by permission of the publisher.

Recreation. The educated person is participant and spectator in many sports and other pastimes.

Intellectual interests. The educated person has mental resources for the use of leisure.

Esthetic interests. The educated person appreciates beauty.

Character. The educated person gives responsible direction to his own life.

The objectives of human relationships are:

Respect for humanity. The educated person puts human relationships first.

Friendships. The educated person enjoys a rich, sincere and varied social life.

Cooperation. The educated person can work and play with others.

Courtesy. The educated person observes the amenities of social behavior.

Appreciation of the home. The educated person appreciates the family as a social institution.

Conservation of the home. The educated person conserves family ideals.

Homemaking. The educated person is skilled in homemaking.

Democracy in the home. The educated person maintains democratic family relationships.

The objectives of economic efficiency are:

Work. The educated producer knows the satisfaction of good workmanship.

Occupational information. The educated producer understands the requirements and opportunities for various jobs.

Occupational choice. The educated producer has selected his occupation.

Occupational appreciation. The educated producer appreciates the social value of his work.

Personal economics. The educated consumer plans the economics of his own life.

Consumer judgment. The educated consumer develops standards for guiding his expenditures.

Efficiency in buying. The educated consumer is an informed and skilled buyer.

Consumer protection. The educated consumer takes appropriate measures to safeguard his interests.

The objectives of civic responsibility are:

Social justice. The educated citizen is sensitive to the disparities of human circumstances.

Social activity. The educated citizen acts to correct unsatisfactory social conditions.

Social understanding. The educated citizen seeks to understand social structures and social processes.

Critical judgment. The educated citizen has defenses against propaganda.

Tolerance. The educated citizen respects honest differences of opinion.

Conservation. The educated citizen has regard for the nation's resources.

Social applications of science. The educated citizen measures scientific advance by its contribution to the general welfare.

World citizenship. The educated citizen is a cooperating member of the world community.

Law observance. The educated citizen respects the law.

Economic literacy. The educated citizen is economically literate.

Political citizenship. The educated citizen accepts his civic duties.

Devotion to democracy. The educated citizen acts upon an unswerving loyalty to democratic ideals.

Perhaps the outstanding contribution of this statement of objectives lies in the fact that it focuses attention on the necessity for education to foster learning other than knowledge, which received the major emphasis in traditional education.

Objectives on the concrete social level serve to bridge the gap between broad social objectives which define education and the operational levels of objectives which include program and instructional objectives.

Obviously, music educators do not generally participate in the formulation of either level of social objectives; rather, they use both as a basis for developing program and instructional objectives. Objectives on the broad social level are properly viewed as sources of philosophical orientation. Thus, music education programs in the United States should reflect the broad concern of American education for providing equality of opportunity and for transmitting all phases of our cultural heritage.

Statements of objectives on the concrete social level properly serve as points of departure for the statement of program objectives. It is a common error to assume that music education can and should contribute to the attainment of all objectives on the concrete social level. Nothing could be further from the truth. In developing program objectives, music educators must make a logically defensible selection of the objectives on the concrete social level to which music education can make a valid contribution. For example, it would appear obvious, with reference to the statement of objectives prepared by the Educational Policies Commission, that music education can contribute most significantly to three objectives of self-realization—those having to do with aesthetic interests, recreation, and intellectual interests. Using these objectives as a point of departure, music educators must then define the musical competencies which will enable students to use music both as a source and a focus for aesthetic interests, recreational resources, and intellectual interests. Music education can contribute to the attainment of these concrete social objectives only when it results in the development of people who are musically educated, that is, people who have developed musical resources and musical competencies which enable them to make music a vital and moving force in their lives.

PROGRAM OBJECTIVES

Program objectives are on the operational level and give explicit direction to the total program in a subject-matter area, for example, the social studies program, the physical education program, or the music education program. Objectives on this level should include all the different types of learning involved in a particular subject—knowledge and understanding, mental and motor skills, attitudes and appreciations, and initiative. There is a great tendency in all subject-matter areas to give preponderant attention to objectives related to the accumulation of knowledge. This is no doubt due, at least in part, to the fact that textbooks provide a readily available and convenient context for learning knowledge and that testing and evaluation of knowledge are much more direct, simpler, and easier to defend than the other types of learning mentioned. Furthermore, the weight of tradition is strongly in favor of teaching facts, even when the relationship of those facts to life activities is tenuous and obscure. As a result, many teachers feel more comfortable and secure in treading the narrow but firm path of knowledge rather than in embarking on the rocky road to more intangible values inherent in understanding, appreciation, attitudes, and so on.

Exclusive attention to learning knowledge can rarely bring about successful results in any endeavor. In the first place, there is little doubt that successful learning of knowledge itself depends upon the learning of proper attitudes and appreciations. Furthermore, if knowledge is to function, understanding is essential. Likewise, unless rewarding and worthwhile habits are learned, all other types of learning remain essentially useless.

Knowledge refers to any body of facts gathered by study, investigation, or observation. Understanding applies to the comprehension of facts and the ability to apply knowledge in a problem-solving situation. These definitions imply that knowledge alone has little value and that it can be put to use only when accompanied by understanding. For example, a student may *know* that the key of E major has four sharps in the key signature and may be able to name them. Taken by itself, however, this verified piece of knowledge has little meaning or use in a person's musical life. It gains real meaning only when he *understands* the function of the key signature, the effect of the key signature on the scale beginning on E, and the relationship of the key of E to other keys in the tonal system. Nevertheless, much time in music classes is spent developing this very piece of knowledge, and many children become able to recite key signatures with rapidity and precision. Because of their lack of understanding, however, the knowledge does not function in their musical pursuits and, in the absence of use, is forgotten much more rapidly than it was learned.

Attitude refers to a generalized emotional reaction for or against a specific object. Attitudes have a direct effect on learning of all kinds and have much to do with the efficiency with which knowledge and understanding are developed. They are also products of education; progress toward any objective in music education depends upon the attitudes developed in children as a result of their musical experience. Many people resist contemporary music, for example, because they have a negative attitude toward any music differing from the traditional mode of musical expression. This attitude, like all others, is learned. It may result from exclusive exposure to traditional music over a long period of time;

it may be a reflection of a similar attitude on the part of music teachers or parents; or it may be due to a lack of understanding of the nature of musical expression. In any case, such an attitude impedes learning of all kinds. The objectives of music education must include positive attitudes on the part of students.

Appreciation refers to a positive emotional reaction to an object and includes some degree of enjoyment and perception of the aesthetic qualities of the object. Any level of appreciation assumes keen enjoyment, and the higher levels of appreciation imply discriminative enjoyment of aesthetic qualities. The development of a high level of appreciation is of utmost importance in music education. For example, the most detailed and precise knowledge of music history and literature does little to illuminate the art of music, unless it is accompanied by a high level of appreciation of and responsiveness to the aesthetic quality of music as it has developed through succeeding stylistic epochs in the history of the art. Music education attains its supreme value when it is first and foremost aesthetic education and when it results in the development of the abilities necessary to enjoy music with perception and discrimination.

The ultimate criterion for judging the success of learning lies in the kinds of initiatives that are developed. Does the learner pursue learning further on his own? Does he habitually put to use in life activities the learning that has accrued from his education? More specific to music education, does he habitually participate in music with ever-increasing pleasure? Does he constantly seek to refine his musical learning? These things can happen only if his learning has included sound initiatives which draw upon and expand his accomplishment in all the different types of learning considered here.

Thus it can be seen that in developing program objectives for the music program, the teacher must give consideration to all the different products of musical learning: knowledge, understanding, attitudes, appreciations, skills, and initiative.

The Statement of Program Objectives

It has been pointed out that one of the unusual characteristics of the concrete social objectives formulated by the Educational Policies Commission is that they are stated in terms of desired behavior. Even with this precedent, however, program objectives of music education continue, for the most part, to be stated as abstract concepts. It is only when program objectives specify and define desired musical behavior that they give direction to teachers in formulating instructional objectives. The guiding principle for the formulation of program objectives is to analyze the behavior of a musically educated person and state specifically the knowledge, understanding, attitudes, appreciations, skills, and initiatives it is desirable and feasible to develop in the course of the total program of music education.

The Importance of Internal Consistency and Continuity in Program Objectives

One of the grave difficulties facing music education at this time is that continuity is lacking from one level of the school to the other. For many years most music education programs operated with a highly organized course of study based upon a precise division of musical knowledge and skill. The sum total of musical competence was, so to speak, divided up and placed in eight, ten, or twelve large capsules, each of which was to be gradually consumed by students during one year of the music program. Supervisors planned the work with utmost care and provided strict supervision to ensure that the schedule was maintained at such a rate that all of each capsule would be consumed by the end of the year. This plan for teaching music, however neat and precise, failed to take into account many important factors, including individual differences among pupils, variations in different classes, and the varied competencies and personalities of teachers. Furthermore, it very often emphasized unduly the learning of knowledge and skill and neglected other learning products. Recognition of these deficiencies has brought about almost complete abandonment of the uniform course of study.

Regrettably, although the music program has escaped from the straitjacket imposed by the uniform course of study, it now often exhibits a perilous lack of unity and coherence. Pupil experiences are often selected and conducted at random, with little comprehension by either teacher or pupils of relationship of present experiences to what has come before and what is to follow. Many music programs lack any goal-directed sequence and fail to bring about continuous progress in the development of musical competencies. For this reason many administrators rightly question the continuation of general music in the secondary school when it is a rehash of the elementary school experience. Many are likewise dubious about the benefit of several years in the band or chorus when successive years of these activities bring about no significant new experience for the student.

Another unfortunate aspect of the present situation is that the different phases of the music program frequently lack common goals and sometimes even work at cross-purposes. For example, an instrumental teacher, who is rightly concerned about the development of music-reading competence, finds that the general music teacher gives little attention to this important objective. Likewise, one teacher in a system may work sincerely and devotedly for the development of musical responsiveness and, to that end, use the finest and most beautiful music possible, while another teacher, principally interested in the development of technique, may flood the pupils with the most barren and mechanical exercise material conceivable. The only result of such situations is confusion on the part of the pupils and the hindrance of their musical development.

The solution to the dilemma lies in the development of program objectives which apply to all levels and phases of the program and in the development of understanding by each teacher of the contribution to those objectives that his particular level and phase of work should make

INSTRUCTIONAL OBJECTIVES

Instructional objectives serve to give direction to day-to-day teaching and learning in the classroom. If they are to function properly, they must exhibit the utmost in specificity and concreteness. Instructional objectives must be geared most definitely to the needs and interests of the particular group of pupils involved.

In the formulation of instructional objectives, consideration must be given to teacher objectives and pupil objectives. This implies the need for pupil-teacher planning of all aspects of the learning experience. Adequate instructional objectives result only when teacher objectives and pupil objectives can be merged. To formulate his objectives the teacher must know and understand all the other levels of objectives and must shape his own objectives so that there is consistency between them and the other levels. It is especially important that he recognize the role of his particular phase of instruction in attaining the overall program objectives. Each level of objectives makes its own unique contribution to the crystallization of thinking on the part of teachers, to determining the direction of instruction, and to influencing the practical achievements of instruction.

Teacher objectives should take into account pupil objectives, and although the two may never by synonymous, they must be compatible. Pupil objectives are usually the immediate things the pupil wants to accomplish. For example, a first or second grader may want to sing a song for his parents. It may be of little importance to him or to his parents whether he sings it in tune or in proper rhythm or with pleasant tone quality. The pupil's immediate and personal objective, however, presents the teacher with a priceless opportunity for attaining his own objectives, which require that the pupil sing a beautiful song, accurate as to tune and rhythm and with the loveliest tone quality of which he is capable. The attainment of this objective in turn contributes to the teacher's long-range instructional objectives of enabling his pupils to enjoy good music, to use their voices well and expressively, and to develop a repertory of worthwhile songs.

THE WORK OF THE SCHOOL

The work of the school includes a number of definite but interrelated processes. The terms commonly applied to these processes are curriculum, instruction, administration, supervision, and evaluation. Each of these is defined and discussed briefly in this section. Later chapters treat fully principles pertinent to each of the processes, with definite application to music education.

Curriculum

Curriculum deals with the selection of desired educational outcomes and learning experiences to achieve these outcomes. Curriculum building in music education includes the formulation of objectives for the music education program, the organization of classes and activities in which to achieve the objectives, and the selection of experiences that are appropriate to the classes and activities and will contribute to pupil growth toward the objectives. The task of selecting experiences also implies concern with the selection of teaching materials.

To illustrate the scope of curriculum building, let us assume that a group of music educators in a school is embarking on such a task. Working cooperatively with administrators, teachers of other subjects, school patrons, and pupils they develop a statement of the objectives of the school's music program. In defining desired musical behavior accruing from the music education program they arrive at the following objectives, among others. The musically educated person:

1. sings with expressive and beautiful tone
2. sings in parts by ear and from the score

3. participates in home and community music activities
4. sings a variety of fine songs from memory
5. recalls the factors necessary for making valid value judgments of songs and song performance

The objectives would indicate the organization of singing activities of various kinds at all levels of the school. The curriculum planners would provide singing as part of the general music program in the elementary school and secondary school, plan choruses, choirs, and voice classes in the secondary school, and assembly singing and informal singing in small groups throughout the school.

Their next step would be to determine what kinds of experiences within the activities are most likely to lead to the objectives previously determined. Thus, the experience of hearing beautiful singing tone from the teacher and from recordings would provide the aural concept essential to the development of beautiful singing on the part of the pupils. The experience of using the ear to sing a harmonizing part to a known melody would lead to the attainment of that objective. The curriculum planners would also need to decide approximately when in the school program this experience should begin.

Another aspect of curriculum planning is the selection of appropriate materials consistent with the objectives and the varying levels of musical growth found in the school.

Curriculum planning involves logical, philosophical thinking that begins with the social objectives of education and progresses to the actual classroom situation. Curriculum planners in music education must have a thorough understanding of all levels of educational objectives. They must understand the nature and needs of children, the unique qualities of music and the contribution that music can make to the development of the human personality, and they must comprehend the nature of the musical experience, the role of music in the life of the human being, the relationship of music to other phases of the school program, and the technique of working in a democratic group.

Instruction

Instruction relates to the conduct and organization of learning experiences, the actual methods of teaching used in the classroom. Teaching methods refer to the variety of ways in which learning experiences may be organized to achieve the most effective results.

The primary basis for the selection of teaching methods must be the objectives of instruction. The question which every teacher must consider in determining methods of teaching is: how should the learning experiences of this group be organized to achieve most efficiently the desired outcomes expressed in the stated objectives? Results must be of prime concern; they represent the final criterion for determining teaching success and the validity of the method used. No method of teaching, however entertaining to students or satisfying to the teacher, can be considered successful unless it achieves the desired results. The relationship between objectives and methods of teaching may be clarified by an example from the area of choral music.

Let us assume that two choral teachers are working with groups at the same level and that both are planning to present public programs of choral music. For Teacher A the presentation of the highest-quality program possible is the primary objective. Therefore, he selects the compositions for the program on the assumption that he is best qualified to make such a selection. In order to prepare a program of the quality he deems essential, he selects quite difficult music that meets his own adult standards. Because of the difficulty of the music the chorus must spend a long time preparing for the program, and several extra rehearsals are required toward the end of the preparation time. The director teaches the parts by rote and conducts intensive drill sessions in order to achieve accuracy on the difficult music. Both he and the students are very intense during their preparation, and the extra rehearsals intrude upon the students' other schoolwork. He exercises his own judgment in the interpretation of the music and in the order of presentation on the program. Eventually the chorus is highly trained in the singing of these few songs and presents a creditable program. Thus, in relation to his objective his teaching methods have been successful. The fact that the students have missed many other important musical experiences and may have slighted their other studies is unimportant to him—he has attained his primary objective. One cannot take exception to his methods of teaching; their consistency with his objective is direct and obvious. One may, however, take great exception to the narrowness of his objective.

Teacher B, on the other hand, while planning a public program, has a broader view of the objectives of choral music. He wants learning of the following kinds to accrue as a result of the choral instruction: acquaintance with a variety of music literature, the ability to read music, discrimination of quality in music, the ability to choose music for a well-balanced program, the ability to make value judgments concerning musical performance, and the greatest possible enjoyment of singing. Teacher B conducts the learning experience in a manner far different from that of Teacher A. He provides his students with a wide variety of music on many levels of difficulty, much of which they can read at sight. He encourages students to suggest songs to learn. He provides fine recordings of choral music for the group to hear. He discovers the students' musical interests and uses them as a starting point for his instruction. He provides opportunities for student conductors and student accompanists. He interprets music in different ways and assists students in making valid value judgments concerning varying interpretations and in understanding the factors essential to such judgments. He does some singing for pure enjoyment. He makes provision for student choices in planning the program and causes students to participate in the administration of the program. In the last weeks before the public performance the group works together to select the best program possible from all the songs they have studied. These are perfected more easily because of the broad insights developed by the students, and the group presents a creditable program. The results of Teacher B's instruction are far broader and more relevant to the musical growth and learning of his students than are Teacher A's. Both groups have had the advantage of a public performance. The first group has accomplished little else, the second has accomplished a great deal more.

Administration

The task of administration is to provide the setting for learning. Administration includes the provision of facilities, equipment, and personnel, and the scheduling of classes, activities, and other functions necessary for supplying optimum conditions for attaining the purposes of the school. Objectives represent the only sound guide for administrative policies and procedures. Administration should never be viewed as an end in itself but always as a means to the most efficient attainment of objectives.

Clear-cut and defensible objectives provide the best means for music education to obtain favorable administrative policies and procedures. For example, if a music education program has as an objective the provision of opportunity for all students to play an instrument, the necessity for purchasing a sufficient number of instruments to avoid denying this opportunity to any student can be clearly demonstrated. Likewise, clearly stated objectives which have the approval of students and parents provide the best means for obtaining the flexibility in scheduling essential for optimum operation of a music program.

Supervision

The purpose of supervision is to improve instruction. The accepted contemporary function of supervision is to promote cooperative efforts among teachers, supervisors, and administrators to improve all the conditions affecting the learning experiences in the school. Supervision refers to the expert technical service which provides the leadership to accomplish this purpose and function.[4]

Modern supervision is concerned with the total teaching-learning situation. This means that supervision seeks to improve every facet of the educational process: teachers, curriculum, materials of instruction, administrative policies and procedures, and evaluation. Modern concepts hold that supervision is the province not only of supervisors and administrators but also of teachers and, to a limited extent, of pupils and parents. Barr, Burton, and Brueckner hold that "the improvement of teachers is not so much a supervisory function in which teachers participate as it is a teacher function in which supervisors participate."[5] The supervisor's role is to provide leadership in structuring a situation in which the abilities of all concerned will be released and in which the competencies of every person can be brought to bear on the identification of problems and their solution.

Like all processes in education, supervision should be objectives-oriented. Competent supervision results in the delineation of valid objectives for education and in the attainment of optimum conditions for their fulfillment.

Evaluation

Evaluation is the process of ascertaining the extent to which the objectives of education are achieved. The primary purpose of evaluation is the improvement of instruction. Evaluative procedures are used to determine status so that progress toward educational goals can be appraised. Evaluation also provides data for grading and marking, may serve as a means

[4] William H. Burton and Leo J. Brueckner, *Supervision: A Social Process*, 3d ed., Appleton-Century-Crofts, Educational Division, Meredith Corporation, New York, 1955, p. 11.

[5] A. S. Barr and others, *Supervision*, D. Appleton-Century Company Inc., New York, 1947, p. 10. Reprinted by permission of Appleton-Century-Crofts, Educational Division, Meredith Corporation, New York.

of motivation for students, and is an essential technique of research.

The evaluative process includes three steps: (1) the formulation of objectives, (2) the collection of data, and (3) the interpretation of data. Objectives must be clearly stated before evaluation can take place because of the fact that any status has only relative value and its significance can be determined only in relation to desired goals. The formulation of objectives involves philosophical analysis and the use of inductive and deductive reasoning.

The collection of data may be accomplished through the employment of a variety of procedures of two general types: (1) quantitative tools, the tools of measurement, and (2) qualitative tools, observational and judgment techniques of various kinds. Measurement tools include standardized tests, teacher-made tests, achievement scales, score cards, rating scales, and so on. The data secured from measurement tools are precise and objective. They are reported in terms of time, number, amount, and other quantitative symbols and are capable of statistical treatment.

Evaluation by qualitative procedures uses observations, logs, interviews, case histories, diaries, and other tools through which observations are made and subjective judgments recorded. Valid and reliable measurement tools are generally superior to qualitative tools for use in areas for which they have been developed. Because of the fact, however, that many objectives of music education are not adequately accounted for by presently available measurement tools, evaluation must make extensive use of the best appropriate qualitative techniques.

Competent music educators must have a complete understanding of the evaluative process, skill in collecting accurate and relevant data, and the ability to interpret the data scientifically and with common sense. It is especially important that they have sufficient understanding to avoid arriving at untenable conclusions when the evidence is insufficient to make valid judgments.

SUMMARY

Music education can make a unique contribution to the total work of the school, but many music programs fall far short in their accomplishments. Success can only be achieved if music educators develop a sound philosophical orientation concerning education in a democratic society and the role of music in that education.

Objectives are clear statements of values, goals, or directions in education. They provide the only sound basis for all aspects of the school's operation. Objectives operate on four levels: broad social objectives, concrete social objectives, program objectives, and instructional objectives. Each level has a unique contribution to make to the operation of the school, and teachers must understand all the levels. The work of the school includes several separate but closely related processes: curriculum, instruction, administration, supervision, and evaluation

The Role of Principles
in Music Education

2 There is a principle, generally accepted among educators, that learning activities in the school should have a direct relation to the problems and situations to be faced by the student both now and later. This principle is often grossly misinterpreted in the belief that future problems can be identified and the student can be instructed in the necessary techniques and devices for solving them. This is not enough, however. The music teacher is seldom served by the knowledge of established procedures to follow when the clarinet players are out of tune; he must have some personally tested conclusions for diagnosing and solving intonation problems, based upon an acquaintance with instrument construction and embouchure development.

The wise music educator, therefore, does not seek to develop a "bag of tricks" but to create his own solidly based pattern of instruction. He realizes that true professional competence in the field of music education is acquired by virtue of a threefold process:

1. investigation of the facts and beliefs pertaining to the field
2. formulation of valid principles

3. testing of the application of these principles in authentic situations

This is how human beings operate; it is for the school to assist and refine the process. This is the import of the study of foundations and principles of music education.

PRINCIPLES DEFINED

A principle is a rule of action based upon all pertinent information. In educational circles it is a fundamental truth regarding the relationship of factors with which a teacher deals. The principle serves to express the meaning of a fact or set of facts so that one can decide what course to pursue.

Generalizations arise at any point where several instances will allow an inference to be drawn. A principle is really a generalization of a very high order, being formed in a conscious search for relevant data, and tested in terms of cause and effect. A well-related series of principles is conceived as a code of conduct or as guidelines for action.

The Ten Commandments provide a useful example. These were obviously based upon observation of human behavior and its consequences in innumerable situations. Certain kinds of action, it became clear, resulted in harm to society or to the individual, while others were found to be helpful in the context of that time. Thus evolved a set of *principles* to guide the behavior of the Israelites.

Since there is much similarity and continuity among most educational situations, principles governing music educators are logically similar. Each person, however, has a somewhat unique background and motives, and therefore evolves his own set of principles. A certain band director, for example, might dismiss a member of his band for rowdy conduct, on the principle that rehearsals should be concentrated, undistracted learning sessions. He would base this conclusion on his experience in bands and upon the fact that attention and purpose are necessary in the learning process. A different teacher, cognizant of the factors of interest span, motivation, and individual differences and operating on the principle that rehearsals should be conducted in relaxed and flexible fashion, might never be faced with an intrusive discipline problem.

SOURCE OF PRINCIPLES

Education is concerned with human beings and with the infinitely complex social and cultural pattern which they have built; herein lies the source of principles. Nothing lasting can be accomplished in the school which is in contradiction to man's biological nature. Neither can his psychological makeup be ignored. These conditions are basic and relatively fixed, even though our knowledge here is far from complete. As a further source of principles there is the vast societal structure, accompanied by a moral and ethical system and aesthetic values. The educational system itself becomes a source of guiding principles for music education, having evolved to meet basic human and societal requirements.

If it were possible to ascertain the truths and exact relationships among all these areas, trustworthy principles would result. But even these principles would need regular amendment in view of the changes which occur in society and in the value system. In addition to this, old facts are constantly being disproved or reinterpreted and fresh areas uncovered. It is no wonder that educational principles need steady refinement.

For example, many public school music teachers have operated on the principle that the primary task was to achieve technical proficiency in their students, which would produce better sounding musical groups and eventually result in more and better university music majors and symphony players. More and more directors, however, are seeing that such narrow goals tend to restrict musical opportunity to the musically elite. Moreover, emphasis on sheer proficiency can damage sensitivity to other musical values. A better principle is to give primary attention to the students' musical understanding and tastes, with the result that those potential music majors and symphony players can maintain their love for music and will have an audience to listen to them.

BASES FOR PRINCIPLES

If a principle is to be established or modified, its basis in fact must be determined. There are three routes to this information: scientific experimentation, expert opinion based on logical reasoning, and personal or collective experience.

It can be seen that the results of scientific experimentation will be most trustworthy. For instance, researchers into music reading and reading readiness have provided a basis for new principles in that field. Such data, along with the considered opinion of recognized authorities, are made known through publications, conferences, and symposia. These may, for example, underline significant shifts in population, in the economic situation, in educational policies, and in musical styles and tastes which will affect music instruction. Many principles are based simply upon local and national tradition as expressed in common usage and practice.

The most accessible basis for principles, however, is the first-hand experience of the individual music educator. Each has undergone and practiced certain patterns of music instruction, and he will tend to regard these as standard operating procedure. His principles will reflect that fact. This is all very well so long as the individual cultivates an open mind to differing opinion. For example, on the basis of experience and expert opinion, one might well adopt the principle that piano study should be *encouraged* as a preliminary to the study of an orchestral instrument. But wisdom would dictate that piano study should not be *required* as an invariable prerequisite to further musical study, in view of the great number of successful musicians who did not so begin and might have been lost to the profession under such a rule.

FORMULATING PRINCIPLES

The process of deriving working principles is one of investigation and reconstruction. One must examine findings in the realms of biology, anthropology, psychology, sociology, philosophy, education, and music education. The resultant facts and opinions, through the process of logical analysis, may be cast in the form of principles.

Principles are stated as laws or concepts. On the basis of psychological and philosophical evidence, it might be flatly asserted that a music program consists of individual, educative experiences with music. On such a fundamental point there can be no reservations—either it is so or it is not. This type of statement is more than a definition. It is a law of action, and there can be no doubt that its deliberate application can have tremendous consequences in instruction.

A more conceptual form of statement is employed in most cases. Since it is a fact that all human beings are inherently responsive to music, it could be proposed that the music program should offer some type of active participation to all students, of a kind which is compatible with their backgrounds, needs, and desires. Sometimes the facts upon which a principle is based are included in the statement as a prefatory clause. There is also a style in which the concept is reduced to a bare minimum, for example, *the principle of interrelationship.* In this case, a previous understanding is assumed, or one must explain that he is referring to the belief that the meaningful experience is one which is tied in with past and future experiences.

LEVELS OF PRINCIPLES

From the examples previously given it should be obvious that not all principles are of the same kind. Some seem to affect a great area, some are clearly subsidiary. This is primarily due to the different degrees of generalization required. In other words, inferences from a great number of facts must be organized in order to produce the sort of principle which may apply in a variety of instances. Such a principle carries a rather timeless, epic quality.

Music education should promote the expressive values of music would be an example of the top-level kind of principle. This statement derives from aesthetic values, several aspects of human need, psychological theory, and broad educational aims. It should affect every phase and level of music education, resulting in less emphasis upon technique, drill, showmanship, and public entertainment. Other principles are more limited in scope. *Objectives should be stated in terms of behavior*, for example, refers specifically to the process of developing objectives. *The material used for drill should be drawn from music students have experienced*, on the other hand, pertains to one small aspect of methods of teaching.

Actually, the number and variety of principles are infinite, and this creates the need for a degree of systematization. Since a single fact might become a source for several principles, there is a tendency for principles to overlap and conflict. There is an additional difficulty in that principles can relate to different aspects of the same thing. For example, the music supervisor not only needs principles to help him define and establish his supervisory program but also needs principles to guide its operation.

Thus it becomes a problem for the music educator to reduce that confusion among principles which can clog his mind and lead to inconsistent actions. He must formulate top-level principles concerning the role and purposes of music education and relate subsidiary principles to both the developmental and operational phases of instruction.

THE USE OF PRINCIPLES

Everyone operates on the basis of principles, even though they may not be expressed or consciously understood. Even the hardened criminal has developed some basic beliefs about society and human nature and what he should do about them. That his code of operations is unacceptable to society at large does not negate the fact that he has it and uses it. Principles are a natural result of information received and generalized. The process may not be conscious, but in any casual conversation the common use of principles may be observed. The best means of discovering another's principles, of course, is by observing his actions. The music teacher who talks at great length about the importance of music in the curriculum, but makes no provision for those who fail to make his picked organization, is clearly unconscious of his true principles. The useful principle must be consciously formed and applied.

Another music educator may go to great lengths to establish his principles. He will investigate several related areas of knowledge and create a series of quite logical statements of principle. At this point, the process stops, for the teacher is not really convinced of his statements. Useful principles are not "paper principles"—they are matters of personal, hard-won conviction.

What is to be done with principles should be quite clear: they are direct guides to the planning of every aspect of instruction. For example, if it is held that objectives should relate to actual social circumstances, the teacher must consider the changing cultural setting of music. He will be concerned that his students react with discrimination to the music of the great mass media—radio, television, motion pictures, and recordings. He will be much more concerned with this than with good concert manners. He will consider skills to be used in family and community music groups more important than the ability to follow field-formation charts for the marching band. Through further application of principles, the program will be organized to develop the students' taste and useful skills. It will be taught, administered, supervised, and evaluated on that basis.

When a music educator's basic principles are consciously established by thorough investigation and hard thinking, when they express his true convictions covering each aspect of his work—that individual will have an operating code. He will have an immeasurable advantage over his equally well-meaning colleague. He will be able to perform the function of a good teacher, namely, to establish objectives which can consummate the large purposes of education and to create the learning environment which can lead to those specific behaviors on the part of his pupils.

If, in addition, a significant proportion of music educators were to meet this responsibility, the position of the profession would be greatly enhanced. There would surely be an appreciable gain in professional vitality and stability and more significant participation in the total educational structure. Many incidental benefits would accrue as a matter of course, affecting status, salary, facilities, and general support.

This job is not a simple one. It is useless to pretend that all truths pertaining to the field of music education can be gathered into a single system of principles. If that were possible it would have been accomplished many years ago. It would be highly presumptuous to prescribe them here, to say nothing of the fact that only personally achieved principles are at all effective. The thing that can be done is to describe and illustrate and to promote the kind of background from which principles will arise. By this means the music educator may be enabled to develop a system of well-founded principles.

SUMMARY

The truly practical way to professional competence in music education is through extensive investigation and the formulation and application of specific principles. Principles may be regarded as fundamental truths upon which one may chart his actions. They are derived from all pertinent information concerning man's biological and sociological inheritance.

Nevertheless, these factors are not constant, and principles must, therefore, be revised. The necessary facts are uncovered by scientific experimentation, expert reasoning, and personal and collective experience. One must investigate and generalize his findings in the various disciplines.

Principles are stated as laws or concepts and are concerned with different levels and aspects of the teacher's work. Because of the infinite variety of principles, it is necessary to devise a systematic code which will apply to each phase of instruction. Such principles, if they are truly a matter of personal conviction, should enable one to discharge his full responsibilities as a teacher. Moreover, well-principled music educators would improve the profession's position within the schools. This is an individual task, since no person has complete information or perfect insight. Each teacher must be able to establish his principles.

QUESTIONS FOR DISCUSSION

1. What are principles? Why are they indispensable to music educators?
2. Are educational principles unchanging? From what sources do they arise? What authority can we accept?
3. How are principles stated? Give some examples relating to the different levels and phases of music education.
4. What does the music educator accomplish with his principles? What benefits may result?
5. What effect do current changes in the music, life style, and education of Americans have on the professional principles of music educators?
6. State your most cherished principle of music education. What is its source? What is your basis for holding it? How successfully can you defend it?
7. Why is it important to specify one's professional principles in writing?

SELECTED REFERENCES

Childs, John L. *American Pragmatism and Education*, Henry Holt and Company, Inc., New York, 1956.

Dewey, John. *The Quest for Certainty*, Minton, Balch & Co., New York, 1929.

Lewis, C. I. *Analysis of Knowledge and Valuation*, The Open Court Publishing Company, La Salle, Ill., 1946.

Mursell, James L. *Principles of Democratic Education*, W. W. Norton & Company, Inc., New York, 1955.

Robinson, Daniel S. *The Principles of Reasoning: An Introduction to Logic and Scientific Method*, Appleton Century-Crofts, Inc., New York, 1937.

PART 2 FOUNDATIONS OF MUSIC EDUCATION

Music education is a global enterprise. It is rooted deeply in the history of the human race and in the minds and hearts of people. The work of thousands of musicians, historians, philosophers, and psychologists has a bearing on music education. In their accomplishments and insights lie the foundations of music education.

The study of history does not solve problems, but it can help us understand the historical ingredients of the present day and inform us about the problems of the past and the ways in which music educators solved or attempted to solve them. Chapter Three seeks to help the music educator of today view his profession in the context of the past and to discover clues to current issues in the record of the past.

Chapter Four looks to aesthetics and philosophy for insights into the nature of music and the aesthetic experience as a basis for developing a philosophy of music education. Chapter Five explores the psychological foundations of music education, presents principles of musical learning, and proposes a program for research into musical learning.

Historical Foundations
of Music Education

3 Beginning with earliest times, each new belief and practice in music education has developed in context with prevailing institutions and conditions. New directions were constantly established and then modified as other influences were brought to bear. The current scene is simply the point to which the past has brought us. A general grasp of the unfolding story of music education, therefore, builds understanding of the present stance of music in the American schools. It also provides some basis for prognostication of future directions.

The story of music education is inextricably associated with the cultural history of mankind. Culture is the manmade part of one's environment—it constitutes the way of life of a particular group of people. Furthermore, it is a vital concern of any such group to transmit the valuable features of their way of life to the succeeding generation. Evidence from ancient artifacts and from all contemporary cultures underlines the point that making music is a regular pastime of man, and was probably one of his earliest accomplishments. Essential musical skills and traditions have thus been passed along from generation to generation, moving naturally into the curriculum when the necessity for formal schooling finally arose. The ensuing changes in social and educational structure nave dictated modifications in the purposes and methods of music education. Without doubt, the issues in music education today have been met in other forms by our predecessors. It is thus desirable to re-create those scenes with a view to useful inferences which may be extracted.

THE BEGINNINGS OF MUSIC EDUCATION

By definition, the musical prehistory of man must be largely surmised. The attempt to reconstruct it has been made by cultural anthropologists and comparative musicologists, largely through study of contemporary nonliterate societies. No human society has been found which has not practiced the art of music and music education. Indeed, in primitive societies music fulfills a basic function as an accessible agent of tribal tradition, aesthetic meaning, and personal expression in which all participate. It is also regularly employed by individuals and groups at work and at play as an apparently unstructured, spontaneous outgrowth of the activity at hand. There seems to be much meaning which is inarticulate except in the form of music and ritual. In order to maintain social continuity such musical understanding and skill must be passed on, along with all other common cultural elements. This can be done by simple educational methods. Since primitive societies are not organized for much specialization of activities, formal schooling is seldom required.

The educational practice of one "untouched" tribe, the Manus of the Admiralty Islands, is illustrative of the normal pattern:

> Whenever there is a dance there is an orchestra of slit drums of all sizes played by the most proficient drummers in the village. The very small boys of four or five settle themselves beside small hollow logs or pieces of bamboo and drum away indefatigably in time with the orchestra. . . . Girls practice less, for only one drumbeat, the simple death beat, falls to their hands in later life. . . . Singing is also learned through imitation of

older children by younger children. It consists in a monotone chant of very simple sentences, more or less related to each other. A group of children will huddle together on the floor and croon these monotonous chants over and over for hours without apparent boredom or weariness.[1]

From all evidence at hand, music education was handled in this general fashion by our primitive ancestors. The objective was clearly that the youth should be able to carry on the elaborate ceremonial traditions. Instruction was no less vital because there was no school; indeed, there was the utmost social pressure and unlimited opportunity to achieve the necessary musical education in connection with tribal activities. Undoubtedly, effective musical participation was generally more widely diffused in primitive societies than has often been the case in civilized communities.

MUSIC EDUCATION IN THE CLASSICAL ERA

As civilization developed in the Mediterranean area, music education became a more formal undertaking. Artifacts, sacred writings, and mythology reveal extensive use of music in the old civilizations. It had plainly developed into a high art for accompanying poetry and dancing and was a special accomplishment of the priestly class. When the Greek tribes invaded the area, during the second millenium B.C., they manifestly absorbed much of this musical culture but exhibited their peculiar genius for purification and organization. We must rely chiefly upon secondary sources for our knowledge about ancient Greek music. Only a few written examples of Greek music can be examined, in contrast to the extensive remnants of the plastic arts. Nevertheless, the abundant reference in Greek literature to music and music education testifies to its importance in their system.

[1] Margaret Mead, *Growing Up in New Guinea*, William Morrow & Company, Inc., New York, 1930, pp. 43-44. Reprinted by permission of the publisher.

Evidence exists that the original structure of Greek education was built on music and gymnastics, although music and poetry were considered one art. Music was for the soul, while gymnastics were prescribed for the body. This was the objective of education: to build citizens of character, stamina, and grace. Accordingly, Lycurgus decreed regular education in music for every Spartan, and Solon recommended music training for all youthful citizens of Athens.

The most characteristic instruments were the harplike lyre and cithara and the aulos, a louder and more sensuous instrument of the oboe type. The aulos was used to accompany the dance, the dramatic chorus, and military exercises. It was associated with the indigenous peoples and the ancient Dionysian cult. The stringed instruments provided a natural background for poetic texts done with solo voice or small groups. It was this last style which Plato called "good" music, which could promote virtue and graciousness.

As Greek civilization deepened and spread, the school curriculum also expanded to include writing, drawing, and other subjects. The position of music was perhaps threatened, and one authority was impelled to write: "About music . . . it is not easy to say precisely what potency it possesses . . . . does it serve for education or amusement or entertainment?" The merits of the case were clear to him however: "there is a form of education in which boys should be trained not because it is useful or necessary but as being liberal and noble . . . . the point is proved by music."[2]

By the fourth century B.C., music education had apparently reached the height of its influence. It has never since played so important a role. Music contests and festivals abounded, concert societies and artists' unions were formed, and the great philosophers were unanimous in its praise. The art itself was subjected to research, so that Aristoxenus and Pythagoras were able to establish music theory on a firm basis.

[2] Aristotle, *The Politics*, translated for the Loeb Classical Library by H. Rackham, Harvard University Press, Cambridge, Mass., 1932, pp. 643, 645, 649. Reprinted by permission of the publisher.

These very developments, however, seemed to lead to the decline of music. There was an adulteration of musical style and taste partly attributable to economic and political degeneration and cultural admixture. Music became separated from poetry, and virtuosity was prized. The simple melodies disappeared and larger ensembles with complex instrumentation became fashionable. Musical mathematics was studied for its own sake in the secondary schools. These are exactly the characteristics of music as a Roman art.

Music education in pagan Rome gradually assumed the aspect of an intellectual discipline. Regardless of Nero's supposed musicianship, performance was ordinarily for slaves and foreigners, to be used for entertainment of highborn Romans. A curriculum gradually evolved, based on writings by Plato and Aristotle, in which music was bracketed with arithmetic, geometry, and astronomy. These constituted the quadrivium, the upper level of the "seven liberal arts." The pattern was well established by the fifth century A.D.

MUSIC EDUCATION IN THE MIDDLE AGES

The Christians resisted the pagan educational system until the Church assumed control of education. The pattern was considered useful by St. Augustine, however, and became entrenched until the humanistic awakening. In the sixth century Boethius prepared five books, *De musica*, and these, plus ancient manuscripts collected by Cassiodorus, provided the point of reference for the music curriculum in the cathedral and monastery schools. Under the influence of these texts, music was studied as pure science, requiring absolutely no understanding of live music nor any skill in performance. By the eleventh century this body of theory was so obviously obsolete that new and more practical texts were used, and a revision and condensation of Boethius's work by Johannes de Muris appeared.

There was necessarily a parallel development in music education, since music was fortunately a vital aspect of the mass. Schools for the education of choristers, called *scholae cantorum*, were established in fourth century Rome and were greatly expanded by Pope Gregory toward the end of the sixth century. Hampered at first by an awkward system of notation, limited intervallic relationships, and a paucity of developed forms, the musicians of the church labored long centuries in establishing a flourishing art. The ability to deal with this music was accomplished by instruction in singing, playing, and the elements of harmony and composition. The situation called for practical preprofessional methods.

The essential pattern of the liberal arts was carried into the universities, the special academic corporations which made their appearance during the twelfth and thirteenth centuries. Thus, music was included in the requirements for the baccalaureate degree, a necessary preliminary to the study of the higher faculties of law, medicine, and theology. There is some evidence that by this time the practical study of music was used to supplement the purely theoretical.[3]

During all this time the common people maintained their musical heritage, by one means and another, as they have always done. They had little or no contact with liberal education or cathedral choirs. Practical musicianship was passed from father to son and from one member of a traveling troupe to another. The rise of the troubadours and trouvères was one manifestation of the power of this secular trend in music. The Meistersingers themselves were guild musicians, who became a self-perpetuating class of professionals through the deliberate selection and training of apprentices in the musical art.

MUSIC EDUCATION IN THE RENAISSANCE

With the impact of humanistic philosophy and the advent of Protestantism, the necessity for universal music education became more evident. Music was no longer considered only a scientific discipline, a setting for the mass, or a practical

[3] Nan Cooke Carpenter, "Music in the Medieval Universities," *Journal of Research in Music Education*, 3 (2):136-144, Fall 1955.

trade; it was prized for its intrinsic beauty and worth and for being naturally expressive of religious feelings. Music instruction thus became standard in the court schools and parochial institutions.

Luther and Calvin insisted on the need for vernacular schools, so that not only the leaders of society but the common people would have the background to enable them to interpret the Scriptures and to become good citizens. Following the prescription of these church leaders, School Regulations were established in 1559 by Christopher, Duke of Württemberg, and these were adopted in substance by the Electorate of Saxony in 1580. A system of elementary schools developed in Germany and Western Europe, nominally state-controlled but regulated by the clergy and taught by the sacristan or parish clerk. The subjects of instruction comprised reading, writing, catechism, and singing. As for the secondary schools, Paulson points out that the instruction in singing and music formed an essential pattern of instruction in this type of educational institution which, closely connected with the Church, aspired to be *seminarium ecclesiae*, a seminary of the Church.[4]

The invention of printing had a stimulating effect on music education. Seven years after Martin Luther pinned his theses to the door in Wittenberg, the first Protestant hymnbook was published. Composers wrote more and more music for educational purposes. As a matter of fact, this period saw the development of music as an amateur art and the production of a great variety of music for the madrigalists and similar chamber groups.

These advances, far from signaling the success of music education, were only aids in attacking the public's musical inertia. The common people were still poorly schooled, and their musical development must have been on a lower level than we can imagine. The situation was quite grim in sixteenth-century England:

[4] Friederich Paulson, *German Education*, translated by T. Lorenz, Charles Scribner's Sons, New York, 1908, p. 77.

Although it is doubtful that more than a few parish churches had organs and choirs, many congregations probably raised their voices together in metrical psalms. Unaided by instruments, hobbled by the illiterate who sometimes made "lining out" (reading each line before it was sung) essential, congregations must usually have found their psalm singing almost wholly a spiritual exercise, and very little musical. . . . It did not require formal training, but it may have been, for the literate, a gateway to musical knowledge.[5]

As to formal schooling in music, it was by no means universal in English society of this time. Half a dozen private schools included music in the curriculum and it was also offered in the cathedral and collegiate church schools. Some children of the court obtained instruction from members of The King's Musick. Canterbury Cathedral and other large churches maintained masters of choristers, who were paid to feed, clothe, and educate a handful of children in music and other subjects.

The most widespread system of musical education at this time occurred in connection with the organized guilds of musicians. The training of musical apprentices flourished. In many instances, the business had actually evolved into a kind of day school. In Elizabethan England it was the only means to professional secular music education.

In spite of such meager opportunity, music education continued to advance in Europe. The thriving of opera, instrumental performance, and new forms during the Baroque era was accompanied by a corresponding widening and deepening of musical literacy. Before the colonization of America was far advanced, the roots of the contemporary pattern of European musical training had been established.

[5] Walter L. Woodfill, *Musicians in English Society from Elizabeth to Charles I*, Princeton University Press, Princeton, N.J., 1953, p. 156. Reprinted by permission of the publisher.

OUTLINES OF THE MODERN EUROPEAN SYSTEM

It must be understood that each European nation has taken its individual course. However, certain basic educational trends can be noted. The work of the guilds has been inherited by the conservatories. These institutions give preprofessional training of high concentration. They are essentially a broad form of the private studio. Their objective is to create high-caliber musicianship.

The tradition of music in the seven liberal arts has been carried into the universities. These institutions originally offered music. Then its study underwent a period of eclipse, but it was reinstated in modern times. Today, European universities grant advanced degrees in music, based largely upon philosophical and scholastic study.

The various types of parochial schools have continued. Their concern has been with the student's general musical training and his development of powers useful in the service of the church. Parallel with these institutions, the various states have created and extended systems of public education. Based as they are upon the examination plan, these schools have the effect of graduating the youth into the vocational specialties or into secondary schools of an upper-class, intellectual orientation. Since many pupils will thus receive no further musical schooling, the state-controlled elementary schools emphasize musical literacy and the general values of music.

The system that has been described has undoubtedly made music a powerful force within its culture and has produced a great number of famous composers and performers. In the twentieth century the curriculum has been broadened and enriched. However, no energetic expansion has appeared in school music to compare with that in America. Exclusiveness and preprofessionalism seem largely to have retained their hold on European music education. General musical training tends to be offered only up to a point. Then, if the student shows professional promise, he is put through a thorough and detailed course of study which guarantees his proficiency.

Notable exceptions are found in a few European countries where the musical education of all students has become a matter of national policy, especially Hungary and, to a lesser extent, Russia. In the former country, the efforts of Zoltan Kodály resulted in a systematic and well-supported system of music education which utilizes the total musical resources of the country and its indigenous musical heritage. The Hungarian system is not only bearing fruitful results in that country but is a strong influence for change in our own program.

Americans have long envied European musical leadership and its tradition of active amateurism, but in most countries the system has apparently not kept up with the times. The American system can safely stand comparison with Europe in terms of the quantity and quality of its product and has far outstripped European countries in the development of school performing groups.

BEGINNINGS OF MUSIC EDUCATION
IN THE UNITED STATES

The early colonists brought with them to America certain notions about musical training. Such beliefs were naturally based upon the European system as it had developed up to that time. These people, however, were in the process of creating a new culture, in keeping with a new environment, and certain differences in their approach were bound to occur.

It is true that they were met with the indigenous musical culture of the Indians and later absorbed influences from the Spaniards to the south and the French in the north. Nevertheless, the settlers of the thirteen Colonies were isolated in a very real sense and were forced to establish their own pattern of music education. The institutions which they created evolved directly into the present system of music education.

Many colonists came to these shores for religious freedom. As soon as possible they set up religious services, and hymn singing played a vital role. As a matter of fact, the *Bay Song Book*, in 1640, was the second book to be printed in America.[6] The Calvinistic Puritans wanted only plain and simple worship without organs, stained glass, and the like. The people were keenly aware of the shortcomings in their singing, but little could be done at first to improve it. The need to do so steadily built up pressure for more adequate musical instruction.

The European institutions which could support musical education were not available in the Colonies. There were no large cathedrals, employing choirmasters and choristers, which could serve to underwrite the creation of a professional class of musicians. Neither were there princely courts, with their establishments of musicians, or musicians' guilds to guide the training of apprentices.

There was little room, indeed, for any but the most productive occupations. For many years people were necessarily concerned with pioneering, fighting Indians, and producing the necessities of life. Although these conditions soon abated in the more settled areas, the environmental struggle has been a continuing one in America. Perhaps this is responsible for a certain materialistic, nonartistic climate of opinion which still persists.

By scarcely perceptible degrees, music in the churches advanced. The Episcopal Church of Port Royal, Virginia, imported a pipe organ in 1700. In 1712 the Reverend John Tufts of Newbury, Massachusetts, published the first practical instruction book in singing. Not long thereafter, several New England town churches took steps toward singing "by

---

[6] This edition included only the text. The ninth edition, published in 1698 included thirteen tunes.

rule or art," as music reading was called. The better singers in the congregations tended to sit together and gradually formed themselves into choirs.

The singing schools originated in attempts to found and improve these choirs. They first appeared in New England in about 1720, and the idea was copied throughout the Colonies. Operation of such a school was usually a part-time venture for the director, who held evening sessions in home, church, or schoolroom for a modest fee. Among singing school masters were men such as Francis Hopkinson, William Billings, and Lowell Mason. They were concerned with developing the ability to read music and to interpret a variety of choral works. Thus, the rudiments of music and sight singing were the basic subjects, and public concerts were prepared whenever possible.

For a century the singing school was the primary institution for the musical training of the citizen. Other than this, a few individuals picked up such instruction as they could from a handful of private teachers or through foreign study. It must not be forgotten, incidentally, that many an immigrant had received his musical education before arriving in America. In this way, Europe continued its contribution to American musical life.

The power of these early efforts in music education is indicated by increasing musical activity. Musical growth was cumulative and results took many forms. In 1752 an orchestra was employed in the production of *The Beggar's Opera* at Upper Marlborough, Maryland. A symphony society was formed in New York as the nineteenth century began, and the Handel and Haydn Society of Boston was founded in 1815. The sizable performances which these and other such groups were able to sponsor clearly suggest that an extensive interest and acquaintance with music had been developed.

From these large musical enterprises it was but a step to the organization of mass singing schools, or music conventions. The first gathering to be so named occurred in Concord, Vermont, in 1829, and the idea attained great vogue during the middle years of the nineteenth century. These conventions were in the nature of festivals or short courses, lasting three or four days and dealing with methods and materials, vocal problems, elementary harmony, and conducting. Like-minded group effort and a concentrated, direct attack on musical problems characterized these Chautauqua-type assemblies. This sort of thing immediately appealed to Americans, and the pattern has been extended to twentieth-century teachers institutes, music conferences, festivals, and summer camps.

The kind of society which gave rise to the music convention was also ready for public school music. Actually, some teachers had already included some singing as part of general classroom activity. Its value was recognized in theory, but it was generally felt that music was not a practical necessity like reading, writing, and arithmetic. This policy was overthrown, however, by the increasing power and combination of the forces that have been described. That is to say, the singing schools, musical societies, choral and instrumental productions, and music conventions had not only been doing a job of music education but had convinced a number of people that music was important in the school curriculum. This was particularly the case in New England and its capital city of Boston. So it was that a citizens' committee made repeated petitions to the Primary School Board. Their plan was finally reported and approved, and music was included in the curriculum at Hawes School in 1838. Lowell Mason, who had been instrumental in this drive, was given the responsibility for the work.

It is interesting to note that these pioneers for school music firmly rejected the theory of talent selection and preprofessional training and aimed rather toward a citizenry versed in music as part of the common cultural heritage.[7] This philosophy could only have been the result of a long period of tribulation such as has been described. Music in society had been developed by the most makeshift methods,

---

[7] Edward Bailey Birge, *History of Public School Music in the United States*, Oliver Ditson Company, Philadelphia, 1928, pp. 44-45.

with no stable institution to foster it. Now, at last, every child was to be educated. Jacksonian ideals were to be realized. This was the time of Horace Mann and the great expansion of the American public school system. Free public education itself had been long in coming, but as soon as these schools were established in principle and in fact, music quickly assumed its place in the curriculum.

As a matter of fact, music was the first subject of nonacademic type to achieve full public school status. Fortunately, Pestalozzi's ideas were spreading among educators during this same period. This sytem placed great emphasis on direct sense experience as "the only true foundation of human instruction."[8] Pestalozzi made a clear distinction between "real knowledge and book knowledge" and regarded education as a means to the development of the child's powers and talents.[9] There was a corresponding modification of the purely academic, nationalistic, and society-centered aims of the schools.

Although Pestalozzi himself did not stress the place of music in the curriculum, the logical extension of his principles called for an expansion in this field. What activity offered more direct opportunities for sense impression and development of individual talents? Neef, coworker of Pestalozzi, opened a school in Philadelphia in 1809 in which music was "regarded as an essential study in the elementary school course,"[10] and the following outline of Principles of the Pestalozzian System of Music was presented to the American Institute of Instruction meeting in Boston in 1830:

[8] Johann Heinrich Pestalozzi, *How Gertrude Teaches Her Children*, translated by Lucy E. Holland and Frances C. Turner, 2d ed., C. W. Bardeen, Syracuse, 1891, p. 316.

[9] Ibid., pp. 46, 258.

[10] Will S. Monroe, *History of the Pestalozzian Movement in the United States*, C. W. Bardeen, Syracuse, 1907, p. 93.

1. To teach sounds before signs and to make the child learn to sing before he learns the written notes or their names;

2. To lead him to observe by hearing and imitating sounds, their resemblances and differences, their agreeable and disagreeable effect, instead of explaining these things to him—in a word, to make him active instead of passive in learning;

3. To teach but one thing at a time—rhythm, melody, and expression to be taught and practiced separately, before the child is called to the difficult task of attending to all at once;

4. In making him practice each step of each of these divisions, until he is master of it, before passing to the next;

5. In giving the principles and theory after the practice, and as induction from it;

6. In analyzing and practicing the elements of articulate sound in order to apply them to music, and

7. In having the names of the notes correspond to those used in instrumental music.[11]

By implication, these were reforms of practices then current, and it is interesting to note the force which some of these principles have maintained even to this day.

One who helped spread these ideas was Lowell Mason, who visited Europe in 1837 and again in 1853 in order to observe methods of music instruction in the Pestalozzian schools and published several books, including the *Pestalozzian Music Teacher*. Moreover, as a close friend of Horace Mann, Mason was engaged as lecturer and demonstrator at many teachers' institutes and normal schools, where these principles were passed on to teachers in the developing public school system.

[11] Ibid., p. 145.

It now appears that Mason little understood Pestalozzian principles. His *Manual of the Boston Academy of Music* was actually a plagiarized translation of a non-Pestalozzian songbook.[12]   Nevertheless, Mason was identified with the educational fad of that day—Pestalozzianism—and deliberately organized the Teachers' Class of the Boston Academy of Music to promulgate those principles as he understood them. This teachers' class, in turn, became the model for the New England music convention.

Music instruction in the schools spread rapidly during the nineteenth century. It was first introduced into the upper grades and was later extended to the primary and secondary levels. Of first concern was the general state of musical illiteracy, so that music reading was greatly emphasized. Materials included both sacred and secular forms. Instruction was handled by music specialists, since many grade teachers were as little skilled as their pupils.

EARLY TRENDS IN MUSIC EDUCATION

As the United States became settled from sea to sea, as communication became easier, and as provincialism gradually subsided, new influences were brought to bear on society and the educational structure. One of these was the advent of the touring concert artist. Jenny Lind, Ole Bull, the Germania Orchestra, and many similar attractions had an immeasurable influence on future directions. The schools had succeeded somewhat in ameliorating musical illiteracy, and the public sought something more than hymns and folk songs. Musical taste and discrimination were not high, but public concerts were events of great importance in many communities. The traveling artists could not have been sustained had that not been the case.

[12] Howard E. Ellis, "Lowell Mason and the Manual of the Boston Academy of Music," *Journal of Research in Music Education,* 3:3-10, Spring 1955.

Not only did famous artists come to America, but foreign-trained orchestral musicians joined with native musicians to form concert orchestras and bands. Of inestimable importance was the orchestra of Theodore Thomas, which planted the flag of instrumental music throughout the country. Thomas was followed by Damrosch and the bands of Gilmore, Reeves, Conway, and Sousa. Many town bands were organized. The Metropolitan Opera Company was formed, and symphonies were established in some of the large metropolitan areas.

These professional artists owed much to school music. In turn, they helped to create a demand for the enrichment of school musical activities. They were influential in proving that the ultimate goals of music education lay beyond that of music reading. Additional opportunities for professional growth were opened to music teachers. Music education at the college level began with the establishment of the Boston Academy of Music in 1832. Oberlin Conservatory was established in 1835 and the same year Oberlin College announced a Professorship of Sacred Music. In 1837 New England Conservatory of Music, Boston Conservatory of Music, Chicago College of Music, and Cincinnati Conservatory of Music all opened their doors. Music departments were functioning at Harvard in 1870, at Vassar in 1873, at the University of Pennsylvania and Smith College in 1875, at the University of Illinois and Ohio Wesleyan University in 1877, and at the University of Michigan in 1879. The first summer normal institutes were held prior to the Civil War and evolved into permanent, year-round normal schools. These schools expanded and deepened their programs, providing more and more elementary teachers who handled music instruction in their own classes. As music instruction became more universal and intensified, teachers organized to control and stimulate their activities on district and state levels. In 1876 the Music Teachers National Association was formed.

On the heels of all this development came a new system of thought which greatly enhanced the position of music in the schools. Pragmatic philosophy, an especially American creation of Charles Peirce, William James, and John Dewey, provided the basis in theory for the progressive education movement. Few people credit sufficiently the role which this movement played in justifying and enlivening music instruction. In Europe and America music had been considered an enrichment of the basic curriculum. To the progressive educator it was a medium of the most practical sort, a natural means of pupil activity and expression.

The system is based on the belief that knowledge is used instrumentally, to guide behavior; its truth is established only by testing it in action. If this is so, then education cannot be a process of factual assimilation but rather one of investigation and activity developing from the felt needs of the pupils.

The principles have led to various experiments with activity and core curricula and to extensive use of the problem-solving method. The ideas represent such a radical departure from traditional practice that they have been vigorously attacked and only partially applied. Nevertheless, the face of American education has been greatly changed.

Music, more readily than the academic disciplines, complied with the principle of experience made useful in actual performance. It is possible in music to assimilate facts and principles unrelated to their use, but it is more natural to place the student in concrete situations. In musical performance, at least, there is constant application and instant evaluation of many facts and beliefs. Successful music teaching has always been "progressive" in nature.

Whatever its basis in truth or its effectiveness in practice, the new movement in the schools helped to increase the number of culturally important offerings and established a certain tolerance toward the development of the individual's interests. Music education has thrived in consequence.

DEVELOPMENTS IN MUSIC EDUCATION SINCE 1900

Much development was necessary before instrumental music could be established in the schools. Until the twentieth century, public school music meant vocal music. That this was so is not surprising, in view of the original purposes of school music, the training of the music teachers, and long-standing tradition. But the examples of instrumental music in out-of-school life and the forces for an expanded curriculum were bound to have their effect.

Another factor was the increasing percentage of students who attended high school. This reduced the hold of the classical curriculum geared to the needs of the dedicated scholar, and encouraged the inclusion of new subjects.

Several high school orchestras were organized during the first decade of the twentieth century. Truly, the term orchestra was often loosely used to designate almost any heterogeneous instrumental group. The effort to emulate professional organizations, however, resulted in the establishment of some school orchestras which did honor to the name. There was a steady improvement in instrumentation.

These first school orchestras, like the town bands, had their origin in musicians who had been developed by out-of-school means. It soon became apparent that some means of recruiting and training instrumentalists had to be found. Just as colonial Americans devised the singing school to meet their need, the twentieth-century music teacher responded with the system of class instrumental instruction in the schools. In a sense, instrumental classes were not new. It has always been natural for musicians to gather in groups and ensembles, and a sort of class instruction develops around the most proficient players. However, the deliberate organization of classes for the training of band and orchestra players is an institution of the public schools of twentieth-century America. In spite of resistance in some quarters it has proved remarkably successful.

Because of the very specific goal of class instruction, that is, to prepare players for the advanced organizations, procedures were also quite specific. Student volunteers were screened into groups on the same age level and instrument. This is the homogeneous method. Teachers usually promoted skills step by step: care of the instrument, position or embouchure, easy tones, and extension of range, keys, and rhythms as regulated by carefully graded materials. Other teachers have favored the heterogeneous approach, establishing what amounted to beginning string or wind ensembles.

Since it takes years to develop proficiency on a musical instrument, class instruction was generally undertaken in the upper grades. In many instances these groups developed directly into full-fledged elementary school orchestras. But it was found that the most rapid progress could be made on the wind instruments. Thus, the first school bands made their appearance in the years immediately preceding World War I.

The school band was a most spectacular development in American education. The war itself stimulated interest in bands, and their usefulness in connection with outdoor events was apparent. School authorities soon found that bands were relatively easy to develop, seemed to foster creative, cooperative group learning experiences, and teamed excellently with the competitive sports. In effect, the tremendous popular enthusiasm which developed for inter-high school and collegiate athletics carried the band program along with it. The band soon established its public relations value. It has been a primary point of contact between school and public.

Additional support to the school-band movement came from commercial sources, such as the instrument and uniform companies. Possibilities for expanded sales of many types of equipment were obvious, and these agencies fostered and encouraged every phase in the development of school bands.

The rapid expansion of musical activity in the schools led to the formation of various new organizations for music teachers. Music sections of the National Education Association met in district and state units, and in 1907 a more general meeting at Keokuk, Iowa, resulted in the organization of the Music Supervisors Conference, later known as the Music Educators National Conference. These groups, and others, stimulated more useful professional relationships, and their meetings and activities have been centers of inspiration for their members.

The contest movement was a very natural outcome of this growth. The idea was strongly supported by the organized teachers' groups and the commercial interests. Gaining strength in the twenties, it swept the entire country, enlisting tremendous support for the cause of music education. In 1928 the first official national contest was sponsored by the Music Educators National Conference and the National Bu reau for the Advancement of Music.

In the same year a new force was established which was to temper the spirit of competition with that of cooperation. The National Music Camp was founded at Interlochen, Michigan, and the idea has spread to many other locations. In these camps students gather from many schools, forming organizations and receiving instruction in the most stimulating setting. This same pattern has been adapted to the numerous all-state bands, festival choruses, and so on, which so often form part of the activity at clinics, festivals, and conventions.

In recent years the music contests have been subjected to attack from several directions. It has been claimed that they have served their purpose and that they contribute to false musical values—competitive spirit, limited repertoire, and an undue emphasis on showmanship and pure technique. This criticism has not led to the abandonment of contests but rather to a modification of the more objectionable features. They have been decentralized, a more extensive repertoire has been fostered, and performances are rated instead ot being placed. In some instances, criticisms are given without the ratings. The future course of the contest movement is difficult to predict.

TECHNOLOGICAL DEVELOPMENTS

The influence of recent scientific discoveries upon music education is often underestimated. The mechanical devices that have been developed are usually relegated to the status of audiovisual aids to classroom teaching. They are this and more: these gadgets have made of America a huge sounding board for music. Simply put, the musical experience is no longer limited to the performer and others who happen to be in the same room. Through the media of radio, television, recordings, and motion pictures, a single performance may affect millions of people, and repeatedly. In fact, it is estimated that the total attendance in person during the entire history of the New York Philharmonic Symphony is surpassed by the audience for one broadcast. This kind of mass dissemination affects the schools. Not only may the schoolchild's performance be so used, but his own school experiences are affected by his constant exposure to music in out-of-school situations.

In the early days of radio serious-music programs represented an important segment of the broadcasting schedule, but the amount of serious music on commercial stations has diminished steadily to such an extent that some stations provide no programs of fine music. Fortunately, however, a few excellent programs such as the Metropolitan Opera and the New York Philharmonic Symphony broadcasts are still available on AM radio. In addition, educational stations and a number of commercial FM stations broadcast several hours of serious music daily. Furthermore, there has occurred recently on television an encouraging increase in serious-music programs of high quality. The production of such programs as Leonard Bernstein's *Omnibus* series and his *Young People's Concerts* indicates that musicians, the television industry, and the public are ready to support music programs of the highest quality.

It must be recognized, however, that much mechanically produced music is cheapening in its influence. The advent of mass audio devices has coincided with the creation of new idioms of popular music. This fact, coupled with the profit motive upon which these media operate, plainly tends toward the promotion of vulgar art. Regardless of the sincere beginnings of jazz and western folk music, their force has been channeled into this commercial use.

It is difficult to make comparisons between present and past levels of musical taste. Historical investigation has been particularly concerned with significant evolutionary developments within a special musical class. The musical taste of the masses has only recently demanded serious attention. But there is evidence that our forebears were greatly taken with embellished operatic arias, the technical display of Franz Liszt, and the emotional style of the Victorian period. It would seem that there is little need to despair of the present level of public taste as compared with that of former times.

The continued mass promulgation of music, in spite of the preponderance of miseducative material, may have its beneficial points. Popular music is manifestly popular because it is simple and direct, for the public at large has insufficient musical experience to respond to more complex and worthwhile examples. A variety of musical experience is likely to produce a more sophisticated response. Given this variety through technological means and well fortified with good music in the schools, the public may well develop considerable powers of discrimination.

The sale of "classical" records has risen to fifteen percent of the long-play market. Many films are now accompanied by high-quality original scores, and serious-music programs are to be found on educational radio and television and even occasionally on commercial stations. As to quality of performance, the market for high fidelity recordings and stereophonic equipment is highly indicative. If nothing else, the public has been educated to demand music of technical polish and authentic texture.

Electronic Music

The most esoteric product of the new technology is electronic music. Sounds are either generated independently or picked up from the world of natural sound. Captured on magnetic tape, they are filtered, mixed, spliced, and altogether reshaped into a final product which is limited only by the composer's imagination.

The art owes something to early experiments involving artificial preparation of movie sound tracks. The creation of new sound via electronic organ, prepared piano, and newly invented instruments contributed to the developing concept. But the refinement of the magnetic tape recorder gave electronic music its basic tool and provided the impetus for creative growth during the 1950s. Today, electronic music is gaining adherents at a rapid pace, and promises to become a major factor in music and music education.[13]

The new technique has not only given limitless tonal resources to the composer, but it has given new dimensions to rhythmic and dynamic patterns. Of special importance is the fact that the composer is his own performer.

At the same time, electronic music is highly effective as one part in an ensemble of traditional instruments. The concerto for magnetic tape provides freedom and interest without giving up the audience appeal of the living performer.

RECENT METHODOLOGICAL IMPORTATIONS

American schools have long been prone to adopt and adapt foreign innovations. Pestalozzi, Herbart, Froebel, and Montessori are familiar to us as founders of such educational systems. Among the most recent importations affecting school music are the methods of Kodály, Orff, and Suzuki.

Along with fellow Hungarian Bela Bartók, Zoltan Kodály developed an early interest in the folk music of his country. Kodály was also greatly concerned with the education of children and was able to install a strong system of music instruction in the schools. Basically, this involved reliance upon singing and an early attack upon music reading using the tonic sol-fa syllables. Hand signals are coordinated with the use of syllables. The stress is upon unaccompanied, a cappella work, and part singing is introduced at a very early stage. Melodic and rhythmic dictation and improvisation of parts represent integral features of the system. Pentatonic scales are used extensively because of their important relation

[13]See *Music Educators Journal* 55(3), November 1968, which is entirely devoted to the topic of electronic music.

to Hungarian folk material and as a stepping stone to the smaller intervals used in other scales.

The Kodály ideas have been introduced to American music teachers through summer workshops, demonstrations, and publications.[14]

Another kind of program for elementary school music has been instituted by the German, Carl Orff. The Orff system also uses the pentatonic scale, but emphasizes the use of instruments. A number of these, the so-called Orff instruments, are new creations reminiscent of the familiar rhythm band instruments. These are used, along with singing, to individualize certain rhythmic, harmonic, and melodic functions. Such renditions tend to develop through elaboration and improvisation, thus extending the creative experiences of the students. One criticism of Orff's plan is that it is based upon reenactment of music history and is thus "out of tune with today's world."[15]

A special approach to teaching the violin has been developed by Shinichi Suzuki of Japan.[16]   In the original form, it is essentially a special style of individual instruction, staffed by Mr. Suzuki's large corps of approved teachers. The pupils begin at preschool age and each lesson is audited by one of their parents who is to listen and supervise the following week's practice. The early stages are taught by rote, with much listening and direct imitation of the teacher. The characteristic patterns for beginners are short, choppy figures with rapid bow strokes, which are easier to manage than long legato bowings and phrases. Pupils are occasionally brought together for festivals where several will play in unison the various compositions included within the standard course of study and already memorized.

The possibilities of the Suzuki plan have been recog-

[14] Mary Helen Richards, *Threshold to Music*, Fearon Publishers, Palo Alto, Calif., 1964.

[15] Marion Flagg, "The Orff System in Today's World," *Music Educators Journal*, December 1966, p. 30.

[16] John Kendall, *Talent Education and Suzuki*, Music Educator National Conference, Washington, 1966.

nized and several advocates have demonstrated the techniques in various clinics. In America, essentially, we have established Suzuki as a beginning method for classes of pupils in the primary grades. The parents are not generally involved beyond the very early stages. What remains of Suzuki is an emphasis on an early start, learning by imitation and drill, and certain improvements in the design and sequence of material to be learned. Thus, the Suzuki method strikes at conservatory traditions long associated with string teaching, and may serve to modify and extend the school string program. Certainly, something is needed to restore the proper balance between the school band and string programs.

The Orff and Kodály systems have also been altered when applied in American school situations. But disciples of any such plan are bound to profit much from the reexamination of their aims and procedures, the new music employed, and the enthusiasm which they develop in process. Any new, experimental situation is likely to secure such advantages. In this sense, the Orff and Kodály systems have worked to improve the general quality of elementary music instruction in America, and this influence should tend to continue.

CULTURAL EXPLOSION

Certain social scientists have invented the term *cultural lag* to express the strain produced by rapid technological advance without commensurate changes in the nation's social and cultural arrangements. The pace has obviously quickened, however, in terms of our musical life, during the sixties. In retrospect, there appeared to be a reaction against the excessive concern with practical and scientific matters that had been triggered by Sputnik and the race to the moon. Large philanthropic foundations supported projects for music such as the Ford Foundation's Contemporary Music Project. A number of young composers-in-residence were subsidized and assigned to qualified public schools where they composed for the musical groups at hand and secured public performances. Various pilot projects in creativity were also sponsored in selected public schools and seminars were organized on college campuses.

The Arts and Humanities program of the United States Office of Education has also been instrumental in supporting various research projects and seminars related to school music. And the impact of Federal aid to education has gradually made itself felt in numerous local music programs through equipment grants under various titles of the Education Act.

Increasing collegiate enrollments have also enhanced the strength of most college and university music departments sufficiently to enable most to exert the calibre of leadership they have long sought. In several states and localities, too, Arts Councils have been established. These groups have managed to secure and channel funds to community choral and symphony societies, to opera groups, and to support and commission various musical activities in such a way as to expand the structure of musical enterprise.

The organized music teaching profession has exhibited an accompanying surge of activity and interest in new directions. During the summer of 1966, an International Seminar in Teacher Education in Music, held on the campus of the University of Michigan, generated an awareness of similarities and differences among the school music programs in all nations, and a determination to mount an attack on the more critical problems facing us. The Tanglewood Symposium met during the summer of 1967 and seemed to express music educators' growing tolerance of today's popular music. There is also an increasing interest in ethnomusicology and a recognition that music from all lands must play a larger role in American school music of the future.

These trends have been accompanied by a steady rise in the number and proportion of people who participate actively in music making. The yearly *Reports on Amateur Instrumental Music in the United States*, issued by the American Music Conference, indicate a steady broadening of the base of musical skill, to the point where nearly fifty million of us, or twenty-five percent, play an instrument at least occasionally. About half of these are piano players and, surprisingly, well over two million play one of the orchestral stringed instruments. All this has produced over fifty thousand school bands, around eight thousand school orchestras, and fourteen hundred community and professional orchestras.

THE STATUS OF SCHOOL MUSIC TODAY

Music education in the United States has many a new path to travel—it has not reached the apex of its development. It does seem, however, that past influences and the efforts of uncounted teachers and pupils have achieved certain clear gains.

The cultural universality of music is at last being reflected in the education of our youth. The great expansion of free public education in this country, taken together with the farsightedness of pioneers in school music and the effects of modern educational philosophy, have put this goal within reach. Today, practically every child has some opportunity to extend his musical responsiveness within the schools.

It is conversely true that many a child misses that opportunity, having undergone musical experience that is abortive. Too often the aims, methods, and means of instruction do not measure up to this task of enhancing the musical responsiveness of every child. In fact, innumerable school children have learned to look upon music as a mechanical act or as a trade for which they have no talent. As adults, these individuals avoid music and certainly provide no support for the music program in the schools.

Music teaching has become more effective, on the whole, because the profession has reached a certain level of maturity. Music teachers may no longer be classed simply as musicians who could not succeed as professional performers. State certification requirements and expanding graduate programs in the universities and conservatories have led to more and more extended preparation. The frantic promotional

stage in school music has largely passed, having been subli-
mated in larger causes. There is evidence of a healthy concern
with teaching the values inherent in music and with acquiring
the know-how to get that job done.

One evidence of growing maturity is the rapid development of interest in research. The Society for Research in
Music Education, launched in 1960 as a child of the Music
Education Research Council, has grown to include some
twenty to twenty-five percent of the membership of the
Music Educators National Conference. The Society's publication, *The Journal of Research in Music Education*, has
meanwhile doubled the number of issues and articles. The
various MENC regional and state organizations now have
research committees and there are several state publications
devoted to reporting research in music education. All this is
reflected in and supported by an increasing profundity of
professional literature.

In many ways, school music has had a large part in the
encouragement and improvement of worthwhile American
composition. From a period of utter dependence upon
European art, the time has arrived when the American
composer, conductor, or performer has a hearing and can
gain a respected position as an artist. It is not long since it
was the fashion to consider the aspiring American composer
as some sort of imposter. The schools have largely supplied
the major symphonies and choral groups with performers and
have taken eagerly to the production of native American
opera.

Many composers have contributed to the band's literature, so that the point has almost been reached where a
school band's entire repertoire can be chosen from good,
original band music. The gradual removal of the band's
former reliance upon orchestral transcriptions, however,
emphasizes the need to supply more widespread opportunity
for orchestral training so that the great symphonic heritage
will remain available.

A recent and noteworthy influence on American composition has been that of the Contemporary Music Project,

funded by the Ford Foundation and administered by the Music Educators National Conference. This effort has included the support of composers-in-residence in public secondary schools as well as the sponsorship of experimental projects in the restructuring of traditional patterns of instruction in music theory and related subjects.[17]

IMPLICATIONS FOR FUTURE DIRECTIONS

One of the more obvious developments in music education is that the schools have assumed nearly the whole responsibility for the citizen's musical training. Before the creation of schools, society itself accomplished music education. Then, when music in the schools failed to perform the necessary educational functions, other agencies were forced to do so. That is, when the medieval schools were concerned only with musical mathematics, the churches trained their own performing musicians. When the church schools taught only sacred music, the guilds were able to teach the secular. School music now covers all these areas, being committed to the principle that every aspect of music must be its concern.

It follows that music educators must be alive to the value of their instruction; school music must affect out-of-school activities. The measure of its worth lies in the answer to this question: does the school enable the individual to participate fully in the musical life of his time?

Indeed, where music education has flourished, it has always contributed directly to social unity and development. Its objectives were specifically drawn in terms of values important to society. The Greeks supported music education because it attempted to produce a rounded individual—one of strong character and of physical and intellectual grace. In America, music was admitted to the schools for the specific purpose of establishing a common musical literacy, useful in the sacred and secular life of the time.

[17] See *Contemporary Music Project, Experiments in Musical Creativity*, Music Educators National Conference, Washington, D.C., 1966.

Music education has undergone many trying periods simply because it became separated from the primary social values. In times past music education has been used to further the aims of clericalism, authoritarian ideology, or a particular social class. Democratic values, however, demand that school music concern itself with elevating the useful powers of every individual. Music education can no longer pride itself on widening the horizons of a selected few—if the rest are to be left in musical delinquency.

The inherent purposes of music in society can never be achieved, however, when music educators fail to stay in tune with cultural change. Greek music educators retreated to musical mathematics when confronted with new musical usages and henceforth lost effective contact with the art. It would be just as perilous to ignore the fact that the modern American spends much of his time watching motion pictures and television programs and is surrounded by radios and jukeboxes. The light and popular music which emanates from such machines is necessarily a concern of the school.

It is apparent that American society has been undergoing some critical readjustments which are going to affect the work of the schools and of the school music program. The former preoccupation with the cold war and with scientific values has been succeeded by successive reforms in the area of civil rights. The war in Vietnam re-created strong currents of pacifism and isolationism. Riots and assassinations followed in the wake of continued economic inequality and urban racism. A large segment of the youth turned its back on older values and traditions to create the passive hippie movement on one hand, the militant campus activists on the other hand.

School music has survived these developments. In fact, it may well have profited in relative position, since there seems to be more interest in ideas and aesthetic values and less in materialistic goals. The demand is to "tell it like it is."

One of the principal difficulties school music faces is to be fair to the diverging values of rich and poor, old and young. The music of any one segment of society is not always acceptable to the other segments. The problem is to maintain contact with the rapidly evolving musical life of the times without abandoning our musical heritage. As teachers, what kinds of music can we most usefully employ? The most honest answer, it would seem, is to use whatever music of today seems to possess the most aesthetic merit, along with that of the past which can still speak to the youth.

For it is another lesson of history that school music strengthens itself by its contributions to the musical art. If the school is to take unto itself the major responsibility for cultural transmission, then it must make sure that the vital elements are preserved and strengthened. The schools must not repeat the error of the quadrivium. They must promote good American popular music and serious compositions; they must supply discriminating musical artists and orchestral musicians; they must provide audiences which are appreciative of worthwhile musical advances. Above all, the schools must resist degenerative tendencies in all these areas. In this regard, it seems essential to widen instruction in the string and keyboard and folk instruments.

Possibly the most recurrent error in the past has been the failure of instruction to remain consistent with the nature of the art. It must be evident that music is neither an intellectual pastime nor a display of technical acrobatics. It should be equally clear that the speedy "ten easy lessons" plan is actually impractical. Rigid short-cut methods simply cannot cope with the amazing subtlety of man and music. The true objectives of school music require a type of instruction which highlights the aesthetic experience with music itself—a methodology of breadth, patience, and inspiration.

School music has sometimes betrayed a sense of insecurity. Teachers may be found who will join every new band-wagon. If people want size and magnitude, these teachers will supply it. If showmanship is the thing, they will excel in it. Surely it is necessary first to consider the nature of music. It has always been found to be an intimate thing, ill-served by high-pressure methods.

Such inconsistencies may be a natural consequence of

the long-standing tradition that musicianship is a highly skilled trade. At least, this has been a common belief since the time of Alexander the Great. It is also quite true that people constitutionally avoid the status of beginner or incompetent. To convince such people that they are not musically incompetent, the music teacher surrounds his activity with a facade of rapid progress and massive achievement.

This sort of thing has never been found to serve the cause of music education. Music is *not* a specialty reserved to the talented; it is universally important to every human being and his culture. It can be taught frankly on that basis. History proves that even the higher branches of the profession of music—teaching, musicology, composition, and professional performance—are not mutually exclusive. How much more important it is to realize that every child can be provided all the ingredients of authentic musical experience. This is the historic mission of music education.

SUMMARY

Long before man entered the spotlight of history he had established music as a cultural factor and had an effective method of music education. Youth imitated their elders in performing the various ceremonial customs. As schools developed in ancient civilizations, music was a natural subject of instruction, and the Greeks regarded music as a central element in creating the stable, gracious citizen. Schoolmen in pagan Rome and in Europe during the Middle Ages numbered music as one of the seven liberal arts, treating it as a mathematical science. It fell to the musicians of the Church and among the common people to maintain the necessary practical and creative instruction in music. Renaissance society saw in music an art of intrinsic beauty and ennobling qualities. Its instruction was also valuable in meeting the needs of hymn-singing Protestant congregations. Music guilds developed their own preprofessional instruction pattern.

These forms evolved directly into the modern European system, with its rather split-track plan of musical training.

The American colonists had no such institutions and were forced to set up singing schools in the interests of better religious services. The musical life of the nation slowly advanced, and with the establishment of the free public schools, music was installed in the curriculum. Music in the schools was greatly aided by Pestalozzian principles, by the touring European artist, and by improved teacher preparation. The progressive education movement provided an additional stimulus to school music. During the twentieth century the instrumental program made its great advance, allied to the system of class instruction and the school band. Music teachers organized and developed the pattern of contests, festivals, and music camps. The mass dissemination of music has affected recent efforts in music education. Today, music education offers its benefits rather universally and has maintained its cultural influence in several important respects.

There are many implications in the record of music education which may serve to illuminate future paths. The historical foundations of music education point up the increasing responsibilities of the profession in regard to both society and the inherent qualities of music.

QUESTIONS FOR DISCUSSION

1. What is meant by *culture*? What is its relation to music and to music education?
2. What was the purpose of music education in primitive times? How was it accomplished? How extensive was it? Are there any parallels in contemporary society?
3. What was the position of music education in ancient Greece? Upon what basis was it justified? Do you think their objectives are legitimate for today's schools?
4. How was music taught as one of the "seven liberal

arts?" What kind of musicianship resulted? Why were the *scholae cantorum* established? How was education in practical secular music conducted in the Middle Ages? What training institution was developed?

5. What were the implications of humanism for music education? What were the results?

6. Why was musical literacy important to leaders of the Reformation? Would you say their measures were successful?

7. What are the main institutions and purposes of music education in Europe today? Can you identify the roots from which they have grown? Describe the possibilities open to European youth in music education.

8. Why was music important to the American colonists? What difficulties did they face in this regard? What institution evolved to meet their need?

9. What were the music conventions? What modern phenomena do they resemble?

10. Upon what premise was music established in the public schools? Why did Pestalozzian theory assist in its entrenchment within the curriculum?

11. Describe the growth of professional music in America. What long-term effect did the traveling artist have upon school music?

12. How did music fit in with the idea of progressive education? What influence has this movement had upon music in the curriculum?

13. How did instrumental music arise in the schools? How did the system of class instruction favor the formation of school bands? What other influences aided in building the school-band movement? Trace the development of music contests and of professional organization of music teachers.

14. How do radio, television, recordings, and movies affect school music? On the whole, would you consider them more useful than harmful? What is likely to be the long-term effect of these technological factors?

15. How would you describe school music today? To what extent are the benefits available to the school population? How adequate are its teachers and their facilities?
16. What does history teach us about the goals of school music? What dangers must be avoided in the future?
17. State your position on the place of youth music in the school music program. What are the relative roles of the music teacher and students in conducting instruction in this style of music? Is this style of music worthwhile in itself or as a means to understanding other styles?
18. What would constitute a reasonable attitude on the part of American music educators toward methods developed in other countries such as Orff, Kodály and Suzuki?
19. To what extent should music programs in inner city schools differ from programs in suburban, small city, and rural schools?
20. What possibilities do you see for using electronic music and other types of experimental music for stimulating creativity in students?

SELECTED REFERENCES

American Music Conference. *Report on Amateur Instrumental Music in the United States*, American Music Conference, Chicago, 1968 and each ensuing year.

Barzun, Jacques. *Music in American Life*, Doubleday & Company, Inc., New York, 1956.

Birge, Edward B. *History of Public School Music in the United States*, Music Educators National Conference, Washington, 1966.

Britton, Allen P. "Music in Early American Public Education: A Historical Critique," *Basic Concepts in Music Education*, National Society for the Study of Education Fifty-seventh Yearbook, Chicago, 1958, Part I, pp. 195-211.

Carpenter, Nan Cooke. "Music in Medieval Universities," *Journal of Research in Music Education*, 3(2):136-144, Fall, 1955.

Davison, Archibald T. *Music Education in America*, Harper & Brothers, New York, 1926.

Ewen, David. *Music Comes to America*, Thomas Y. Crowell Company, New York, 1942.

International Conference on the Role and Place of Music in the Education of Youth and Adults. *Music in Education* United Nations Educational, Social and Cultural Organization, Paris, 1954.

Kaufman, Helen L. *From Jehovah to Jazz*, Dodd, Mead & Company, Inc., New York, 1937.

Lahee, Henry. *Annals of Music in America*, Marshall Jones Company, Boston, 1922.

Lang, Paul Henry. *Music in Western Civilization*, W. W. Norton & Company, Inc., New York, 1941.

Lang, Paul Henry, ed. *One Hundred Years of Music in America*, G. Schirmer, Inc., New York, 1961.

Lehman, Paul R. "Federal Programs in Support of Music," *Music Educators Journal*, 55:1, September 1968, pp. 51-53, 117-120.

Nettl, Bruno *Music in Primitive Culture*, Harvard University Press, Cambridge, Mass., 1956.

NEA Research Division *Music and Art in the Public Schools*, Research Monograph 1963-M-3, National Education Association, Washington, 1963.

Rockefeller Panel Report *The Performing Arts: Problems and Prospects*, McGraw-Hill Book Company, New York, 1965.

Rusk, Robert R. *The Doctrines of the Great Educators*, Macmillan & Co., Ltd., London, 1954.

Scholes, Percy A. *The Puritans and Music in England and New England*, Oxford University Press, London, 1934.

Woodfill, Walter. *Musicians in English Society from Elizabeth to Charles I*, Princeton University Press, Princeton, N.J., 1953.

Philosophical Foundations
of Music Education

4 Webster defines philosophy as follows: "Literally, the love of wisdom; in actual usage, the science which investigates the most general facts and principles of reality and of human nature and conduct; specifically, . . . the science which comprises logic, ethics, aesthetics, metaphysics, and the theory of knowledge."[1] This definition encompasses the subject of technical philosophy, and a student majoring in philosophy at a university studies all these fields. Technical philosophy represents an exacting discipline and an almost boundless area of knowledge far beyond the scope of this chapter. All these fields of study do have relevance for developing a philosophical foundation for music, however, and the serious student is urged to do extensive reading in each of them.

When we speak of a philosophy of music education, we refer to a system of basic beliefs which underlies and provides a basis for the operation of the musical enterprise in an educational setting. A philosophy should serve as a source of insight into the total music program and should assist music

[1] By permission. From Webster's New International Dictionary, 2d ed., © 1959 by G. & C. Merriam Co., Publishers of the Merriam-Webster Dictionaries.

teachers in determining what the musical enterprise is all about, and how it should operate. A definitive philosophy is useful, even essential, for an operation as complex and as important as music education because concepts, theory, and practice rely on one another.

Traditionally, Americans have been suspicious of philosophy and have prided themselves on being practical people. Likewise, music teachers often grow impatient with theoretical considerations and commonly accept practice more readily than theory. The growing complexity of the technology of our society and the increasing reliance of the society on theory and basic principles, have, however, caused a dramatic change in attitudes toward philosophy. Everyone realizes, for example, that a precise theory preceded the splitting of the atom and the development of atomic energy. The achievement would have been inconceivable without an underlying basis in theory.

In recent years music educators have begun to realize that a systematic philosophy could be one of the most practical things a teacher can have. When problems arise for which the music educator has no ready answers, he can turn to his philosophical foundation for clues to appropriate solutions. Having a reasoned philosophy enables a teacher or administrator to behave rationally rather than on naive impulse or ingrained habit. Theory and practice have a relationship of mutual dependence: practice checks the soundness of theory by putting it to work and testing it out, theory checks the soundness of practice.

Everyone reading this book seriously is committed to a career of teaching music on some level. What is there about music that impels us to spend our lives and our substance preparing to teach it? What is there about music that can sustain us through a liftime of contact with it? What is the nature of the aesthetic musical experience? What qualities do music and the musical experience have that justify their inclusion in the school curriculum? In summary, *why teach music?* The answers to these questions constitute the framework for a philosophy of music education, and the purpose of this chapter is to present ideas relevant to answering these questions.

THE PURPOSE OF A PHILOSOPHY OF MUSIC EDUCATION

The questions that have been asked are not academic. Having sound answers to them is of primary importance to everyone teaching music or preparing to teach music. What can a body of sound underlying beliefs, that is, a philosophy of music education, do for the music teacher?

In the first place, having a sound philosophy of music education inspires and lightens the work of the music teacher. Every teacher encounters difficulty and discouragement in the course of his work. Involvement in teaching day after day presents highly complex problems, some of which appear to be insoluble at the time. Even the most skillful teacher encounters failure in teaching. Some classes or individual students present most discouraging problems and appear to make little or no progress. The discouraged or beaten teacher of music is a total loss. The very nature of the subject requires constant enthusiasm and inspired teaching. A body of underlying beliefs about music and passionate enduring faith in its worth, to which the teacher can turn for inspiration and guidance, are essential for a lifetime of music teaching.

Second, a philosophy of music education serves to guide and give direction to the efforts of the teacher. All teaching is an application of the philosophy of the teacher. If his philosophy is vague and ill-defined, his efforts are likely to be random, unfocused, and inconsistent. A well-formulated and comprehensive philosophy, on the other hand, permeates every aspect of his teaching. It serves as an important source of principles and helps him decide whom to teach, what to teach, and how to teach. Objectives, curriculum content, course content, methods of teaching, supervision, and administration are all a direct reflection of the philosophy of the school and the teacher.

Third, a sound philosophy of music education helps the music teacher clarify and explain the importance of music to his colleagues and to laymen. Support for music from all people concerned with the school—administrators, other faculty, and parents—is essential if the music program is to extend or even maintain its present status and accomplishments. This is especially essential in times of educational crisis such as these when there is constant pressure for undue emphasis on the utilitarian, the technical, and the material aspects of life to the detriment of the moral, emotional, spiritual, and human values. Forces are increasingly at work which threaten the music program. In the minds of many, education in music and the other arts is not an essential part of basic education but a peripheral area to be tolerated if convenient and to be done without when difficulty arises. The fate of music programs during the depression years and in the current crisis of American schools gives ample evidence of the importance of this function of a philosophy and the necessity for having music educators who are prepared to defend the music program and garner support for it.

Thus, it can readily be seen that in order to be equipped for his profession every music teacher must base his professional life on a firm philosophical foundation. Let us now proceed to an examination of the areas pertinent to the formulation of a philosophy of music education.

BUILDING A PHILOSOPHY OF MUSIC EDUCATION

John Dewey cites the common isolation of art products from the human conditions under which they were created and says that the first task of one who is writing on the philosophy of fine arts is "to restore continuity between the refined and intensified forms of experience that are works of art and the everyday events, doings and sufferings that are universally recognized to constitute experience."[2]

Many forces in present-day society tend to broaden the chasm between ordinary experience and aesthetic experience. All the arts are generally relegated to a special place of limbo, a "higher" place to be sure, but the higher the pedestal on which they are placed, the more remote they become from the everyday life of the people and the more the average man tends to disassociate himself from art objects and experience with them. Music is relegated to the concert hall; plastic arts, painting, and sculpture, to the museum. Even many devotees of the arts tend to compartmentalize their lives and think of their aesthetic experience as being apart from their ordinary existence, and the common man is prone to consider the aesthetic world a never-never land in which he has little or no interest or stake, something so precious and strange that he has no need for it. He thinks of art objects and art experience as being the sole property of a small, rather peculiar set of people of whom he is rather suspicious and whom he understands almost not at all. This situation exists at a time when mass media and mass music education serve to bring unprecedented numbers of people into contact with music, but the passing years have seen a steady decline in the amount of serious music on radio and television channels. It is clear that casual contact with great art does not develop an art-conscious person.

Now this has not always been so. In earlier civilizations aesthetic activities, objects, and ideas played a significant role in the life of the community. Everyday life was enhanced by a wide range of expressive activity. Household utensils and instruments for war and hunting were fashioned with extreme concern for the delight of the senses. Religious rites and celebrations were marked by dancing and pantomime.

[2] Reprinted by permission of G. P. Putnam's Sons from *Art As Experience* by John Dewey. Copyright 1934 by John Dewey. Copyright renewed 1962 by Roberta A. Dewey.

Drama, music, painting, sculpture, and architecture were closely woven into the fabric of everyday living.

In the earlier years of our own culture aesthetic experience and ordinary experience had a close relationship. Harvest celebrations, frontier country square dances, and so on, were shot through and through with aesthetic import. The singing school, the singing convention, and the family and group songfests which dominated our musical life in an earlier day were likewise manifestations of a need for aesthetic experience. None of these was remote from life nor were they considered effete or effeminate. On the contrary, they were vital, highly charged forces in the sentient life of the people.

These facts give us important clues to the understanding of the aesthetic experience, namely, that all art experience is closely connected with the qualities of ordinary experience and that ordinary experience can grow naturally and normally into aesthetic experience. There is a continuum between the two.

THE FORM OF EXPERIENCE

For the conception of the aesthetic experience as being closely connected with and related to ordinary experience to have meaning, an understanding of the quality of ordinary experience is essential. The life of every living creature consists basically of reaction to its environment. If the environment contains elements to satisfy basic needs, the creature may thrive and find fulfillment in living. If the environment lacks the conditions and qualities essential for survival, the creature perishes forthwith. Even in a favorable environment all living creatures encounter dangers and threats to their well-being and must draw upon the environment to satisfy their needs. Hunger for food, for example, indicates a lack of adjustment with the environment, and the hungry creature must reach out into the environment to satisfy its hunger and return itself to a stage of adjustment or equilibrium. The process of life then consists of a constant flux between lack of adjustment and adjustment, a constant movement between disequilibrium and integration with the environment. Mere existence is accomplished when basic needs are gratified. Life is enhanced when, as a result of reaching out into the environment to restore its equilibrium, the creature attains a more highly integrated and more satisfying adjustment with the environment than it previously enjoyed.

Dewey emphasizes the fact that the basis for aesthetic experience is found in the rhythm of ordinary creature existence:

> These biological commonplaces are something more than that; they reach to the roots of the esthetic in experience. The world is full of things that are indifferent and even hostile to life; the very processes by which life is maintained tend to throw it out of gear with its surroundings. Nevertheless, if life continues and if in continuing it expands, there is an overcoming of factors of opposition and conflict; there is a transformation of them into differential aspects of a higher powered and more significant life. The marvel of organized, of vital adaptation through expansion (instead of by contraction and passive accommodation) actually takes place. Here in germ are balance and harmony attained through rhythm. Equilibrium comes about not mechanically and inertly but out of, and because of, tension. . . . Form is arrived at when a stable, even though moving, equilibrium is reached.[3]

Even though this rhythmic movement between the loss and restoration of integration is characteristic of all living creatures, it is with man that the movement becomes conscious, and it is from the material of this rhythm that man forms his purposes. Man has the cognitive capacity to recognize the sources of equilibrium and disequilibrium in his environment and finds conscious satisfaction in overcoming obstacles which disrupt or threaten his equilibrium. Man's thinking

[3] Ibid., p. 14.

takes place at two junctures in his experience: (1) he contemplates all the conditions of his environment and identifies immediate and potential problems and threats to his equilibrium, and (2) when confronted with the discord implicit in disequilibrium, he reflects on the means of attaining equilibrium. The entire rhythmic movement is emotionally charged. Emotional excitement accompanies each break, either actual or impending, in the equilibrium he has achieved. He values the inner peace and satisfaction that come from making terms with his environment and prizes the struggle he experienced in coming into adjustment with the conditions of existence. Each experience not only brings about a period of equilibrium but also gives man new resources for gaining an even more propitious and satisfying adjustment. Thus, each period of adjustment marks not only the end of the past search for equilibrium but the beginning of a new search. At times a person may attempt to "rest on his laurels" and try to prolong unduly the period of consummation of a past experience. That gives him no satisfaction, however, because such prolongation represents withdrawal from experience and an inevitable loss of vitality.

The thing that sustains man in his constant struggle with his environment and pushes him on to fresh strivings to overcome obstacles is his all-pervading memory of that satisfaction that comes from fulfillment in experience. Thus, from birth to death man glories in experience, struggles with his environment, overcomes obstacles, attains new purposes, plots new courses of action, and finds intense satisfaction in the fulfillment of his purposes. This ordinary experience, when it includes anticipation of, and participation in, conflict leading to consummation, has within it the roots of aesthetic experience.

Prizing the rhythm of experience and finding fulfillment in experience, man has interest in objects which exemplify the conditions surrounding the realization of fulfillment or harmony For this reason he receives aesthetic pleasure from natural objects and natural phenomena which exhibit the stress-release, want-fulfillment, ebb-flow rhythmic pattern of his own experience. He finds fulfillment and pleasure in contemplating the surf as each wave gathers energy from a remote source and moves relentlessly to the beach or rocks, in a bolt of lightning flashing across the sky followed inexorably by a clap of thunder, and in the countless other natural phenomena which we call *beautiful*.

AESTHETIC EXPERIENCE

The same conditions in man that enable him to gain aesthetic pleasure from natural phenomena embodying the struggle-fulfillment rhythm also account for his capacity to fashion concrete objects of artistic import which express the struggle-fulfillment concept. The artist, prizing highly the phase of experience in which union is achieved, "does not shun moments of resistance and tension. He rather cultivates them, not for their own sake, but because of their potentialities, bringing to living consciousness an experience that is unified and total."[4] The capacity of man to respond to art objects likewise is due to his ability for conscious contemplation of the rhythm of life experience. When an artist fashions an art object, whether it be a sculpture, a painting, or a piece of music, he is expressing his conscious concept of man's experience embodying the rhythm of struggle and fulfillment. The object is both the result of such experience and the expression of the experience, and it serves as a vehicle by which other men can find additional meaning in experience and undergo new experience. It serves both the artist and the viewer as a symbol of the struggle-fulfillment rhythm of experience.

The heightened quality of man's experience in comparison with animal experience Dewey ascribes to man's excelling in "complexity and minuteness of differentiation." As a result, man has capacity and necessity for more comprehensive and exact relationships among the constituents of his

[4] Ibid., p. 15.

being. According to Dewey, "As an organism increases in complexity, the rhythms of struggle and consummation in relation to its environment are varied and prolonged, and they come to include within themselves an endless variety of subrhythms. The designs of living are widened and enriched. Fulfillment is more massive and more subtly shaded."[5]

Langer,[6] on the other hand, identifies a basic need peculiar to the human being but notably absent in all but the more highly developed animals, namely, the need to symbolize experience. She characterizes man as a symbol-making, symbol-using, symbol-responding creature who transforms experience by means of symbols.

Schoen[7] recognizes the close relationship of ordinary experience and aesthetic experience and provides a meaningful analysis of the two. According to Schoen, ordinary experience (the world of common affairs) encompasses knowing and feeling for the sake of action. Knowing and feeling in ordinary experience are prized for their survival value. The roots of intellectual experience and aesthetic experience lie in knowing and feeling in ordinary experience. The difference is that in intellectual experience knowing is prized for its own sake and in aesthetic experience feeling is prized for its own sake.

Aesthetic experience, like ordinary experience, has qualities of undergoing and doing and embodies the rhythm of struggle and fulfillment. Ordinary experience has aesthetic qualities if it is vital and conscious of movement through obstacles toward fulfillment. Ordinary experience has practical, emotional, and intellectual properties. It is practical in that the person is interacting with his environment; it is intellectual in that the person finds meaning in it; it is

---

[5] Ibid., p. 23.

[6] Susanne K. Langer, *Philosophy in a New Key*, New American Library, New York, 1948.

[7] Max Schoen, *The Understanding of Music*, Harper & Brothers, New York, 1945.

emotional in that perceptive feeling binds all the parts of the experience into a whole. Ordinary experience is either mainly practical or intellectual depending upon the purposes that initiate and control it. The consummation of a practical experience is valued for the concrete results attained. Thus, the farmer transforming an uncultivated patch into a field undergoes a practical experience. He operates under the impulsion of the need for a crop and struggles with obstacles to his purpose. He reflects on the best way to clear and plow the field. He garners his past experience to assist him and uses his knowledge about such things as climate, type of soil, the market, etc., to decide what and when to plant. These constitute the intellectual element of his experience. He is conscious of the results of his efforts, can conceive of the finished product, and anticipates the consummation of his experience. These constitute the aesthetic element of his experience.

The consummation of an intellectual experience is valued for the conclusion reached, a formula or truth which adds to the sum of knowledge and which can be used for subsequent inquiry.

In a work of art, on the other hand, there occurs no self-sufficient, discrete conclusion. The end is significant not in itself but only in relation to all the other parts. The recapitulation is not the movement in sonata allegro form. It has importance only as the culmination of all that has come before in the movement. We do not value the recapitulation of a sonata movement as an entity in the way we may value the field that the farmer produced or the formula that the scientist developed. This provides the clue to a distinctively aesthetic experience, namely, that it is a complete experience on its own account. Its worth depends not on our discovering the "deposit" of the experience but on our perceiving and undergoing the producer's expression of his own doing and undergoing in visual or aural materials. An experience is aesthetic when resistance, tension, excitement, and emotion are transformed into a movement toward fulfillment and completion.

THE MUSICAL EXPERIENCE

The question of the nature of the musical experience has occupied the attention of countless philosophers and musicians. Discussions of the question fall roughly into two categories: those based on a romantic conception of musical art, and those based on an empirical conception.

According to the romantic conception music, along with the other arts, is part of a transcendental world, an almost supernatural phenomenon, which has an existence all its own with little or no relationship to the world itself. The artist is considered an inspired being who alone has connection with the world of art and who through inspiration and genius is called to interpret the artistic sphere for ordinary human beings. Thus, the artist is infallible and never subject to the control or criticism of ordinary mortals. An artist is the sole arbiter of quality in art, and the proper role of the ordinary man is to accept, revere, and try to understand the results of the artist's divine inspiration. Artistic inspiration is on somewhat the level of religious inspiration and worthy of the same type of reverence and unquestioning acceptance. In the view of the romantic conception the capacity to approach the condition of the artist and to find meaning in art is dependent upon the amount of "sensitivity" with which a person has been endowed. Art in full measure is only for a few and others can only worship from afar or remain untouched by it.

The previous discussion must have revealed that the romantic conception of art and music is unacceptable to the present authors. They hold, on the other hand, that music and all the arts are human phenomena growing out of human experience and having roots in ordinary experience.

Music is an expression of the struggle-fulfillment rhythm of human living. Tone affects all the bodily processes—respiration, heart beat, blood pressure—musculature, the visceral system, and the nervous system. This physiological sensitivity to tone provides the basis for the responsiveness of all human beings to music. Coupled with this basic responsiveness to tone are these psychological factors: (1) man's consciousness of the rhythmic pattern of life processes, (2) his responsiveness to objects which symbolize the struggle-fulfillment rhythmic pattern, and (3) the delight that he receives from perceiving symbols which embody the fulfillment-directed experience.

All human experience is composed of movement taking place in time and space, and all experience is accompanied by feeling. The function of the arts is to symbolize the feeling of movement in time and space. The movement in actual experience takes place in actual time and actual space. The space involved in a picture is not actual space in the same sense that the space of a natural landscape is actual. The space involved in a picture is unrelated to the space of actual experience and is called "virtual."[8] Likewise, music takes place in time, but it is not actual time in which we arise, eat our breakfast, and go to work. The time in music is again virtual time, and what music does is give us an illusion of the passage of time. "Musical duration is an image of what might be termed 'lived' or 'experienced' time—the passage of life that we feel as expectations becomes 'now' and 'now' turns into an unalterable fact. Such passage is measurable only in terms of sensibilities, tensions and emotions; and it has not merely a different measure, but an altogether different structure from practical or scientific time."[9]

All human experience, including experience of feeling, has form. To designate the form of experience the extremes of experience are labeled with such words as growth and decay, birth and death, ebb and flow, intensity and resolution, struggle and fulfillment, excitement and calm, and so on. Such is the pattern or form of the life of feeling, and "the pattern of music is that of the same form worked out in pure, measured sound and silence. Music is the tonal analogue of the emotive life."[10]

Music fulfills the essential relationship to the life of

---

[8] Susanne K. Langer, *Feeling and Form*, Charles Scribner's Sons, New York, 1953, pp. 169-187.

[9] Ibid., p. 109. Reprinted by permission of the publisher.

[10] Ibid., p. 27.

feeling that any symbol must bear to what it means, i.e., the symbols and the object symbolized must have some common logical form. It likewise fulfills other requirements of an operating symbol, i.e., (1) music is easier to perceive and to handle than human feelings; and (2) musical forms can be invented, altered, repeated, uttered, and recalled at will. Human feeling is subject to none of these manipulations. "Sound is a negotiable medium, capable of voluntary composition and repetition, whereas feeling is not; this trait recommends tonal structures for symbolic purposes."[11]

The present authors maintain with Dewey that the aesthetic experiencing of music is closely related to ordinary experience, and with Langer that "the function of music is not stimulation of feeling but expression of it; and furthermore, not the symptomatic expression of the feelings that beset the composer but a symbolic expression of the forms of sentience (i.e., feeling) as he understands them. It bespeaks his imagination of feeling rather than his own emotional state and expresses what he *knows about* the so-called 'inner life.' "[12]

If music is a symbol, what does it symbolize? To clarify the answer to this question a basic understanding of the symbol function is essential. There are four elements in the symbol function: (1) the subject, the person using the symbol; (2) the object, the thing symbolized; (3) the symbol itself; and (4) the conception of the object.

To use an example from language, let us assume that you and I are the subjects; the object is an article that people sit on; the symbol is the word *chair*. Your and my conceptions of *chair* may vary somewhat, but both of us have a common concept of what a chair is, namely, something to sit on. Thus, we can use the symbol *chair* to think about and talk about an object of which we have a common concept even though the object is not present and our conceptions of

[11] Ibid., p. 27.
[12] Ibid., p. 28.

the object may not be identical. The word *chair* has been applied to the object by common agreement and usage and denotes a particular class of object. The essence of language is denotation, the application of a symbol to an object.

Music likewise is a symbol, but of a different order, what Langer has called "an unconsummated symbol."[13] Music does not function denotatively. The tone C has no assigned meaning; nor does the C chord, C-E-G; nor does a melodic pattern moving either up or down from the dominant tone to the tonic. Thus, music can have no assigned connotation. It does, nevertheless, have all the other earmarks of a symbol. In music the symbolic elements function as follows: (1) the subject is a person (composer, performer, or listener); (2) the object is the ways or forms of human feeling; (3) the symbol is tonal motion in virtual space; and (4) the conception of the object (the ways of human feeling) varies from one subject to another as a result of the differences in the experience each has undergone and the understanding each has developed.

In summary, then, the tonal motion in music symbolizes the subject's conception or understanding of the ways of human feeling.

Recognition of music as a symbol has brought many people to grief because of the cultural pervasiveness of our most highly developed symbol system, language. They have been led to the conclusion that, if music and language are both symbolic, it should be reasonable to impute to music many of the characteristics of language. Thus, we hear much talk about "the language of music" and such romantic phrases as "music, the universal language." If this error in thinking led only this far, it would not be disastrous; but it has led many musicians and especially music teachers to damaging conclusions and highly questionable practices. These include the notions that music has definite meanings, that music can convey specific emotions, that the best road

---

[13] Langer, *Philosophy in a New Key*, p. 240.

to music appreciation is verbalizing the "meaning" of the music, and that musical structure may be defined in terms of the structure of language.

Music is not a language simply because, unlike language, the elements of music do not have an assigned meaning and the essence of language is the assignment of meanings to words. Musical elements do not function in this way, and any imposition of the function of language on music inevitably confuses musical understanding. But, you may ask, if music is not a language, what is it and what does it mean? The answer is simple. Music is a form, a form which has significance as a symbol of the rhythm of life experience. The form of music bears a close analogy to the life of feeling, and since the material of music is sensuous material to which the human being is responsive, it is capable of having import. "This import," writes Langer, "is the pattern of sentience—the pattern of life itself, as it is felt and directly known."[14]

RESPONSES TO MUSIC

The characteristics of the musical experience having been sketched broadly, attention must be given to some specific questions which inevitably arise in a consideration of the musical experience. First of all, what is a musical response to music? Some people operate on the assumption that any response to music is a musical response and attach small significance to the various kinds or levels of response. It is well known that people respond to music in highly different ways. For example, one person may habitually tap his foot on hearing music and find great pleasure in highly rhythmic music but find no basis for response in a composition in which rhythm is not the dominant characteristic. Another may attend the melody closely, try to hum along with the performance, and desire to recall the melody of each compo-

[14] Langer, *Feeling and Form*, p. 31.

sition he hears. Such a person would be likely to reject all compositions lacking a singable melody or a composition in which the melody was out of his vocal range. Another person may find pleasure in day dreaming while listening to music and judge all music by the kind of opportunity it provides him for fantasy making.

The first two of these responses are directly related to musical elements while the third actually has little to do with the music itself. Although no one would wish to deny to any person the mode of responding to music that brings him pleasure, it is believed that responses which depend on attending music elements are preferable to responses to which music is only incidental.

Responses to music, then, can be categorized as unmusical or musical. Unmusical responses include associating music with images, memories, specific feelings, moods and stories and scenes. Because of the very nature of music—its abstractness, the effects of tone on the whole body, the possibility of associating natural sounds and language sounds with musical sounds—and because of the fact that certain kinds of music become culturally associated with daily life situations, this is admittedly a "natural" way of responding to music and may be a proper mode of response for all people some of the time. It is not, however, acceptable for any person all of the time because it fails to take full advantage of the potentialities of music for abstract experience on an aesthetic level divorced from the mediocrity of ordinary experience. From the music educator's point of view these are not responses to be cultivated. In fact they need no cultivation; they occur almost universally without guidance or organized learning. If the music education program can have no result that would not take place in the ordinary course of events without music education, then it has no reason for existence.

At the other end of the scale lies another response to music which often occurs as a result of extensive training in music. This has been called the technical or critical response. Many musicians have developed this kind of response to the point that they do not really like music except for the opportunity it gives them to criticize each performance they hear or participate in. They complain about tempo, pitch, balance, tone, or some other aspect of each performance they encounter. This is not to imply that there is not a place for technical criticism in the life of the musician. It denies vehemently the primacy of the critical response and contends that unless a felt response to the musical expressiveness precede and endow the critical response, the musician or critic is divorcing himself from the art of music and, furthermore, is undermining the authenticity of his criticism.

Responses to music differ in level and degree of subtlety, but they have one common characteristic, namely, they rely on human responsiveness to tonal materials and to tonal patterns by means of which music symbolizes struggle-fulfillment rhythm, the form of human feeling. Musical responsiveness is universally present in the human species. Although they differ in the degree of sensitivity to the musical stimulus, all persons can respond musically and aesthetically to the tonal stimulus. The primary objective of music education must be to develop the innate musical responsiveness of every individual to the highest possible level and to nurture and expand his potential for aesthetic experience.

The primary characteristic of musical responses to music is the quality of conceiving and reacting to the expressive form present in every musical composition. Expressive form refers to patterns of tension and release which enables us to conceive the emotional idea expressed by the composer. The term *expressive form* used here differs from structural form, which has to do with the organization of the parts of a musical composition. Hearing and feeling patterns of intensity and release constitute the first requisite of musical hearing and musical performance. Without this the listener perceives nothing and the performer expresses nothing. The first task of music education must be to develop this sensitivity without any intrusions, intellectual, mathematical, or critical. Unfortunately, this task is one frequently neglected at all levels of musical education. Excessive talk about music, excessive concern with technique, and reliance on extramusical factors to gain the interest of students all represent practices inimical to the development of sensitivity and responsiveness to the expressive form of music. Widely practiced teaching methods such as baiting each piece of music with a story or descriptive account and telling stories about composers and musicians are not conducive to developing responsiveness to music. The former represents a distorted view of the nature of the musical response; the latter can have meaning only if prior expressive experience with music has created a desire in the pupil to know something of the composer and the circumstances surrounding the composition of the music

The following chapter on musical learning treats musical meaning and perception, and the chapter on methods of teaching deals at length with techniques for developing musical responsiveness. But it is appropriate here to point out the essential character of teaching focused on this objective. What should be done is to provide a rich musical environment in the school in which every child has experience, both as a performer and listener, with a wide variety of expressive music of a difficulty consistent with the developmental level of the child and performed with the highest possible level of musicianship.

MAKING VALUE JUDGMENTS IN MUSIC

Almost everyone proceeds on the assumption that music varies in quality, that some music is better than other, that one composition is superior to another. This assumption is borne out by the fact that some musical compositions have gained and maintained a place in the permanent repertory while others, although they may achieve singular popularity for a time, are soon forgotten and revived only for their historical interest. It is also true that some music affects listeners and gives them pleasure while other music lacks appeal and leaves listeners unaffected. Thus, music does vary in quality, and the qualities that contribute to this variance are considered here.

All good music is expressive in that it embodies the composer's conception of the stress-release form of human experience. This represents the first criterion of quality in music: do its tonal patterns exhibit the rhythm of struggle and fulfillment which is analogous to the form of human feeling and in which the performer or listener can find emotional import? If a piece of music fits this criterion, it is good music. The presence of this quality is what makes such widely divergent musical compositions as "Home on the Range," "The Tennessee Waltz," "The Stars and Stripes Forever," and "St. Louis Blues" all good music. The absence of this quality makes the Czerny *Velocity Studies*, "Arkansas Traveler," or an elementary-series song written to exemplify the descending chromatic all poor music. The former group all have as their purpose and function to excite feeling. The latter group are expressive of little or nothing, their purpose is to exemplify technical problems or to provide a steady beat.

Another characteristic of good music is that it is put together with expert craftsmanship. Craftsmanship facilitates expression, but it never replaces it. Thus, music constructed by formula, such as many of the dreary products of the Schillinger system, a great deal of the music written for the movies, and the recently publicized music written by Illiac are not good music.

Having gone this far, can we go further in determining quality in music? Or, is all expressive, well-crafted music equally good? We must, and can, go further. Otherwise, efforts to improve taste and to educate people musically are a sham and a waste of time, and we may as well close up the music education shop except for developing performers.

What is it then that makes the "Leibestod" a better piece of music than "I Love You Truly" and Beethoven's *Sixth Symphony* better than Sinding's "Rustle of Spring?" All four are adequately crafted and people find expressive value in all of them, but two of them are considered ordinary and two are conceded to be great music.

Good music and great music differ in two essential characteristics: (1) the subtlety of expression and (2) the abstractness of expression. Popular music, most hymns, semi-popular music, and most folk music lack subtlety. The melodies are obvious and easily comprehended. A musical person can learn the melody in a hearing or two, and even the less musically adept can do so with limited casual contact. The harmony, likewise, is trite, straightforward, and easily antici-pated. The rhythm and structure are regular, lacking in devel-opment and variation. The thematic material of good music usually has an essential simplicity which limits the possibilities for development and variation. Some lack of development may be due not to the nature of the thematic materials but to the genre of the composition or the limited resources or intentions of the composer.

In good music, furthermore, one of the musical ele-ments usually receives predominant emphasis. In a senti-mental ballad, the melody is the significant element; in dance music, the rhythm; in mood music, perhaps the harmony or tone color. There exists a lack of integration among the elements which limits severely the expressive value. As a result, good music does not hold the interest for long. The musical person can plumb its depths easily and quickly, and it does not bear repeated hearings or contact over a period of time unless through association with an event, mood, memo-ry, emotion, and so on, it takes on meaning outside its musical meaning. For example, "The Star Spangled Banner," a good but not great piece of music, is associated with patriotism and love of country and has become an important source of symbolic experience and an important piece of music in the United States, but it is of only passing interest to citizens of other countries. Likewise, "I Love You Truly" and other songs usually associated with weddings become for many people symbolic of their feelings about their courtship and marriage and occupy an important role in evoking memo-ries and feelings of great value and significance to them.

Good music has limited expressive value in itself but may serve as a vehicle for evoking strong feeling through its association with an extramusical factor with which it becomes associated. This explains the survival of "God Bless America" after its introduction during World War II, even though it had had only passing favor when first published years before with different words.

Great music and music tending toward greatness exhibit much more subtlety both in the musical ideas themselves and in the treatment of the ideas. Melodies require closer attendance for apprehension. Ranges may be extreme, germinal ideas may be developed and varied in countless imaginative ways. In great music the thematic material, even though simple in its bare statement, has possibilities for development, variation, and manipulation that give full sweep to the imagination and inventive skill of the composer. The composer furthermore adopts for the composition the form and medium of performance that provide scope for the most artistic unfolding and presentation of the full significance of the musical idea. Harmony may likewise be complex and full of surprises. Anticipating the harmonic movement is difficult. Highly tensional harmonic movement may pervade the composition, and remote key relationships increase the intensity and heighten the fulfillment that comes with a return to the original key center. The rhythms are complex and highly developed. Complexity of form and subtle relationships among the different parts are present. And finally, all the aspects of the music—melody, harmony, rhythm, and form—are integrated into an expressive whole in which no one element predominates but all play their logical role in the expression of the struggle-fulfillment rhythm of human feeling.

Good music and great music also express different degrees on a continuum from specificity to abstractness. Both appeal to the life of feeling and call forth a felt response. Good music appeals to specific feeling on much the same level as the feelings of ordinary experience. Listening to good music may make one feel patriotic, merry, solemn, penitent, affectionate, devout, amused, inclined to dance, or whatever. Good vocal music excites highly specific feeling owing to the influence of the words. Thus, the feelings expressed by hymns, most popular songs, many folk songs, and semiclassical songs are most direct and specific. Likewise, instrumental music such as marches, highly programmatic music, dance music, and mood music calls forth specific feelings.

Great music, on the other hand, instead of calling forth specific feelings expresses the "life of feeling," a general state of feeling. Great music does not give us moods and emotions but insight into the form and structure of human feeling. To appreciate a great piece of music is to perceive the composer's and the performer's conception of the human emotional life. Great music expresses symbolically the life of feeling which cannot be expressed through language or any other medium of human expression.

What does the establishment of these standards mean in evaluating different kinds of music? It means that the more subtle and the more abstract the musical expression, the greater the piece of music. Thus, "Smoke Gets in Your Eyes" is a better piece of music than "Dark Town Strutters Ball"; "The Sounds of Silence" is better than "Home on the Range"; "St. Louis Blues" is better than "Something Stupid." "Ich Liebe Dich" is better than "I Love You Truly," but both are good music while the "Liebestod" is great music. "Funeral March of a Marionette" is good music but the "Marche Funèbre" from Beethoven's *Third Symphony* is great music.

Program music, along with film music, music written for ballet, and music incidental to a play, is unlikely to be great music. None of these kinds of music result from purely thematic thinking and development. The composer supplements his musical idiom by imagined or actual situations, subjects, or events that hold a mood or specify an emotion The quality of the music is usually directly related to the degree of restriction imposed by the situation. The composer who is required to write music conforming in intensity to a film may, if he is skillful, heighten the emotional import of the film; but his music is often insignificant when considered on its own. On the other hand, some composers do their finest work when their imaginations are stirred by an extra-musical idea. Stravinsky may be cited as one notable example. If the program or situation restrains and structures his thematic thinking and development, however, truly great music can never result. This explains the superiority of his *Orpheus* to his *The Rite of Spring*. In the former the subject gave flight to his musical imagination; in the latter the involved program inevitably intruded. In the same way a broad programmatic idea undoubtedly enabled Beethoven to write in his *Sixth Symphony* a great work embodying a fresh concept of feeling different from that found in any of his other compositions. He warned us, however, against becoming immersed in any program in connection with the symphony.

The fact is that program music must be evaluated in terms of the music itself without reference to the program. If the music is expressive and has deep emotional import in its own right, it is great music. If it requires the program to gain import, it can only be inferior music.

In addition to these standards for evaluating music on one's own, there are two important sources of value judgment which must be considered: cultural acceptance and the judgment of musical experts.

Musical taste is culturally shaped. A composition highly regarded in the Orient may evoke no response at all in the West, but the fact that generations of Orientals have found expressive value in it indicates it is either good or great music for them. We can rely somewhat on the survival of a piece of western music as an indication of expressive appeal and value. Music in which one or more generations have found significance must have expressive power and musical appeal. Unless sociological, technological, or intellectual developments have cut us off entirely from the era in which the music found favor, it will still have value for us at the present time.

For new music we must arrive at value judgments by applying our own standards and by relying on the opinions of musical experts. The critic with intensive and extensive musical experience and with accumulated skill and insight into the worth of musical compositions represents a valuable source of guidance to laymen, music students, and teachers of music in judging the worth of new music. Reliance on mass taste to select great new music cannot be seriously considered. The forces of musical tradition are strong enough to make mass acceptance of a composition that departs significantly from tradition very unlikely. Responding fully to great music requires repeated contact and familiarity. One of the unique characteristics of great music is that it bears familiarity and knowing well, and to evaluate it without contact over a period of time is unfair and dangerous.

THE POPULARIZATION OF GREAT MUSIC

A discussion of musical values directed toward teachers of music must consider attempts to make great music popular by adulterating it. Such attempts usually take the form of putting words to highly melodic passages or "jazzing up" the music. The difficulty with such practices is that they destroy the integrity of the composer's conception and pull great music down to the level of good music or worse. The addition of sentimental words to a great piece of instrumental music distorts the expressive power of the music by making the music expressive of specific feeling. Thus, "Tonight We Love" may be an attractive popular song, but it certainly is no better than hundreds of legitimately composed popular songs. Furthermore, singing the words neither brings about interest in or understanding of Tchaikovsky's music in its original form nor represents a sound beginning point for such interest and understanding.

"Jazzing" great music usually means speeding up the tempo, giving additional emphasis to the rhythm, or using instruments normally used in dance bands. Treating great music in this way may attract the transient interest of students, and they may tap their feet when listening to it and dance to it with pleasure. Exposure to music of this kind, however, can never result in the understanding of great music. Experience with great music from which the greatness has been removed accomplishes the same results as experience with ordinary popular music and nothing more.

The notion that the popularization of great music leads to a comprehension of it is based on a naive concept of the transfer of learning completely unjustified in the light of research on the subject. If the purpose of the music education program were to entertain students, jazzing great music and the addition of sentimental words to it might be in order. If, on the other hand, the development of the aesthetic potential and of musical understanding is involved, neither practice has a place in the program. Casual concern with trivial music can never achieve great purposes in music education.

THE NEW MUSICS

The aesthetic position on which the previous discussion of philosophy of music education is based may be characterized as Absolute Expressionism. It is a soundly based position and true to the nature of traditional music and responses to traditional music. It must be recognized, however, that it does not apply with the same force to recently developed music as to traditional music.

The face of music has changed and is changing so fast that it staggers the mind of the traditional musician. Only a few years ago one could talk about music and refer honestly to one essentially cohesive body of material. There is no longer *a* music. Now there are *musics*, and the new musics operate within different aesthetics.

The new musics consist primarily of two streams: (1) music based on Afro-American musical forces that maintains the elements of traditional music but in a different mix; and (2) that music, usually called experimental (Cage, Stockhausen, and others), which denies all of the traditional musical verities.

Musical developments during the mid-twentieth century have raised a new philosophical problem for music educators: what is the role of the new music in the music education program? Youth music and experimental music have become potent forces in the musical life of the world and cannot be ignored in the construction of a philosophical orientation for music education.

Youth Music

The contemporary folk music movement represents a musical and cultural phenomenon that is unique in modern times. Young people all over the country are tuned to and participating in music with an enthusiasm and devotion that are unparalled in this country. Music seems to be operating as a real social force, going far beyond the purposes of popular music of the past. Furthermore, much of the new popular music has a musical and ideological sophistication far beyond that of the typically trite popular music of the past.

Modern troubadors are writing and performing their own folk music, music which treats life and confronts the issues of the present day. The blending of rhythm and blues and country and western, initiated by Elvis Presley and refined by the Beatles and other groups, has resulted in rock in all its forms and styles. Jazz has continued to develop in new directions. The result is the first truly indigenous music of the United States: Afro-American music.

Afro-American music represents a departure from music in the European tradition in which melody and harmony were dominant with rhythm usually playing a subsidiary role. In Afro-American music the beat is the message. This music has a quality of spontaneity long missing from music in the European tradition. It is participative music, not consumable music. As such it harks back to Renaissance music which was also participative in nature. This new music represents a departure from the producer-consumer dichotomy which has dominated our concern with the music of the seventeenth, eighteenth, and nineteenth centuries even though only the music of the nineteenth century was actually based on this dichotomy. As a matter of fact, the music of the sixteenth, seventeenth, and eighteenth centuries placed great emphasis on improvisation and was influenced by musical forces both from above and below.

It should be recognized that the music program as it has operated has been based on the consumer-producer dichotomy. The essential point is that the producer-consumer dichotomy is fast losing its dominance in the world of music, and the music program needs music which is participative. Music in the Afro-American tradition fits this criterion.

Furthermore, from a sociological standpoint it is significant that with Afro-American music blacks are entering and creating a mainstream of American culture. Bringing this music into the school music program could well make a significant contribution to unifying our society.

The school music program can no longer ignore this music which has unique vitality and relevance for young people in our time. The best of it must be brought into the school music program. It can and does provide an avenue for aesthetic experience for many young people because it represents a living music of good quality which has meaning for the new generation.

Experimental Music

The field of serious music is rife with experimentation and change. A whole new concept of musical expression is emerging. Electronic music, aleatory music, new vocal sounds, and new instrumental sounds achieved both through altering traditional instruments and developing new instruments represent only a partial listing of new directions in music. The invention of magnetic tape opened up an entirely new horizon for music in which sounds are valued for their own sake, the limitations of performers do not limit the imagination of the composer, and the composer becomes one with the performer. This music operates within an entirely different aesthetic context from that of traditional music.

While it is admittedly difficult to comprehend and evaluate the results of this experimentation and change, there can be no doubt that the face of music will be changed by it. Experimental music is a part of the contemporary musical scene, and as such it deserves a place in the school music program.

WHY SHOULD MUSIC BE INCLUDED IN THE SCHOOL CURRICULUM?

Music has been included in the curricula of schools from the beginning of recorded history, and widely varying reasons for its inclusion have operated at different times. Much of the time music has been justified for the extrinsic value of musical activity, and participation in music has been considered a means to achieving ends essentially unmusical. Plato, for example, held that the great value of music lay in its usefulness in achieving social results which he considered desirable. He went so far as to proscribe the use of certain modes as immoral and lascivious. The Romans included music as one of the seven liberal arts because the mathematical aspects of music seemed fit for celestial beings, along with arithmetic, geometry, and astronomy. During the Renaissance and Reformation, Protestant elementary schools brought music into the curriculum to develop religious feelings and to save souls. Children in these schools sang hymns to further the religious objectives of the schools. Music was used in the eighteenth century to heighten the nationalistic spirit and feelings of patriotism. In American music education, extrinsic values have tended to dominate the thinking of music educators and administrators from Lowell Mason to the present day. Typically, it is claimed that music education:

includes activities and learning which develop the social aspects of life.

develops the health of the student.

aids in the development of sound work habits.

instills wholesome ideals of conduct.

aims to develop good citizenship.

improves home life.

Although all these claims have an extramusical conception of the value of music behind them, they are not all
equally farfetched. Music can be a social asset, provide a
focus for group work, and represent a rewarding endeavor in
the home. Some of the other claims, however, border on the
ridiculous. Musicians have never been known to have better
health than other people, and their posture and health habits
are not demonstrably superior. The claim for the development of work habits depends upon a highly specific view of
transfer of training which has long been proved unsound. The
claim for developing wholesome ideals of conduct apparently
stems from a notion that music has a transcendental goodness
about it that may rub off onto musical participants. The idea
that music contributes to development of citizenship seems
extremely naive since music groups do not demand a democratic way of life. Actually, they are likely to be the most
authoritarian groups in which one ever finds himself.

The authors cannot accept extrinsic values as the basis
for the function of music in the life of the human being or in
the school program. While certain values of this kind may
accrue, they do not provide the raison d'être for the music
program. Furthermore, reliance on extrinsic values inevitably
perverts and distorts the art of music and debases its true and
enduring values.

Reliance on the extrinsic values of music has provided
music education with a flimsy, unconvincing argument, because none of the claimed values are unique to music and the
musical experience. Even if music did develop better health, a
good physical education and health program would undoubtedly be more efficient. Developing wholesome ideals of conduct, at best a peripheral accomplishment of music participation, can take place more directly through religious training

and other facets of the school program. Likewise, the development of citizenship can best be achieved through civics classes, history classes, and citizenship education projects. And no reasonable person can believe that work habits developed in music are more likely to operate in other fields of endeavor than those developed in shop, home economics, and algebra classes.

In addition and most regrettably, reliance on extrinsic values of music has provided cover for scanty musical achievement, minimal musical learning, and low musical standards. The music teacher who teaches little or no music is often excused on the grounds that the children are happy or are good group members. These results are good, but they are not a direct corollary or outcome of musical experience and have little or no relevance for conducting and evaluating the music program.

After many years of justifying music education in the public schools on extramusical grounds and on extrinsic values, there has been a definite trend in recent years toward justifying the music program on the basis of the values of music itself. The intellectual leadership of the music education profession became increasingly skeptical of the worth of a philosophy for music education based on extrinsic values. Evidence of discontent appeared in articles in professional journals and in the statements of speakers at professional meetings. Furthermore, many people became aware of the increasing alienation of music education in the public schools from music programs at the college level, which resulted in a growing dichotomy in the music education enterprise based on educational level, along with a growing schism between music education and professional music. It became obvious that a program operating on the basis of extrinsic and extramusical values was inevitably incompatible with programs operating on the basis of music for its own sake and its intrinsic aesthetic value.

Other factors were influential in the discontent with a philosophy of music education based on extrinsic values. First, there occurred a tremendous increase in the number of students entering graduate programs in music education and a significant improvement in the quality of those programs. Music educators became increasingly sophisticated and learned not only in music but in philosophy and psychology. They came to understand the need for a comprehensive philosophy of music education and were no longer satisfied with having no basic beliefs or a naive theoretical framework.

A second factor was the upheaval that struck the entire educational system as a result of the successful launching of Sputnik, which dramatized the educational advances of the Soviet Union. The resulting unprecedented emphasis on science and its related academic subjects, often to the detriment of education in the humanities and the arts, forcefully brought to the attention of musicians and music teachers at both public school and college levels the necessity for closing ranks and joining forces in preserving and extending the music program at all levels.

Does the rejection of extrinsic values as the basis for the inclusion of music in the school weaken the case for music and leave it unsupported in the scramble for curricular time? By no means. Actually, it strengthens the place of music by enabling us to emphasize its positive values and to show the unique role of music education as part of aesthetic education.

Man is unique among all creatures in the extent and quality of his potential. He has physical, intellectual, ethical, and aesthetic potentials. If any aspect of his potential is neglected and undeveloped, he never attains his true stature as a human being. Responsibility for developing his physical potential is shared by the home, medical services, and the school physical and health education program. The focus of most of the school program is on developing his intellectual potential. The school, the home, the church, and community agencies share responsibility for developing his ethical potential. Although other agencies such as the home, mass media, and community influences contribute to his aesthetic development, the school has primary responsibility for helping him attain stature in this realm of meaning in which life gains some of its most worthwhile and enduring values. Through aesthetic education he finds true self-realization, insight into life values which are timeless, culturally significant, and personally satisfying. He discovers means for satisfying a basic and pervasive need of all human beings, namely, the need for symbolic experience.

Music has unique qualities that make it the most desirable medium of organized aesthetic education. Human beings are universally responsive to music and can find satisfaction and meaning through experience with it. Although there are wide variations in musical capacity and sensitivity, every person can find satisfaction and enjoyment not only as a consumer but also as a producer of music on some level and in some medium. Music is unique among the arts in lending itself to group participation. For instance, while the consumption of plastic art is an individual matter, everyone within hearing of a musical performance can perceive its meaning. Likewise, the performance of music is largely a group activity. Thus, music fits into the scheme of education more neatly than any other form of artistic endeavor and must perforce carry the major load of aesthetic education in all organized general education. Herein lies the major case for the inclusion of music in general education. Who can assail the importance of aesthetic experience in the life of the human being? Who can deny the cultural pervasiveness of the musical art? Who can doubt the cultural significance of music from the beginning of recorded history and the richness of the musical cultural heritage? Who can negate the fact that music lends itself admirably to organized instruction and group participation within the school framework? Who can fail to recognize the urgent necessity for aesthetic education in this modern day when there is a constant tendency to emphasize the material, the technological, and the intellectual aspects of life to the detriment of the spiritual and human values?

We are now in a position to state in summary form the basic tenets of our philosophy of music education. They grow out of the preceding discussion, and we believe them to be logically, musically, and educationally sound.

1. Art is the result of man's need to transform his experience symbolically.
2. Aesthetic experience grows out of and is related to ordinary experience. Aesthetic quality is the source of man's highest satisfaction in living, and while all experience that is carried on intelligently has aesthetic quality, man's most valued experience is in connection with art objects consciously and feelingly conceived and contemplated.
3. All human experience is accompanied by feeling. Music bears a close similarity to the forms of human feeling and is the tonal analogue of the emotive life.
4. Music is expressive of the life of feeling in that its movement symbolizes the movement of feeling alternating between struggle and fulfillment, intensity and release, rise and fall, movement and repose, and even, finally, life and death.
5. The import of music is not fixed; it is subjective, personal, and creative in the best sense of the word. We can fill the forms of music with any feelingful meaning that fits them.
6. Since the appeal of music is to the life of feeling, every musical experience and all experience with music must be experience of feeling.
7. Music attains significance only through its expressive appeal, and all work with music must be carried with full cognizance of its expressive appeal.
8. Every person has the need to transform experience symbolically and the capacity for symbolic experience with music.
9. The only sound basis for music education is the development of the natural responsiveness that all human beings possess.
10. The music education program should be primarily aesthetic education.
11. Every child must be given the opportunity to develop his aesthetic potential to the highest possible level through expressive experience with music, including vo-

cal and instrumental performance, listening, and composition appropriate to his developmental level.

12. Music education should be cosmopolitan, employing all kinds of music and giving recognition to the value of all kinds of music.

13. While no type of music can be ignored in the music program, major attention should be given to providing musical experience that is educative in that it leads to an aesthetic response to great music, to the clarification of musical values, and to the development of musical independence.

14. All instructional material should be musical material of the highest possible quality. All teaching should have as its primary objective the illumination of the art of music and should emphasize musical values and not extramusical values.

15. Through extensive experience with music certain extrinsic values inevitably accrue. These include the development of resources for worthwhile use of leisure time, the opportunity to participate with peers in a worthwhile group endeavor, resources for enriched home and community life, and the opportunity to discover unusual talent. Results in these areas can occur, however, only when the primary emphasis is placed on providing musical experience that is worthwhile in itself.

QUESTIONS FOR DISCUSSION

1. How do you justify the inclusion of music in the curriculum of the public school? Formulate a statement that would be meaningful and convincing to a school administrator or a group of parents.

2. This chapter contains a statement to the effect that the way a person teaches is a reflection of his philosophical orientation. Select three teachers of music you have had in public schools or college and whom you remember well. Sketch briefly the philosophical orientation of

each teacher based upon your analysis of his teaching practices and his attitude toward music and toward students.

3. What sources of symbolic experience do you value most in your own life? How do you account for the valuation you place on each type of experience you have mentioned?

4. Richard Strauss is reputed to have said that it would eventually be possible to portray the knives and forks on the table with music. Do you agree or disagree with the statement? Why? Do you think it desirable that such a development in music take place?

5. In what respects does music resemble and differ from language?

6. Do you believe that music educators are justified in attempting to raise the level of musical taste? Why?

7. If music education succeeded in developing in all school children a taste for the best in serious music, would there still be a place and demand for folk music and popular music?

8. What is your opinion of the value of instruction in such instruments as guitars and ukeleles in connection with the school music program? Do you think such instruments should be taught in the music program?

9. In what respects do you believe the music program in public schools has improved in the past ten years? In what respects has it failed to improve, or, perhaps, deteriorated?

10. Is the music education program of which you are a product consistent with the point of view expressed in this chapter? If not, what changes in the program would result if this point of view were put into effect?

11. Formulate as clearly as possible your own philosophy of music education.

12. Do the new musics (Afro-American and experimental) represent works of art? How should their development be reflected in the philosophical orientation of music educators of today and tomorrow?

SELECTED REFERENCES

Broudy, Harry S. "A Realistic Philosophy of Music Education," *Basic Concepts in Music Education*, National Society for the Study of Education Fifty-seventh Yearbook, Chicago, 1958, Part I, pp. 62-87.

Burton, William H. and Helen Heffernan. *The Step Beyond: Creativity*, National Education Association, Washington, D.C., 1964.

Cage, John. *Silence*. The M.I.T. Press, Cambridge, Mass., 1966.

Dewey, John. *Art As Experience*, Minton, Balch & Co., New York, 1934.

Diller, Angela. *The Splendor of Music*, G. Schirmer, New York, 1957.

Edman, Irwin. *Art and the Man*, W. W. Norton & Co., Inc., New York, 1939.

Jones, LeRoi. *Blues People*, William Morrow and Co., Inc., New York, 1963.

——. *Black Music*, William Morrow and Co., Inc., New York, 1968.

Langer, Susanne K. *Feeling and Form*, Charles Scribner's Sons, New York, 1953.

——. *Philosophy in a New Key*, New American Library, New York, 1948.

Leonard, George B. *Education As Ecstasy*, Delacorte Press, New York, 1968.

Leonhard, Charles. "The Next Ten Years," *Music Educators Journal*, September 1968, pp. 36-38.

McMurray, Foster. "Pragmatism in Music Education," *Basic Concepts in Music Education*, National Society for the Study of Education Fifty-seventh Yearbook, Chicago, 1958, Part I, pp. 30-61.

Meyer, Leonard B. *Emotion and Meaning in Music*, University of Chicago Press, Chicago, 1956.

Mueller, John S. "Music and Education: A Sociological Approach," *Basic Concepts in Music Education*, National

Society for the Study of Education Fifty-seventh Year-
book, Chicago, 1958, Part I, pp. 88-122.
Music Educators National Conference. *Electronic Music*, The
Conference, Washington, D.C., 1968.
———. *Perspectives in Music Education: Source Book III*, The
Conference, Washington, D.C., 1966.
———. *The Tanglewood Symposium: Music in American
Society*, The Conference, Washington, D.C., 1967.
———. *Youth Music*, The Conference. Washington, D.C.,
1969.
Pleasants, Henry. *Serious Music and All That Jazz*, Simon and
Schuster, New York, 1969.
Pratt, Carrol C. *The Meaning of Music*, McGraw-Hill Book
Co., New York, 1931.
Reimer, Bennett. *A Philosophy of Music Education*, Pren-
tice-Hall, Inc., Englewood Cliffs, N.J., 1970.
Schuller, Gunther. *Early Jazz: Its Roots and Musical Devel-
opment*, Oxford University Press, New York, 1968.
Seashore, Carl E. *Why We Love Music*, Oliver Ditson Com-
pany, Philadelphia, 1949.
Sessions, Roger. *The Musical Experience of Composer, Per-
former and Listener*, Atheneum, New York, 1962.

Foundations
of Musical Learning

5 This chapter has as its purpose the exploration of musical learning. It begins with a definition of learning, considers the nature of musical meaning, provides an analysis and description of the products of musical learning, and gives attention to the relationship between musical learning and maturation. Succeeding sections of the chapter deal with learning theories, present eleven principles of musical learning, and suggest a program for the future.

The material presented in this chapter is intended to provide a theoretical framework for the delineation of objectives in music education and to establish the basis for the derivation of methods of teaching in music education. Later chapters treat these two topics in detail.

LEARNING DEFINED

Learning is growth; learning is development; learning is experience; learning is something new that has been added; learning is a process that results in change in behavior. These are but a few of the definitions given to learning in the professional literature, but psychologists have not yet agreed on a definition acceptable to everyone. The fact is that the term *learning* has many meanings and no one generalized definition yet devised can apply to all the varied processes by which changes in human behavior occur.

Faced with this plethora of meanings for the term and the necessity for discussing musical learning within the framework of a chapter, one can only devise a definition which has for him the greatest operational value and which makes for a minimum of confusion. The present authors use the following definition for learning in school: Learning is a process which begins with a problem, progresses to the solution of the problem by the apprehension, clarification, and application of meaning and results in a change in behavior.

This definition has several advantages. First, it rightly emphasizes the central role of meaning in learning. Without meaning there can be no learning. The meaning may be obscure or scanty, or it may be of an entirely different order than we desire it to be, but meaning of some kind is an essential ingredient of learning.

A second advantage of the definition is that it implies the developmental nature of learning. Significant learning usually takes place over a period of time during which the learner refines the meaning he has apprehended and develops efficiency and precision in applying the meaning to problems. Learning by "sudden flashes of insight" undoubtedly occurs occasionally, but more commonly, learning is the result of a more-or-less extended period of exploration of a given situation and the gradual emergence of meaning.

A third advantage lies in the emphasis on the problem-solving nature of learning. The process of learning is not complete until the meaning derived from a situation has been applied to a problem. Furthermore, the definition gives recognition to the behavioral component of learning. Finally, it ties one to no particular theory of learning but enables him to use fruitful concepts developed in all kinds of experimentation on the learning process.

MEANING IN MUSIC

Having, by definition, emphasized the central role of meaning in learning, we must give attention to meaning in music. Unless the nature of musical meaning is clear, efforts to control the musical learning situation can never be efficient.

The nature of the meaning that music has for listeners and participants has excited great controversy through the years. Meyer has identified two different types of musical meaning, *absolute* meaning and *referential* meaning.[1] Absolutists hold that the meaning of music lies in the discernment of the complex relationships within a musical work. The referentialists admit the presence of these abstract meanings, but contend that music also communicates extramusical meanings related to actions, concepts, characters, and situations. The question of musical meaning has been further confused by the arguments of the formalists and expressionists. The formalists contend that the meaning of music is primarily intellectual. The expressionists argue that the musical stimulus is capable of exciting feeling.

It seems reasonable to accept the presence of both absolute and referential meaning in music. Furthermore, the capacity of music to excite feeling has been well established. It is, however, difficult to accept the notion that the appeal of music is primarily intellectual. It must be granted that music varies in the amount of its intellectual appeal and that people can be trained to search for intellectual meaning, even to the exclusion of expressive meaning. It may even be possible, as some composers and aestheticians have contended, to write music with a predominately cerebral appeal. We can assume with confidence, however, that most music has an expressive purpose and does indeed excite feeling and that both absolute and referential meanings do exist in music.

A brief summary of the general nature of meaning may

---

[1] Leonard B. Meyer, *Emotion and Meaning in Music*, University of Chicago Press, Chicago, 1956, p. 1.

serve to clarify these two types of musical meaning. Meaning of all kinds occurs as the result of a relationship among three elements in a situation: the stimulus, the consequence of the stimulus, and the observer reacting to the stimulus. The consequence indicated by the stimulus may be of the same kind as the stimulus, or the two may differ in kind. When, for example, the stimulus, thunder, indicates the consequence, rain, both are of the same kind, natural phenomena, and the meaning is called *embodied*. On the other hand, the word fire, serving as a stimulus, may be a signal that something is burning. The stimulus and the consequence differ in kind; the former is a word, the latter an event. This type of meaning is called *designative*.[2]

Both embodied and designative meaning operate in music. From the viewpoint of the absolutist, music has only embodied meaning. That is, the musical stimulus or series of stimuli points not to any extramusical concept or event but to other musical events that are about to happen. "One musical event (be it a tone, a phrase, or a whole section) has meaning because it points to and makes us expect another musical event."[3]

Meyer has shown that embodied musical meaning grows out of expectation. In other words, meaning is the result of the realization of the syntax of musical stimuli. If we learn as a result of musical experience to expect a more-or-less definite musical consequence to a musical stimulus, the stimulus has embodied meaning. If, on the other hand, a given musical stimulus arouses no expectation owing to lack of experience or an attitude of indifference to the stimulus on the part of the observer, the stimulus can have no embodied meaning.[4]

Music also has, for many people, designative meaning of different types. This happens when a musical stimulus points to a consequence that is not a musical event but an event or concept of an entirely different order. Music may have mean

[2] Ibid., p. 35.
[3] Ibid., p. 35.
[4] Ibid., pp. 43-82.

ing as a result of private associations that the listener makes between the music and a memory, a feeling, or an image. For example, a listener in the presence of a particular piece of music may associate the piece with a memory of his childhood, be affected by the association, and impute meaning to the composition. There is no essential relationship between the form and content of the music and the character of the association. The music is a stimulus for meaning, but the meaning is not musical; it is extramusical. The unfolding of the musical idea makes little or no difference. The nature of the meaning and the affect are determined by the "subjective content of the individual mind."[5]

Everyone probably makes associations of this kind, and the result can often be a highly affective experience. There is nothing wrong with such extramusical associations, they are natural and desirable. They are not musical responses, however, and provide no basis for the development of musical responses to music. Meaningful extramusical responses can rarely be passed on from one person to another because of differences in past affective experience.

Associations of another type are those shared by a group or culture.[6] For example, the slow march in a low pitch range has developed for most people in the western world an association with death and grief. Likewise, an individual instrument, type of musical organization, or even a single composition may develop direct associations within a culture. Witness the common association of the oboe with pastoral scenes and the marching band with patriotic fervor and a martial spirit. Especially unfortunate associations have occurred between the "William Tell Overture" and the Lone Ranger and between the sentimental words used in popular songs based on serious music and the serious music itself. Other associations arise as the result of the similarity between musical sounds and natural sounds such as the wind, thunder, and the cry of a person under emotional stress.

[5] Ibid., p. 258.
[6] Ibid., pp. 258-266.

Faced with these different types of meaning arising from music, the music educator must choose which kind of meaning he is going to emphasize in the music-learning situation. Many music educators give primary emphasis to referential meaning and extramusical concepts. Such an emphasis has led to the presentation of a preponderance of programmatic music and to unduly detailed attention to the program. Other common teaching devices which point to referential meaning include telling fanciful stories about all kinds of music, giving verbal descriptions of moods and images to be associated with compositions, connecting rhythmic movement with characteristic animal movements ("This music goes like an elephant.") teaching sentimental words to the melodies of great music, striving for specious correlations, and so on. These represent sincere but largely misguided efforts to reveal the meaning in music. They are based on the erroneous notion that children and untutored adults lack the capacity for finding abstract embodied meaning in musical experience and that they require mental hooks in the way of vivid images or concrete connotations to gain meaning from music.

If it could be established that learning extramusical meaning represented a first step leading to the apprehension of musical meaning, such efforts would be justified. This is not the case, however, for emphasis on extramusical meaning inevitably leads away from the music itself and musical meaning.

We have stated our conviction that music education should be primarily aesthetic education. An essential corollary of this belief is that music education should give primary attention to developing students' abilities to perceive musical meaning.

THE ROLE OF PERCEPTION IN MUSICAL LEARNING

Perception is defined as an act by which meaning is gained from the sensory processes while a stimulus is present. Musical perception is the act of gaining meaning in the presence of musical stimuli. Perception is closely related to learning, but they are not the same process. Perception operates in learning, and learning affects all subsequent perception. But learning, by definition, includes more and goes further than perception. Meaning is central to both perception and learning. The difference between the two processes lies in the mode by which the mind treats meaning. Perception results in the formation of concepts. The data received by the senses are supplemented, interpreted, and given meaning as the mind reacts to the sense impressions in terms of past experience, the present situation, and the purposes or goals with which a person identifies himself.

Concepts enable a person to classify or categorize his experience. The formation of concepts depends upon his organizing his experience and making discriminations among the stimuli that strike his senses. *Concepts are cognitive organizers of experience.*

An infant, for example, very early organizes his experience to discriminate between the sight and sound of people on the one hand, and animals, on the other. Even though he has not yet learned names to apply to these two classes of beings, he nevertheless has concepts of them. Later he is able to make more subtle discriminations, say, between cats and dogs, men and women, and boys and girls. He has developed more discriminating, more highly organized concepts. He also learns the names commonly used to identify these concepts and, as a result, is able to use them to think more precisely and to communicate with other people about his experience.

Musical perception results in the formation of musical concepts (that is, organizers of musical experience). To gain meaning from musical stimuli, a person organizes his experience with those stimuli, makes discriminations about the ways the musical tones move, and categorizes the differing ways in which they move.

When an infant hears his first piece of music, his response to it is, almost surely, purely sensual: the affect is soothing or exciting. As he hears other pieces of music, he perceives differences among them, and his differing physical responses often demonstrate his ability to discriminate among them. (He is soothed to sleep by one piece of music, excited and impelled to move by another.) As time and musical experiences unfold, he begins to make more subtle discriminations. He may perceive differences in melodic shape, rhythm, tempo, or form. He is developing musical concepts even though he has no way to identify them verbally.

He is able to tell one piece from another; he may be able to sing a melody he hears; he may move to the rhythm as he listens or sings. Subsequently, he organizes his experience with music with increasing precision and ever more subtle discriminations. At a later time he may learn to name his concepts. This melody goes "up," this one "down," this rhythm moves "evenly," that one "unevenly."

The essential points are (1) that musical concepts emerge from experience with musical stimuli, and (2) that musical concepts must exist before they can be identified by name.

Children differ greatly in their innate ability to develop musical concepts, but all children have a capacity for such development. Children with a high level of what music educators call musical aptitude, or musicality, develop musical concepts easily and often very early.

As a result of experience with music, one child is able to sing a fairly complex song by the age of eighteen months or two years, and moves in time with the beat when he hears music. Another child, given comparable exposure to music, is much less responsive. He does not sing, and his bodily movement to music is much less rhythmic. The first child has been able intuitively to organize his experience with music and his responses to musical stimuli. He has developed musical concepts even though he has not yet identified them by name. The second child is slower in organizing his experience into concepts. He requires help in organizing his experience with music and in making discriminations concerning it.

Children need to learn to identify their musical concepts

by names in common usage in order to use them more precisely and to communicate with other people about them and about music. Words commonly used to identify basic musical concepts include high, low, up, down, fast, slow, even, uneven, same, different, skip, step, and so on. Once such basic concepts have been established, clarified, and applied through and in experience with music, children should be assisted to combine concepts into generalizations about music in language that is meaningful to them.

Music educators must be aware that the name for a concept is not the concept and that the name can have little or no meaning unless the concept has emerged in the mind of a child as a result of his experience with a variety of musical stimuli. Furthermore, generalizations presented by teachers have little meaning for children and are quickly forgotten.[7]

Continuing musical perceptions result in the formation of more complex musical concepts. For example, when a child perceives meaning in a song, the primary concept has to do with the expressive purpose of the song as a whole. Apprehension of the melody, the rhythm, the harmony, and the form results in the formation of concepts of melodic shape, rhythmic and harmonic movement, and structure. Concepts which emerge from a child's experiencing one song may be clarified and applied as he experiences other songs and other types of music. The result is more efficient apprehension of musical meaning in subsequent musical experience, and generalizations about musical meaning and musical elements gradually emerge.

Perception of musical meaning results from awareness of and responsiveness to the undulations between intensity and release embodied in tonal and rhythmic movement. Musical meaning arises from musical stimuli when the musical observer—listener, composer, or performer—perceives the tendencies activated by a musical stimulus, becomes aware of

---

[7] For an excellent discussion of concept learning, see John P. DeCecco, *The Psychology of Learning and Instruction:Educational Psychology*, Prentice-Hall, Inc., Englewood Cliffs, N.J., 1968, pp. 385-425.

inhibitions of tonal tendencies, has expectations of the way in which the intensity aroused by the inhibition of tendencies will be resolved, and finally, is aware of the actual resolution of the intensity.

Before an observer can find musical meaning in musical experience he must have knowledge of the musical stimulus and he must respond to it. He must "experience the primary illusion, feel the consistent movement and recognize at once the commanding form which makes the piece an inviolable whole."[8] Meyer describes two kinds of expectation in musical perception: one growing out of the mode in which the mind organizes and groups data, the other based on learning. Although the mind always tries to fill in structural gaps, knowledge of what constitutes a gap depends upon experience with a given style system.[9] This knowledge is gained through feelingful experience with expressive music on a developmental level appropriate to the learner. This experience may be had through singing, playing, listening, and creative musical expression. Through musical experience the learner must develop awareness of the modes of arousing tendencies, expectations, inhibition, and resolution acceptable within a given style system.

This is exactly what should happen to children during their first experiences with music. They should become aware of the movement of the commanding line of musical compositions as it moves from the initial idea to the consequence of the initial motif. They should become aware of the expressive function of departures from and the return to the original idea. Out of this type of awareness expectations develop within each style system.

A simple example may serve to clarify this process. Suppose a class of young children is singing "Twinkle, Twinkle, Little Star." After hearing it sung and learning to sing it with expression consistent with its structure they

---

[8] Susanne K. Langer, *Feeling and Form*, Charles Scribner's Sons, New York, 1953, p. 147.

[9] Meyer, op. cit., pp. 43-44.

become aware that the initial idea, "Twinkle, twinkle, little star," arouses an initial intensity which is resolved by the consequence, "How I wonder what you are." They become aware of the intensity generated in the motif and expect some movement to resolve it. The departure, "Up above the world so high, like a diamond in the sky," likewise creates a new level of intensity calling for resolution which is brought about by the repetition of the first phrase of the song.

Thus the children not only learn to sing a song and perceive the meaning of the words, they also develop awareness of tonal movement from intensity to release, and expectations that intensity will occur both within the phrases of the song and within the total song. Furthermore, they begin developing expectations of the ways in which tension may be achieved and resolved. In short, they begin to develop responsiveness to the expressive import of the song and to form essential musical concepts.

The difficulty with much beginning learning in music is that the development of expressive awareness and tonal expectations is neglected. The pitches and rhythm may be learned correctly, and the meaning of the words may be perceived, but the affective nature of musical expression elicits little response and remains unperceived.

The learner can perceive musical meaning only when his musical experience, either as listener or participant, takes place in a musically meaningful and expressive context. It is, therefore, essential to use actual music with true expressive value and highly expressive performance by the teacher, by the learner, and from recordings. Musical perception takes place when the learner sings or plays with an affective response and when he listens delightedly to artistic performances of songs and instrumental compositions within the range of his perceptive capacity.

Once the beginning learner has gained the "big idea" of the expressive quality of music and the nature of musical meaning, he is ready to extend his musical experience to larger forms, new and more complex styles, and more subtle examples of musical expression. He is likewise ready to begin to learn musical information and musical skills and to develop musical understanding.

The crucial point is that he becomes responsive to the expressive value of music and perceptive of musical meaning. Perception of the verbal content of songs, perception of extramusical meaning, and the attainment of superficial knowledge and mechanical skill can never substitute for musical perception.

THE PRODUCTS OF MUSICAL LEARNING

Learning leads to changes in behavior, and any analysis of the learning process must give attention to the types of behavior involved and the kinds of changes desired. The present authors have indicated their belief that the music education program should have as its principal focus the development of a musically educated person. Analysis of the behavior of such a person reveals that he exhibits several different kinds of behavior. He responds to music in a feelingful way; he solves expressive and technical problems he encounters in musical performance; he recalls relevant information about the music he is involved with; he sings and plays a musical instrument; he reacts positively to music and musical performances; he discriminates quality in musical performance; he seeks opportunities to participate in music.

All these behaviors result from musical learning. The following section has as its purpose the definition of the areas of musical learning and the clarification of the learning products of a musical education.

Musical Appreciation

Appreciation is defined as the apprehension and enjoyment of the aesthetic import of music. Appreciation includes responsiveness to all the expressive elements of music such as rhythm, harmony, melody, texture, timbre, tonality, form, and phrase line. To appreciate music is to perceive its embodied meaning, to become immersed in the unfolding and development of the musical idea. Appreciation requires awareness of tonal motion and tonal tendencies, the development of expectations in the presence of musical stimuli, sensitivity to the inhibition of tonal tendencies, and, finally, awareness that one's expectations have been either fulfilled or denied. The basis for the development of appreciation lies in the cultivation of sensitivity and responsiveness to the consistent movement of music, to the undulations between intensity and release, and to the expressive import of the moving line in music.

The term appreciation is used and defined here with full cognizance of the confusion of meaning associated with it. Appreciation regrettably has come to be associated principally with listening and the "music appreciation" class. Appreciation operates in listening but it is also present in artistic musical performance, ranging all the way from the beautiful singing of an elementary school general music class to the highly developed artistry of the concert performer.

Musical Understanding

Musical understanding is defined as the ability to bring accumulated musical learning to bear on the solution of musical problems. It involves the conscious use of information, skills, appreciation, and musical concepts in a cognitive framework when one is involved in such musical endeavors as listening, performing, composition, improvisation, and music reading. The principal ingredient of musical understanding is the ability to apply consciously one's knowledge of and sensitivity to embodied musical meaning, musical structure, and musical style to all types of musical experience. It seems evident that the development of musical understanding, along with the development of musical appreciation, represents a major cornerstone of any serious program of music education.

The nature of musical understanding may be clarified by some examples. An understanding listener, when confronted with a contemporary sonata, brings to bear on his perception of the new sonata his accumulated insight into musical meaning in general, into sonata form, and into contemporary techniques of musical expression. His understanding enables nim to follow the line of the composition and to perceive its expressive content. The listener who lacks understanding, even though he appreciates traditional serious music, may anticipate hearing traditional harmony, texture, and other stylistic characteristics he has come to expect in music and, in their absence, may reject the new composition completely.

Likewise, a child lacking in musical understanding may be able to improvise an accompaniment or add a part to a given melody which harmonizes agreeably, but his creative effort may be inconsistent with the style of the melody and add little or nothing to the expressive effect. Musical understanding, on the other hand, would enable him to secure an expressive melodic line, rhythmic and melodic variety, and a harmonic structure consistent with the style and expressive intent of the melody.

Musical understanding should not be considered as unique to higher levels of musical accomplishment. It can and indeed should come into play at every level of music education. For example, children in the primary grades need a basic level of understanding to develop tasteful and expressive rhythmic accompaniments for songs. An understanding of phrase structure, of the relationship between phrases, and of the expressive intent of a song enables children to develop an accompaniment which enhances the musical and expressive worth of the song rather than mechanically beating time as is so often the case.

Understanding results from perception of musical relationships, the clarification of musical concepts and the application of those concepts to interesting and intelligible musi-ւ al problems. The importance of this phase of musical ιearning cannot be overemphasized.

Musical Knowledge

Knowledge, or knowing, is a *construct* (a complex image or idea resulting from a synthesis by the mind), while recall, or recognition, is the overt behavior from which we infer the presence or absence of the construct. Knowledge about music, when properly associated with the development of musical appreciation, understanding, and skill, represents an important facet of musical learning. Knowledge and information not related to the expressive meaning of music, like most isolated information, have only transient meaning and are very likely to be forgotten.

Knowledge about music may be extrinsic or intrinsic to musical understanding and appreciation. Much of the information included in program notes, record covers, and music appreciation courses is not directly relevant to these behaviors but aids "appreciation by strengthening belief and creating a willing attitude"[10] in the listener or performer. Thus, information about the composer's life, the circumstances and reception of the first performance of a work, and so on, although not essential to musical understanding, does have a place in musical learning. It must be emphasized, however, that such knowledge is a means to the learner's heightened receptivity and not an end in itself. The utility of testing such knowledge is thus open to serious question.

Intrinsic knowledge includes information on the nature of musical materials, knowledge of musical form and musical styles, or knowledge of the descriptive program used by a composer for a given work. Such knowledge is essential to musical understanding and properly merits greater emphasis in music education than extrinsic knowledge.

Musical Skills

Although musical skill is often considered synonymous with musical technique, the present analysis of musical learning is marked by a broader conception of skill, encompassing skills of listening, performance skills, and music reading. Each aspect of musical skill is considered in turn.

Skills of listening. The listening activity frequently goes no further than the development of a pleasurable response to

[10] Meyer, op. cit., p. 76.

music. The listener learns to enjoy rich tone quality, a pleasant melody, or an exciting rhythm. Gurney has called this level of hearing "indefinite."[11] A listener on this level may supplement his musical response with an extramusical response if the music stirs his imagination or arouses a series of images or memories.

Hearing of this type represents a point of departure for musical learning, but we must go further than this. Listening should always be pleasurable, but it should lead to the development of the ability for tonal thinking. The skilled listener has learned to discriminate in matters of melody, rhythm, and tempo, and to apprehend large tonal patterns. His listening skill includes awareness of tonal progression, sequence, phrase, motif, and contrast. He experiences tonal and rhythmic movement in relation to what follows and what precedes. He has expectations of what is to happen tonally and realizations of what has happened. He hears melody not in isolation but in relation to harmony and texture. He anticipates the resolution of dissonances, perceives changes in tonality, and discerns the structure of compositions. These represent desirable and attainable listening skills which can contribute to musical appreciation and understanding.

Listening is viewed by some as a passive, nonparticipative activity, quite discrete from other types of musical experience. Our conception of listening is that it should be an active perceptual process, rewarding in its own right but also integral to all musical activity—playing, singing, and composing. Listening is the basic musical activity and it rightly pervades all others.

Skills of performance.   Mursell identifies two problems in learning performance skills, the problem of control and the problem of action pattern, and rightly holds that the key to both lies in the "musical intention, the musical conception to be realized."[12]

[11] See Max Schoen, *The Understanding of Music*, Harper & Brothers, New York, 1945, pp. 82-84.

[12] James L. Mursell, *Education for Musical Growth*, Ginn & Company, Boston, 1948, p. 221.

Musical understanding, appreciation, and listening skills are basic to the development of performance skills. Mere proficiency or technique, however fluent, cannot function expressively without these basic learnings.

The focus of all efficient learning of performance skill and of good technical practice is upon the musical meaning one desires to express, the musical goal he has in view. This means that the learner must begin performance-skill development with the clearest possible conception of his expressive purposes and shape his technique in terms of those purposes.

Learning of performance skills should be problem-centered, and the logical problem is a piece of music the learner desires to perform. The learning should begin with an aural concept of an expressive performance of the piece he wishes to play or sing. To establish this concept the beginner usually needs to hear a fine performance of the piece by his teacher or from recordings. The more mature musician may begin by hearing such a performance, but he refines his conception, and may initiate it, by studying the score and applying his musical understanding to the problem.

When the aural concept is established, the learner begins work on the essential movement patterns. He plays the piece through and discovers the movement problems. With his musical conception as the guiding force, he gradually shapes his movement pattern to achieve his musical intentions. Through analysis of difficulties he encounters and the practice necessary to overcome them his movement patterns gradually become precise and controlled. Practice materials are taken directly from the music, and any passage presenting a movement problem provides the material for practice. The movement problem is identified, analyzed, taken out of context, practiced on, and placed back in context, always with the purpose of achieving an expressive musical result. This is the essence of meaningful learning of performance skills. The essential point is that learning performance skills proceeds best when approached as conscious exploration of an intelligible problem of musical expression rather than as routine repetition of movement patterns isolated from musical expression and devoid of musical meaning.

To apply this concept of learning to beginning instrumental instruction, the proper approach is through an easy melody the pupil knows and likes. Through his own singing and through hearing the instructor play the melody he arrives at a conception of the expressive purpose of the melody. He develops concepts of its tonal and rhythmic movement, its melodic shape, the tone quality of the instrument, and so on. He explores the instrument, and with the guidance and example of the instructor he gains a basic concept of how to hold the instrument and how to produce tone. He does not strive for perfection in these areas, but as soon as possible he begins to play the melody. His early playing is inevitably crude and inaccurate, but he reflects on each trial to discover what the difficulty is. Passages giving him trouble serve as the source of practice material. He constantly goes back to the music to clarify his expressive intentions, and, with his ear and his musical intentions serving as a guide, he gradually achieves accuracy, fluency of movement, and expressive results.

Music reading. The skill of music reading, a species of performance skill, is properly considered as an outgrowth of musical responsiveness and musical understanding. The development of the skill depends upon awareness of tonal and rhythmic movement in music and the development of concepts of tonality, of the tendencies of chords and tones, of the meaning of notational symbols, and of the relationship between the symbols and the sounds they represent. Like all musical concepts these emerge gradually out of varied musical experience. In early study they are clarified by general analysis and application to the score. Later come specific analysis and application, followed by extensive and more precise experiences in converting notational symbols into the tonal and rhythmic movement they represent.

To illustrate the learning process in relation to music reading, the following two paragraphs describe learning activities and results appropriate to the general and specific phases of the learning process. The description is limited to the development of tonal concepts, but the process is applicable to the development of rhythmic and structural concepts as well. The use of tonal concepts for illustrative purposes does not imply that each type of music concept should be approached separately. Tonal, rhythmic, structural, and interpretive concepts reinforce one another, and their development should proceed hand in hand. Specific attention to a single concept is, of course, appropriate when a problem requiring such specificity arises.

To develop tonal concepts essential for music reading, a child should sing and hear many songs and instrumental melodies. Under the guidance of a skilled teacher, he learns to recognize repetition and contrast in melodic patterns. He becomes aware of the presence of active tones and rest tones in the songs he hears and sings and of the tendency of melodies to end on the tonic tone. He learns to hear and to sing the resolutions of active tones in the scale. Through hearing chordal accompaniments to his singing, playing accompaniments on the Autoharp, and vocal chording, he likewise becomes aware of the sound and tonal tendencies of the fundamental chords. He follows the notation of the song he sings and hears and arrives at a general understanding of the function of notation. He realizes that the direction of the notation and that of the melody coincide and that skips, steps, and repeated tones differ from one another in both sound and notation. These are desirable representative results of the general phase of learning.

In the more specific phase he learns to sing the roots of the I, IV, and V7 chords, to sing the chords in arpeggios, and to name the chords. He sees the arpeggiated chords on the blackboard and discovers them in the notation of melodies he sings and hears. He has practice in setting up the tonality by singing the roots of the I, IV, and V7 chords. He plays, sings, and writes the scale in various keys and discovers the need for and the function of the key signature. He learns to interpret the key signature and to establish the key from the sounded key tone. He learns to relate tonal patterns in melodies he hears, sings, and reads to the tonality and to the tones of the fundamental chords. Finally, he has extensive practice in reading easy songs which contain tonal patterns familiar to him. As he encounters unfamiliar tonal patterns, they are, in turn, differentiated from and related to the familiar patterns.

The complex conceptual framework which music-reading skill requires is best developed through singing, playing, listening, and moving to actual music, with increasingly specific emphasis on hearing tonal and rhythmic patterns and relating those patterns to their notational equivalents, and through extensive experience in reading. As is true with any skill, practice is essential in the maintenance of skill in music reading.

Musical Attitudes

Attitudes are defined as general emotionalized reactions for or against a thing. They may be positive or negative, with intensity ranging all the way from strongly for to strongly against. Attitudes affect the efficiency of all learning, since they form a basic part of an individual's readiness to learn. A student with a negative attitude toward music is certain to make little or no progress in learning music unless his attitude can be changed. Musical attitudes are learned, and a change in attitude represents a change in behavior.

Musical attitudes are acquired through four major means. These include, first, long exposure to cumulative experiences which influence the individual. For example, a student whose musical experience has resulted in pleasure, satisfying accomplishment, and approval from his peers and parents is likely to have a highly favorable attitude toward music. If, on the other hand, lack of success, frustration, and ridicule from parents or peers have attended his musical experience, a negative attitude is equally probable.

A second way in which musical attitudes are acquired is through a vivid or traumatic single experience. For example, the attitude of a student formerly indifferent to music may be transformed by performing under a highly inspirational conductor, or by appearing with success and acclaim in a public recital. Another student may develop negative attitudes toward music as a result of an embarrassing debacle in public performance.

Attitudes are also acquired as a result of emulation of a person or an organization. For example, a child is likely to reflect the attitudes which his parents or other persons he admires hold toward music. Likewise, a band member in a school where the lack of cooperation and mutual regard between the band and vocal departments generates competition and antagonism is likely to have negative attitudes toward vocal music.

Finally, attitudes are formed through association. If a person likes or dislikes one factor in a situation, the entire situation may assume similar coloration. For example, as a result of persistently unrewarding experience with sol-fa syllables in a general music class, a student may develop a negative attitude toward the class, even though he may have found some of his class experiences rewarding. Similarly, through association a student's attitude toward music may reflect his like or dislike of the music teacher.

Musical Initiative

Musical initiative implies active musicianship which eventuates in musical independence. A person who has developed desirable musical initiative does things with and about music. He has a consuming interest in music and has gained the knowledge, understandings, skills, and other musical competencies which enable him to further pursue musical learning on his own and to take responsibility for shaping and enriching his own musical experiences.

Musical initiative develops in music learning situations in which the student has the opportunity to explore music on his own, to exercise his musical preferences, to initiate musical projects, and to analyze his own musical problems and work toward their solution. The development of musical initiative requires interest in and responsiveness to music, coupled with a broad base of musical competencies.

Musical initiative should not be thought of as an end

product which emerges full-blown only after a long period of study. Its development is a continuous process which has its beginnings in the child's early, uncomplicated musical experiences, and we should encourage initiative on the appropriate level from the very beginning of music study. As the child's musical resources grow, his initiative is broadened in scope and refined. As he matures personally and musically, he develops ever-greater measures of musical independence.

MATURATION AND MUSICAL LEARNING

Maturation associated with age is commonly accepted in both learning theory and learning practice. Ordinarily, a child of three is not expected to ride a bicycle, use a typewriter, or play the piano, but such accomplishments are commonplace for ten- or twelve-year-olds. Occasionally, a three-year-old may learn very easily to perform these feats, and most children could do so at the age of three (to a degree) with extraordinary amounts of practice. It is usually more efficient, however, to delay these learnings until the child has reached the age and maturational level which enable him to attain them with greater ease and much less practice.

Wheeler developed a gestalt theory of learning with a strong biological emphasis which attributed all behavior to growth.[13] His theory implied a principle which has been called *stimulation-induced maturation.*[14] The term refers to a kind of maturation, in addition to age maturation, "a supplementary growth process induced by the conditions of stimulation."[15] The second type of maturation depends upon experience in a stimulating environment and may be

[13] Raymond H. Wheeler, *The Science of Psychology*, Thomas Y. Crowell Company, New York, 1929.

[14] Leon R. Doré and Ernest R. Hilgard, "Spaced Practice and the Maturation Hypothesis," *Journal of Psychology*, 4:245-259, 1937.

[15] Ernest R. Hilgard, *Theories of Learning*, Appleton-Century-Crofts, Inc., New York, 1948, p. 238. Reprinted by permission of Appleton-Century-Crofts, Educational Division, Meredith Corporation.

called experiential maturation or simply, for our purposes, *musical maturation.*

Both types of maturation are important in musical learning. Age maturation must be taken into account, for example, in deciding when a child should begin the study of a standard musical instrument. Playing such an instrument well requires a high level of muscular coordination and control, and efforts to learn to play an instrument before such overall control is well established can only demand a quantity and intensity of practice inconsistent with accomplishment. The easy-to-play instruments that require less precision and control are highly appropriate for young children, and most or all of the values achievable in the early years through playing instruments can be achieved on the Autoharp, tone bells, song flutes, recorders, and other easy-to-play instruments.

Of equal importance is musical maturation. Musical maturation results from a child's undergoing a variety of rewarding musical experiences focused on the development of musical responsiveness and musical understanding. The outcomes of this experience should be the apprehension, naming, and gradual clarification of significant musical concepts—rhythmic, melodic, harmonic, structural, notational, and so on. Beginning specialized musical instruction before a child has a background of such concepts places an unnecessary burden on both the child and the teacher and makes significant progress in musicianship and musical playing highly unlikely.

Many problems in musical learning arise through pupils' lack of musical maturation. For example, the presence of nonsingers in the early grades is most often due to the children's lack of previous stimulating musical experience and not to faulty native musical endowment. Such children, for the most part, simply have not developed an adequate comprehension of melodic shape and the coordination necessary to produce vocally the sounds they hear. The teacher's clue in these cases is not to consider the children as problem cases and launch into individual remedial work; such a procedure is likely to compound the difficulty. He should, on the other hand, arrange for the children to have, as part of the total group, varied tonal experience in which they can participate wholeheartedly, with pleasure and without embarrassment. As a result of this musical stimulation they will gradually acquire a more adequate comprehension of pitch differences and of the melodic contour of songs and will learn to sing on pitch.

The high school instrumentalist who plays "mechanically" may have a faulty comprehension of musical expressiveness. The percussionist who fumbles an intricate rhythmic pattern probably does not feel the basic rhythm. And the child-prodigy pianist who has startling technique but fails to communicate musical meaning usually lacks musical understanding. All these kinds of problems are the result of insufficient or one-sided musical maturation. Their solution lies not in tedious mechanical drill on an isolated problem or skill but in clarifying the musical concept involved through varied musical experience appropriate to the learner's level.

Closely associated with the concept of maturation is the concept of readiness which has been employed with excellent effect by language-reading experts. They have developed reading-readiness materials and tests of reading readiness to a high level. Their success has led some music educators to adapt the concept of readiness to music reading. The general idea is that children should have a specified period of general tonal experience during which they sing, listen to music, play simple instruments, use rhythm instruments, move to music, and so on. After such a period the day is supposed to arrive when they are "ready" to read music. At that time, which may vary from the third to the seventh grade, some teachers feel impelled to "get down to fundamentals," which with regrettable frequency means getting bogged down in routine, mechanical and the superficial drill on notational material isolated from music experience.

There are at least four serious faults with the usual practices based on the concept of music-reading readiness. First, since no tests or other evaluative techniques comparable to those used in language reading are available, no sure way exists to determine when a child is ready to read music. Second, the children in a given group are unlikely to be ready at the same time. Third, the practices fail to take into account the fact that musical maturation, like age maturation, is not saltatory in nature but is a continuous developmental process which proceeds gradually from general to specific responses. Fourth, even if the children are ready, work with notational materials divorced from musical experience is unlikely to be rewarding.

The general music program, properly conducted, provides the best means to musical maturation. It should be organized to provide varied musical experiences consistent with the children's age and maturational level that lead to broad musical learnings. The experiences should result in the apprehension and gradual clarification of significant musical concepts. At first grasp the concepts are inevitably apprehended only vaguely and in general terms, but as they are encountered and used again and again in continued experience, their meaning is gradually clarified and becomes more specific. Thus the pupils *grow* into music reading, instrument playing, listening skills, musical understanding, and musical specializations.

The implications of this position are clear and direct. Both age maturation and musical maturation must be taken into account in program planning and in devising methods of teaching. Arbitrarily beginning specialized instrumental instruction at one specified grade level is indefensible. Some children have the physical and musical maturity to profit from such instruction at a given time, but others do not. The indicated solution is to introduce as much flexibility as possible into scheduling specialized instruction and to make the decision for each child on the basis of the maturity he has demonstrated in general music experiences. If instrumental instruction can be introduced at only one grade level, there is good reason for postponing it until the fifth, sixth, or seventh grade, especially if the pupils are receiving a valuable general music experience.

A cyclic approach to planning the music program and to

music teaching is indicated. Thus a given musical concept or piece of musical information is not allotted arbitrarily to one grade level to be learned there and no place else. Rather, musical concepts, musical information, and musical techniques are encountered again and again, and each time they are encountered, the teacher assists the children in apprehending them with increasing clarity and control. Teaching takes the direction of organizing the musical experiences so that the pupils have the opportunity to apprehend, name, clarify, and apply musical concepts with ever-increasing precision and confidence.

TRADITIONAL THEORIES OF LEARNING

The interest of psychologists in the learning process stems from the pioneer work of Ebbinghouse (1885), Thorndike (1898), and others. With the publication of his book *Animal Intelligence*[16] in 1898, Thorndike laid the groundwork for the theory of learning which dominated American education for three decades of the twentieth century and which remains influential today. That theory is generally known as *connectionism*. Other psychologists, including Guthrie, Hull, and Skinner, developed learning theories based on stimulus-response association. Some of these theories represented extension and development of Thorndike's work, but others revealed basic disagreement with him.

The first theory to threaten the dominance of Thorndike in America was the gestalt doctrine, which gained influence as the result of the publication in English of Koffka's *The Growth of the Mind*[17] in 1924 and Kohler's *The Men-*

---

[16]Edward L. Thorndike, *Animal Intelligence*, The Macmillan Company, New York, 1911. (A revision of the 1898 edition.)

[17] Kurt Koffka, *The Growth of the Mind: An Introduction to Child Psychology*, translated by Robert Morris Ogden, 2d ed., Harcourt, Brace and Company, Inc., New York, 1928.

tality of Apes[18] in 1925. The former book aimed direct criticism at the concept of trial-and-error learning as developed by Thorndike, and the latter proposed learning through insight as an alternative to trial and error. Many progressive educators readily accepted the new theory because of its emphasis on intelligent learning, which fitted Dewey's concept that the individual has the capacity to define and solve his own problems. Lewin, Wheeler, Tolman, and others developed and extended the gestalt doctrine with formulations and experimentation of their own.

Thus a situation arose in which the teacher attempting to apply the psychology of learning to his teaching was confronted with a confusing array of theoretical positions, many with fundamental differences. Some of the differences have arisen as the result of genuine theoretical disagreements, but others are due to the development of special terms and concepts and to the wide variation in the nature of research problems.

To reduce the confusion created by the numerous theories of learning, Hilgard groups them into two main families and designates them as (1) *association theories* and (2) field theories.[19] The association theories include Thorndike's connectionism,[20] Guthrie's contiguous conditioning,[21] Hull's systematic behavior theory,[22] and Skinner's descriptive behaviorism.[23] The field theories include the varieties of

---

[18] Wolfgang Kohler, *The Mentality of Apes*, translated by E. Winter, Harcourt, Brace and Company, Inc., New York, 1925.

[19] Hilgard, op. cit., p. 9.

[20] Edward L. Thorndike, *The Psychology of Learning: Educational Psychology*, vol. II., Teachers College, Columbia University, New York, 1913.

[21] E. R. Guthrie, *The Psychology of Learning*, Harper & Brothers, New York, 1935.

[22] Clark L. Hull, *Principles of Behavior*, Appleton-Century-Crofts, Inc., New York, 1943.

[23] B. F. Skinner, *The Behavior of Organisms*, Appleton-Century-Crofts, Inc., New York, 1938.

gestalt, neo-gestalt, organismic, and sign-significate theories developed by Lewin,[24] Tolman,[25] Wheeler,[26] and others.

Hilgard admits that his grouping is not completely consistent but gives ample justification for it as follows:

> The distinctions between the families are not always sharp and there are agreements and disagreements which cut across lines. That is, on some specific issues it would be possible to find association psychologists on opposite sides of the fence, paralleled by field psychologists divided on the same issue. But the total picture does not present such confusion. Although association psychologists do not comprise a single harmonious family, still any one adherent to that position tends to offer explanations more like those of another than like the explanations of any one in the field group. Correspondingly, the members of the field psychology family have in common their opposition to associationist conceptions. It is important to understand this basic cleavage, because there are profound differences in outlook despite efforts of eclectics and mediators to harmonize the opposing camps.[27]

He cites five issues on which associationists and field theorists have different outlooks: (1) environmentalism versus nativism, (2) the nature of wholes and parts, (3) reaction versus cognition, (4) mechanism versus dynamic equilibrium, and (5) historical versus contemporary causation.

The positions of both the associationist and field theories are opposing but consistent on these issues. Associationists tend to attribute more to learning than to native endow-

---

[24] Kurt Lewin, *Principles of Topological Psychology*, translated by Fritz Heider and Grace Heider, McGraw-Hill Book Company, New York, 1936.

[25] Edward C. Tolman, *Purposive Behavior in Animals and Man*, Appleton-Century-Crofts, Inc., New York, 1932.

[26] Raymond H. Wheeler, *The Science of Psychology*, 2d ed., Thomas Y. Crowell Company, New York, 1940.

[27] Hilgard, op. cit., pp. 9-10. Reprinted by permission of the publisher.

ment, consider wholes in terms of their parts, explain present behavior on the basis of past experience, prefer machine models to illustrate the laws to be used in psychological explanations, and concern themselves with observable reactions in their experimentation.

Field theorists, on the other hand, prefer natural endowment as explanatory of behavior, give great emphasis to the wholeness of any phenomenon, give greater attention to structuring the present field than to past experience, prefer to use natural models such as whirlpools or musical melodies in psychological explanations, and emphasize cognitive processes and the occurence of ideation in learning.[28] In recent years it has been increasingly recognized that conflicts in learning theory have been magnified out of proportion to their importance. While there are basic differences among theories, there are also many similarities. Differences in terminology and types of research have been responsible for at least some of the conflict. Research on each theory has, however, affected other theories, and there are signs of progress in moving toward a comprehensive theory of learning. For the forseeable future it seems reasonable to take the position that, in view of the present state of development in learning theory, the wide variety of learning situations involved in music education demands a fairly extensive set of principles drawn from more than one theory.

RECENT DEVELOPMENTS IN LEARNING THEORY

Seashore did excellent pioneer work in serious experimentation to apply psychology and learning theory to musical learning and music teaching. Unfortunately, no one continued experimentation on the basis of Seashore's work, and few music educators have developed new directions for such experimentation. Mursell made an important contribution in

---

[28] These descriptions of associationist and field-theory positions are summarized from Hilgard, op. cit., pp. 9-17

bringing psychological considerations into the consciousness of music teachers by his insightful analysis of the learning-teaching process and by logical application of some general tenets of field theory to musical learning, but he did not take an experimental approach to the problem and his conclusions have yet to be verified by research.

Several music educators have taken an eclectic approach to the psychology of learning and have adopted a few general principles of learning such as the principles of motivation, and reward and reinforcement and applied them to musical learning. It must be recognized, however, that these principles are based almost as much on common sense as on learning theory.

The same situation holds largely true for other school subjects, and it is almost inevitable that it be so. The early efforts to apply experimental learning theory to teaching practice were probably premature. The movement got its start through the efforts of E. L. Thorndike, who, after his early animal experimentation in learning, went into the field of educational psychology. The fact that Thorndike made the leap from experimental to applied psychology may have resulted in the development of unrealistic expectations on the part of educators.

The problem boils down to one of pure versus applied research. The psychologist, unlike some of his fellow scientists, has been placed in a position of having to solve practical problems before the laws of behavior necessary to do so are available.

Melton affirms the difficulty of applying results of experimentation in learning theory to educational practice. "While there have been many impressive advances in psychology and especially in our understanding of the learning process during the past twenty years, the fact remains that there is no unified science of learning . . . and this makes the application difficult."[29]

---

[29] Arthur W. Melton, "The Science of Hearing and the Technology of Educational Methods," *Harvard Educational Review*, 29(2):100, 1959.

While it is essential for the music educator to be aware of the limitations of learning theory and the difficulty of applying experimental psychology to educational practice, several recent developments in the psychology of learning do seem to provide a basis for systematic attack on the application of theory to educational practice in music.

Four men have been selected for brief discussion: B. F. Skinner, Jean Piaget, David P. Ausubel, and Robert M. Gagné. At least two factors have influenced this selection. First, their work seems to have special significance for musical learning. Second, they differ widely in background, orientation, and method of research. Skinner is an experimental psychologist who has bridged the gap between experimental and applied psychology. Piaget, trained in zoology, used the method of the logician to develop his theory of learning and concept formation on the basis of observation of children in learning-task situations. Ausubel is a distinguished educational psychologist with a background in psychiatry. Gagné is a Canadian psychologist now working in the United States.

Skinner

Skinner takes an optimistic view of the possibility of applying results from experimental learning theory to educational practice by means of the teaching machine. He describes the teaching machine as "an example of technological application of basic science"[30] and, in his view, "The laboratory study of learning provided the confidence, if not all the knowledge, needed for a systematic attack on the status quo"[31] (of educational practice). Basically, Skinner has applied his concept of reinforcement to the learning process through use of the teaching machine.

He emphasizes the need for constant and immediate reinforcement of the learner. While the school is not presently without reinforcers, such as the ultimate advantages of

---

[30] B. F. Skinner, "Why We Need Teaching Machines," *Harvard Educational Review*,31(4):397, 1961

[31] Ibid., p. 398.

education, marks, grades, and diplomas, available reinforcers do not specify effective contingencies of reinforcement. The time gap between behavior and such distant consequences is too great.

The teaching machine is efficient because (1) the student can be immediately and frequently reinforced, (2) the student can proceed at his own rate, and (3) the student follows a coherent sequence. (The first two advantages are intrinsic to the teaching machine, while the third depends on the quality of programming.)

Skinner also provides a cue to programming by pointing out the need for behavioral definition of what we are trying to teach. Once this has been accomplished, we are in a position to teach these behaviors directly. Thus, we teach not knowledge in the abstract but behaviors from which we infer the presence of knowledge. The job of programming consists of setting up in a coherent sequence the behavioral repertoire which distinguishes a person who knows something from those who do not.

Machines would seem to have great value in teaching music for several reasons. The traditional teaching of music is often lacking in immediate reinforcement. Furthermore, previous musical background, aptitude, and rate of learning vary so markedly among individuals that, despite our best efforts at individualization of instruction, a learning sequence and pace suited to all students in a class are almost impossible to attain. Furthermore, aversive motivation in the way of avoiding poor grades is not as effective in music as in many other subjects.

Since the technology for devising the most complex machines employing both sight and sound is available, the crux of the matter of teaching music by machine lies in our being able to do a thorough and specific job of defining the behaviors involved in being a musical person. Only then will we be able to program musical learning effectively. We need to analyze the various types of musical learning in terms of specific behaviors and set up programs by which these behaviors can be learned.

For example, analysis of the behavior of a good reader of music would probably reveal that among other behaviors, he maintains a basic tonal orientation, grasps tonal patterns rather than separate pitches, feels the beat as it moves through the measure, and relates rhythm patterns to the beat. A teaching machine could be constructed to call for precisely these behaviors and others involved in music reading on the part of the learner and to reinforce the learning immediately. Machines geared to musical learning represent a fruitful avenue for experimental effort on the part of music educators.

The interest in the programming of learning, which is the logical result of the development of teaching machines, may, in the final analysis, be more important to music education than the machines themselves. Programmed learning demands more careful and specific attention to objectives than has ever been attained in the teaching of music. The job boils down to defining in great detail and with extreme specificity the repertory of behaviors in relation to musical stimuli of various kinds which distinguish the skillful musician from the unskilled, the musical person from the unmusical.

Piaget

Piaget,[32] a Swiss psychologist, has developed a theory of mental growth by observing the behavior of children. His early work, in which he observed pairs of young children in interaction with their environment, focused on the development of language and forms of thinking in the child. Later he extended his method to include close observation of children of all ages, giving older children learning tasks, and varying the circumstances to validate a given interpretation. In addition, he employed the technique of asking the children highly specific questions concerning events enacted in front of them

---

[32] Jean Piaget, *The Language and Thought of the Child*, Meridian Books, The World Publishing Company, Cleveland, 1965.

or concerning their own actions. Thus, his approach is both clinical and experimental. His theory embraces the process of concept formation and the stages which occur in the development of thought processes from infancy to adolescence. The most influential American interpreter of Piaget's position has been Jerome Bruner of Harvard University.

Piaget has delineated four major stages in the development of behavioral and thought processes: sensorimotor, birth to eighteen months; preoperational, eighteen months to the age of six or seven; concrete operations, age six or seven to the age of ten or fourteen; and finally, formal operations.

The preoperational stage is active and the child uses symbols crudely but manipulates reality by intuitive regulation rather than by symbolic operations. In the stage of concrete operations the child begins to manipulate the symbols that represent things and relations in his mind; in the stage of formal operations he does so with growing precision.

An operation differs from a simple action in being internalized and reversible. *Internalized* means that the child can carry out trial and error in his mind without overt action. *Reversible* means that the child is able to regard any set of activities and conceive a corresponding reverse procedure. Central to Piaget's theory of concept formation is the idea of conservation or invariance of substance throughout observed changes in state.

Bruner differentiates between concrete operations and formal operations in this way: "Concrete operations, though they are guided by the logic of classes and the logic of relations, are means for restructuring only immediately present reality. The child is able to give structure to things he encounters, but he is not yet readily able to deal with possibilities not directly before him or not already experienced." In the stage of formal operations, on the other hand, " . . . the child's intellectual activity seems to be based upon an ability to operate on hypothetical propositions rather than being constrained to what he has experienced or what is before him. The child can now think of possible variables and even deduce potential relationships that can later be verified by experiment or observation."[33]

It seems likely that aspects of Piaget's work are directly relevant to music education. In the first place, his theory of concept formation may shed light on the development of musical concepts about which we know very little. Secondly, his description of developmental stages may provide insight into the development of musicality. Conservation of tone patterns and rhythm patterns, for example, is essential to tonal thinking and to an adequate conception of rhythm and tonality. Thirdly, the application of both his clinical and experimental techniques to the study of musical learning and musical concept formation have great possibilities. Marilyn Pflederer Zimmerman[34] has employed both Piaget's theoretical orientation and his research technique in preliminary studies of music concept formation. While her results cannot yet be considered conclusive, they do point to the capability of young children to develop fairly complex concepts and the desirability of more active participation and experimentation with musical materials by children than is generally provided in elementary school music programs.

The research of Piaget and others emphasizes the soundness of the idea that the development of musicianship and aesthetic sensitivity can and must begin in early childhood. There is increasing recognition that in connection with many abilities there is a critical stage that occurs early in the

---

[33] Jerome Bruner, *The Process of Education*, Harvard University Press, Cambridge, Mass., 1962, p. 37.

[34] Marilyn Pflederer, "The Responses of Children to Musical Tasks Embodying Piaget's Principle of Conservation," *Journal of Research in Music Education*, 12:253, Winter 1964.

Pflederer, "Conservation Laws Applied to the Development of Musical Intelligence," *Journal of Research in Music Education*, 15:216, Fall 1967.

Marilyn Pflederer Zimmerman, "Percept and Concept: Implications of Piaget," *Music Educators Journal*, 56 (6) : 49-50, 147-148, February 1970.

development of a child. If education is delayed past this critical stage, the child can never fulfill his potential. There is every reason to believe that there is a critical stage in the development of musicianship and aesthetic sensitivity, which occurs early, probably before the age of nine. In view of presently available evidence, it is arrant nonsense for music educators to continue using the bulk of their financial and human resources on students in high school. A planned program of music education in nursery school, kindergarten, and the primary grades, providing a rich variety of experience with music conducted by well qualified teachers, merits the highest priority in music education program planning.

Ausubel

Ausubel[35] has established a spirited defense of both verbal learning and reception learning and has presented a subsumption theory of meaningful verbal learning and retention. He considers unjustified the present disrepute into which verbal learning has fallen. He attributes the low estate of verbal learning to the fact that subject matter is still presented to pupils largely in rote fashion and to psychological confusion.

"First, psychologists have tended to subsume many qualitatively different kinds of learning processes under a single explanatory category. As a result, it has not always been sufficiently clear, for example, that such categorically different types of learning as problem solving and the understanding of meaningfully presented verbal material have different objectives, and that conditions and instructional techniques facilitating one of these learning processes are not necessarily relevant or maximally efficient for the other. Second, in the absence of an appropriate theory of cognitive organization and of long-term learning and retention of large bodies of meaningful subject matter, various explanatory principles (e.g., retroactive inhibition, stimulus generalization, response

[35] David P. Ausubel, *The Psychology of Meaningful Verbal Learning and Retention*, Grune & Stratton, Inc., New York, 1963.

competition) have been uncritically extrapolated from laboratory findings on nonverbal or short-term, fragmentary or rote verbal learning. It is small wonder, therefore, that teachers nurtured on such theoretical fare have tended to perceive meaningful verbal materials as necessarily rote in Character and, in consequence, have either felt justified in using rote practices or have summarily rejected verbal techniques as unsuitable for classroom instruction."[36]

Ausubel defines the distinction between reception and discovery learning and between rote and meaningful learning. In reception learning the content of what is to be learned is presented in its final form to the learners without any involvement in independent discovery on their parts. In discovery learning, on the other hand, the principal content of what is to be learned is not given but must be discovered by the learner before he can internalize it.

Ausubel points out that the distinction between rote and meaningful learning is frequently confused with the distinction between reception and discovery learning. As a result, many people assume that only discovery learning can be meaningful and that reception learning by its very nature is rote learning. He emphasizes, however, that both reception learning and discovery learning can be meaningful or both may be rote. The meaningful or rote character of learning depends not on whether it is reception or discovery learning but on the learner having a set to relate what is learned to an existing cognitive structure and on there being potential meaning in the learning task.

It is within this context that Ausubel constructs his subsumption theory. "The model of cognitive organization proposed for the learning and retention of meaningful materials assumes the existence of a cognitive structure that is hierarchically organized in terms of highly inclusive conceptual traces under which are subsumed traces of less inclusive subconcepts as well as traces of specific informational

---

[36] David P. Ausubel, "In Defense of Verbal Learning," *Educational Theory*, 9(1):15, January 1961 (a).

data. The major organizational principle, in other words, is that of progressive differentiation of trace systems of a given sphere of knowledge from regions of greater to lesser inclusiveness, each linked to the next higher step in the hierarchy through the process of subsumption."[37] Music teaching practice has emphasized direct experience with music, and the professional literature has emphasized learning by independent discovery. This concept of musical learning, while it is certainly valid, especially in the elementary school and for adults who have had limited musical experience, has two limitations in practice: (1) Like all discovery learning, it is terribly time-consuming, and (2) it has frequently been structured (or unstructured) in such a way that students have failed to develop a cognitive structure to which further learnings are relatable.

Ausubel's theory seems significant and relevant to musical learning for a number of reasons. In the first place, verbal learning should play an important role in overall musical learning; there is a large body of meaningful generalizable musical information which merits being learned. Presently used teaching methods do not emphasize sufficiently the cognitive aspects of musical behavior. Furthermore, we tend to teach music in the same way regardless of the age of the students. Ausubel's theory (reinforced by the import of Piaget's stages) may provide a cue to needed change in the teaching of music at the secondary school level. It would seem to indicate that the elementary school years should be devoted to developing essential musical and verbal concepts in a cognitive structure through direct experience with music and an emphasis on discovery learning. Beginning in the upper grades and, to an increasing degree through the high school and college years, greater emphasis would be placed on reception learning, in which new material is incorporated in the existing cognitive structure through a process of progressive differentiation. New material on entering the cognitive field interacts with

[37] David P. Ausubel, "A Subsumption Theory of Meaningful Verbal Learning," *The Journal of General Psychology*, 66:213, 1962.

and is subsumed under a relevant and more inclusive conceptual system. The measure of meaningfulness is the degree to which the new material is relatable to stable elements in the cognitive structure.

Application of Ausubel's theory could result in significant improvement in verbal learning essential to musical development. It appears obvious that the learning of musical information in general music classes, music theory, and music history is presently largely rote in character and that the learning and retention of such material leave much to be desired. Attempts to fulfill the conditions of subsumption theory would seem to be a promising direction for experimentation and research for music educators at the secondary school and college levels.

Gagné

Gagné has set forth a behavioristic position in learning that is having a profound influence on the thinking of educators.[38] He holds that the key to learning lies in the analysis of human performances and, based on that analysis, in stating the objectives of education as tasks.

The description of human performances must contain a good strong verb—that is, a verb referring to observable human action. The word *appreciate*, for example, does not qualify as a strong description of behavior. It is vague and general and does not represent an observable human action. The implication is that we need to identify observable behaviors that can logically be associated with appreciation and that contribute to appreciation. An objective must describe the smallest unit of performance which can be identified as having a distinct and independent purpose.[39]

Objectives will have varying degrees of generality; that is, some objectives (behaviors) depend upon others. In other words, there are such things as subordinate objectives, behav-

[38] Robert M. Gagné, *The Conditions of Learning*, Holt, Rinehart and Winston, Inc., New York, 1965.
[39] Ibid., pp. 241-247.

iors which are prerequisite to other behaviors. If we are going to have any real sequence in musical learning, we must be able to describe the behaviors we ultimately want to teach and the more specific behaviors which are prerequisite to the more general and more complex behaviors.

Gagné describes eight sets of conditions that distinguish eight types of learning: (1) signal learning, (2) stimulus-response learning, (3) chaining, (4) verbal associate learning, (5) multiple discrimination, (6) concept learning, (7) principle learning, and (8) problem solving. He does not attempt to interpret the results of studies of learning and apply them to the learning process. Rather, he proceeds on the basis of the question, "What are the dimensions of learning phenomena which need to be studied experimentally?"[40]

Gagné's analysis of the conditions of learning and his description of learning structures in a number of school subjects provide music educators with a source of insight into the learning process and cues to the analysis and management of musical learning.

PRINCIPLES OF LEARNING

With full recognition of the difficulties involved in such a task and of the limitations implicit in it, we have sought to derive from learning theory principles of learning which are especially applicable to learning problems in music education. These principles cut across the lines between opposing theories but admittedly have a bias in the direction of the field theories. These principles are stated and applied directly to musical learning.

1. *Efficient learning begins with a compelling and intelligible problem.* The learner must have a purpose in view if his learning efforts are to be more than blind fumbling, and he gains purpose when confronted with a problem

[40] Ibid., p. vi.

he desires to solve. Musical learning can be no exception to this principle. The problem may be playing a piece he wishes to learn, preparing for a recital appearance, hearing harmonic changes in a passage which stirs his imagination, comprehending a chord progression, or mastering a technical difficulty in performance. The essential point is that it be a musical problem directly related to the beauty and expressive import of music. Music itself provides the most meaningful context for the identification and solution of musical problems. All people have a natural tendency to respond to music, and teachers should constantly capitalize on this fact by stressing the expressive import and not the bare bones of musical structure and technique.

2. *The learner must perceive the relationship between his learning experiences and the problem he wants to solve.* A physician of our acquaintance liked music and wanted to learn to play the piano so that he could provide chord accompaniments for his own singing and for family singing. He began private lessons with enthusiasm, but his teacher started him with a beginner's piano instruction book which did not include keyboard harmony and which contained no pieces of interest to the adult student. The physician practiced faithfully for a while the assignments he was given but was unable to see any relationship between what he was doing and the problem he wished to solve. The result, not uncommon in all phases of musical instruction, was that he soon lost interest and discontinued his lessons.

In learning music theory the student must be led to see that the skills and understandings he acquires are applicable to the refinement of his musical behavior. Likewise, the student practicing studies and exercises must perceive the relationship between his practice and expressive musical results. If this is not so, both phases of music study inevitably become sterile, routine, and monotonous and have little meaning for the student.

3. *Motivation is central to efficient musical learning.* Incen-

tives, interest, pressures, purposes, recognition, and rewards are all involved in motivation. Musical learning has an abundance of sources of motivation. These include basic human responsiveness to music, the emotional satisfaction that comes from musical participation, the possibilities for demonstrable progressive success, and the almost universal social approval accorded musical accomplishment.

Motivation may be either extrinsic or intrinsic to music. Extrinsic motivation is not directly connected with music and includes rewards such as gold stars on the pages of an instruction book, the desire for recognition and approval from parents or peers, the desire to become a member of a musical group, and so on.

Intrinsic motivation depends upon the satisfaction and pleasure that come from music itself. An excellent illustration of intrinsic motivation is the third-grade boy who loved the music period and said to his teacher, "Music is the joyfullest time of all." Intrinsic motivation is the most valuable and should be sought, but extrinsic motivation is useful especially at the beginning of specialized music study.

Success provides motivation of the highest quality and intensity. The pupil with musical goals that are achievable but challenging, who achieves regular success with music, who receives praise for his efforts, and who develops confidence in his musical abilities inevitably has a high level of motivation.

The level of goals is a crucial item in motivation. Goals that are too high and remote result in discouragement; too low goals bring about inertia and boredom.

4. *Learning depends upon impressions received by the senses.* In musical learning, hearing, sight and kinesthetic feel are all involved. It appears obvious that hearing merits primary emphasis, but much musical learning is carried on without sufficient attention to musical hearing. Aural awareness is the key to all musical learning,

and the music-learning situation should be constantly focused on ear training. Sight and kinesthetic feel are important but properly come into play only after aural concepts are well established.

5. *Provisional tries must be made in musical learning.* The learner needs the opportunity for provisional tries once he knows what he is trying to do. It should be recognized that he is likely to make more wrong tries than right ones, but he profits from his tries only if he has a conception of the musical effect he is trying to achieve. Learning proceeds from crudeness to precision, and it is a mistake to break patterns up into meaningless bits so that the learner can achieve perfection at the beginning. The pattern for efficient musical learning is (a) an aural concept of what is to be achieved, (b) provisional tries, (c) reflection on what is right and what is wrong, and (d) a decision on changes to be made in the next tries.

6. *The perfection of complicated skills requires correct forms of movement established by practice.* Practice is essential to the development of performance skills, but a great deal of practice is frequently carried on for long periods with no notion of its purpose, and repetition without learning is all too common.

A problem of musical expression should initiate the development of technique, and the best technical practice is carried on in a context of actual music. Once problems of technique have been identified and understood, practice materials may be taken from the piece in which the problem occurred or occasionally from a book of studies. The value of a beginning student's going through an entire book of exercises, however, is open to serious question. Technical problems are solved through analysis and understanding, not through blind mechanical practice.

Practice is likely to result in learning if the following conditions are present: (a) the learner sees the problem; (b) the learner is conscious of the need for practice; (c) the practice material is directly related to the problem; (d) the practice is characterized by reflection, self-criticism, and further reflection; and (e) the learner participates in the selection of practice material.

It is obvious that a good deal of what passes for music practice does not fulfill these conditions.

Frequent short practice periods are likely to be more economical and efficient than long periods. The period may profitably be lengthened as the learner matures, but practice should never be carried on to the point where the pupil has difficulty maintaining interest and concentrating his attention. Too long practice periods bring on fatigue, boredom, and repetition without learning.

Meaningful practice is characterized by purposive and goal-directed work on an intelligible musical problem. It is nothing more nor less than an intensive individual learning experience.

7. *Musical learning has a sequence of synthesis-analysis-synthesis.* Efficient musical learning is always directed at a musically intelligible whole, not toward the bits and pieces of musical structure, musical technique, or musical experience. Once a concept of the whole has been established, there begins the analysis phase during which the parts are differentiated in relation to the whole. This, in turn, leads to a reorganization or restructuring of the whole. As this process is repeated, concepts of the whole, the parts, and the interrelationships among them are clarified.

For example, in learning a new song by rote children should first grasp the expressive intent of the song. They hear the song, become aware of the general contour of the melody, and try to sing it. With repeated hearings and further tries at singing it they gradually refine their concept of the song. If some passages present rhythmic or melodic difficulties, they are taken out of context, worked on, and placed back into the context of the phrase in which they occur. Thus an accurate and expressive performance of the song gradually emerges.

Similarly, chorus members learning a new composition hear a recording of it or listen to the accompanist play it through. They get a general idea of its content, its shape, its harmony, and its expressive purpose. Then they try to read it through with the piano accompaniment. Passages giving trouble are singled out for special attention and immediately placed back into context. They become aware of the relationship between the different vocal parts and hear their own parts in relation to the total harmonic and rhythmic flow. Their performance gradually becomes refined and accurate as their expressive intentions and their musical concepts are sharpened and clarified.

This is in sharp contrast to procedures often followed in learning new choral music. Many teachers begin by playing the soprano part for the first phrase, having it sung, moving to the alto part, then combining the two. Each part is singled out in turn and added to the others. The difficulty is that no preliminary synthesis takes place; the learners have no concept of the whole.

8. *Learning is an active process.* Learning takes place only through activity by the learner. His activity may be mental, physical, or both, but there must be a release of energy directed at the learning problem. Efficient musical learning requires exploration and discovery of musical meaning by the student. The learner must have a sense of personal involvement in the learning problem. Many unsuccessful musical learning situations are characterized by a passive attitude on the part of the learners. For example, listening lessons often entail great activity by the teacher and little by the pupils. As a result, the teacher may learn a great deal with little or no effect on the students.

9. *Learning is highly individualized.* The ability to learn depends upon both native endowment and previous experience which make the individual what he is. In every group there are wide variations in musical knowledge, understanding, skill, and in attitudes and emo-

tions. The same teaching materials, teaching methods, and motivating devices cannot work equally well with all students. Pressure may stimulate some students but retard others. Recitals and contests undoubtedly are advantageous for some students but not for others. The clue to the individualization of the learning situation lies in understanding each student, his motives, his capacities, his purposes, and his personality.

10. *Learning may transfer if generalization takes place.* The question of transfer is of crucial importance in musical learning, because unless transfer does take place, musical independence can never result. It is obvious that musical learning does occur without transfer. Evidence of this is found in the great number of musicians who learn to play a few compositions beautifully while under the guidance of a teacher but who are unable to prepare a performance independently. Likewise, learnings accruing from the music theory class frequently do not transfer to a pupil's performance. Failure to obtain transfer often results from undue concern with specifics and details, without adequate attention to deriving and applying generalizations to all phases of musical experience.

All musical learning should be focused on pupil development and testing of generalizations which can be used in solving musical problems. For example, learning in applied music and music theory should result in the formation of generalizations about interpretation, with reference to such matters as the shape of phrases, resolution of dissonances, and movement toward cadences. Likewise, learning in music history should result in the formulation of generalizations based on an understanding of musical styles which can be applied to the comprehension and performance of compositions in a wide range of styles.

Transfer of musical learnings results not in student mimicry of the teacher or in encyclopedic knowledge but in broad functional musicianship and musical independence.

11. *Learning is affected by the total environment of the learning situation.* Physical and social factors have a direct influence on the effectiveness of learning experiences. The learner is interacting not only with the teacher and the instructional materials and methods but with the total situation. An attractive, well-lighted, comfortable room and good equipment represent important factors in efficient learning. The social climate likewise has a potent effect on learning. The learner works more efficiently under a cheerful, helpful teacher who shows interest in his progress and his problems. A feeling of security and lack of tension are important characteristics of a good learning situation.

A PROGRAM FOR THE FUTURE

Up to the present time, most of the efforts to apply learning theory to musical learning have taken this direction: Because a particular theory of learning (e.g., field theory or associationist theory) indicates such and such to be true, the music teacher ought to do thus and so. This represents a logical application of principles of learning to the teaching and learning of music. A number of learning theorists and educational psychologists have arrived at the conclusion that the time has come to abandon such hortatory tactics. Such tactics have accomplished an admirable purpose. Almost all music teachers have become more or less cognizant of psychological considerations that are relevant to teaching and are aware of at least the obvious implications of learning theory for teaching method. There is good reason to believe that further efforts in this direction can accomplish little more than has already been done.

Current thinking among psychologists has produced what seems to be a more promising alternative, which takes this direction: Because such and such appears to be true, we should determine whether the teacher can be helped to implement principles from learning theory with well-designed instructional material and teaching and evaluative procedures consistent with the nature of the materials. In other words, the shift in emphasis is from logical application of principles of learning to a kind of action research. Such a shift seems timely and promising in the field of music education.

A more fruitful alternative to past practice may lie in subjecting musical learning to searching analysis to determine what different types of learning are involved in musical learning as a whole. Once we identify and understand the different types of learning involved in the development of musicianship, we can then turn to a relevant theory of learning for principles of learning that are applicable to each type and for cues as to how best to structure experiences relevant to each type.

It seems obvious that musical learning is a multifaceted process and that there are several different types of behavior and several types of learning involved in the various outcomes music educators seek. Analysis of musical behavior has resulted in the identification of five different types of behavior in relation to music: knowing, feeling, hearing, discriminating, and performing. Each behavior involves a different type of learning and no one theory of learning can explain all the types of learning involved.

Learning to know, for example, undoubtedly involves perception. It would seem reasonable to adopt a cognitive restructuring approach to learning theory for this type of learning. The teacher would have the task of organizing experiences for the student that would be influential in restructuring the student's cognitive field. He might turn to Piaget, Bruner, or Ausubel for theoretical principles to guide and evaluate his procedures.

Learning to hear, on the other hand, involves at some point in the learning sequence a great deal of conditioning, and a theory which views learning as conditioning would appear applicable. The teacher's task in this instance would be to develop a sequential program of musical tasks which would provide the student with repeated opportunities to respond to cues and to receive prompt reinforcement. In this instance, the teacher might turn to Mowrer[41] or Skinner as a source of theoretical principles.

The program described may be summarized as follows:

1. There are several different types of learning involved in overall musical learning.
2. No one theory of learning can account for all the different types of learning.
3. There is little reason to continue at the hortatory level of drawing implications from learning theory for the teaching of music.
4. A more fruitful approach may be to analyze musical learning, which music educators are in a unique position to do. Learning theorists can assist in the analysis but cannot do it alone. A cooperative effort of learning theorists, educational psychologists, and music educators is indicated.
5. Once we know the different types of learning we are trying to implement, we can choose with greater confidence the theoretical view of learning that is relevant and applicable to each type.
6. Action research and experimental research pointed toward the development of a theory of musical learning, and a technology of music teaching should be initiated at all levels of the program. Music educators, learning theorists, educational psychologists and curriculum specialists should be involved directly in the research.

SUMMARY

Learning is defined as a problem-centered process in which the learner gradually apprehends, clarifies, and applies meaning. Without meaning there can be no learning. Music education is properly concerned with the explication of musical meaning.

[41] O. H. Mowrer, *Learning Theory and Behavior*, John Wiley and Sons, Inc., New York, 1960.

Music has both embodied (musical) and designative (extramusical) meaning. The latter emerges almost without formal musical instruction; the former merits and requires the best efforts of music teachers. The perception of embodied meaning depends upon development of responsiveness to the undulations between intensity and release which take place in tonal and rhythmic movement. This, in turn, leads to the development of expectations and understanding of the ways in which intensity will be resolved. Musical meaning can emerge only from varied experience with actual music performed artistically and expressively.

Musical learning leads to changes in musical behavior. The products of musical learning include appreciation, understanding, knowledge, skills of listening, skills of performance, attitudes, and habits.

Age maturation and musical maturation are both essential to economical learning of highly specific and specialized musical responses, and both must be taken into account in planning the music program and perfecting methods of teaching. A cyclic approach to program planning and music teaching is indicated. Learning theories fall into two main groupings, associationist theories and field theories. Since no one theory of learning can presently account for all the forms of learning which occur, it is essential to develop a set of learning principles which cut across the lines separating the various theories.

QUESTIONS FOR DISCUSSION

1. How would you define learning? What are its essential characteristics?
2. Describe how meaning arises in music. How is it possible for music to have extramusical meaning? What are the implications for musical instruction?
3. Describe the expressive qualities which may arise from tonal and rhythmic movement. Why is it so important to develop the sense of tonal expectation?

4. What types of behavior result from musical learning? In what respect is musical knowledge important? How does knowledge relate to musical understanding and appreciation?
5. Why are listening skills so important in music? How do they affect performing skills? In what ways is practice made effective?
6. What is involved in learning to read music?
7. Describe the chief means to the formation of attitudes. Why is musical independence so important and how is it achieved?
8. What is meant by maturation? Is the rate of maturation affected by experience? Why must maturation be taken into account in planning musical instruction?
9. Describe the essential differences between field theories and association theories of learning. Can you see how such differences might affect the conduct of music teaching?
10. What is the nature of musical problems? Why are they indispensable in learning?
11. Describe several forms of motivation in musical learning. What is the best means of motivation?
12. Illustrate how musical concepts may be formed.
13. Why is "transfer" so important? How is maximum transfer achieved?
14. What are the implications of recent developments in learning theory for the organization and conduct of the music education program?
15. What aspects of musical learning seem to you to lend themselves to programmed learning?

SELECTED REFERENCES

Ausubel, David P. *The Psychology of Meaningful Verbal Learning and Retention*, Grune & Stratton, New York, 1963.

Bigge, Morris L. *Learning Theory for Teachers*, Harper & Row, New York, 1964.

Bilodeau, Edward A., ed. *Acquisition of Skill*, Academic Press, Inc., New York, 1966.

Bruner, Jerome S. *The Process of Education*, Harvard University Press, Cambridge, Mass., 1960 (also, Vintage Books, Random House, New York, 1963.)

DeCecco, John P. *The Psychology of Learning and Instruction,*: Educational Psychology, Prentice-Hall, Inc., Englewood Cliffs, N.J., 1968.

Fitts, Paul M., ed. "Factors in Complex Skill Learning," *Training Research and Education*, Academic Press, Inc., New York, 1962, pp. 244-285.

Flagg, Marion. *Musical Learning*, Summy-Birchard Company, Evanston, Ill., 1940.

Gagné, Robert M. *The Conditions of Learning*, Holt, Rinehart and Winston, Inc., New York, 1965.

Gronlund, Norman E. *Stating Behavioral Objectives for Classroom Instruction*, The Macmillan Company, Collier-Macmillan Limited, London, 1970.

Hilgard, Ernest R., and Gordon W. Bower. *Theories of Learning*, Appleton-Century-Crofts, New York, 1966.

Holland, James G., and B. F. Skinner. *The Analysis of Behavior*, McGraw-Hill Book Company, New York, 1961.

Hunt, James McV. *Intelligence and Experience*, The Ronald Press Company, New York, 1961.

Klausmeier, H.J., and Chester W. Harris, eds. *Analyses of Concept Learning*, Academic Press, Inc., New York, 1966.

Lundin, Robert W. *An Objective Psychology of Music*, The Ronald Press Company, New York, 1968.

Lysaught, Jerome P., and Clarence W. Williams. *A Guide to Programmed Instruction*, John Wiley and Sons, New York, 1963.

Mager, Robert F. *Preparing Instructional Objectives*, Fearon Press, Palo Alto, Calif., 1962.

Meyer, Leonard B. *Emotion and Meaning in Music*, University of Chicago Press, Chicago, 1956.

Mursell, James L. "Growth Processes in Music Education," *Basic Concepts in Music Education*, National Society for the Study of Education Fifty-seventh Yearbook, Part I, Chicago, 1958, pp. 140-162.

——. *Education for Musical Growth*, Ginn & Company, Boston, 1948.

Piaget, Jean. *The Language and Thought of the Child*, Meridian Books, The World Publishing Company, Cleveland, 1965.

Thorpe, Louis P. "Learning Theory and Music Teaching," *Basic Concepts in Music Education*, National Society for the Study of Education Fifty-seventh Yearbook, Part I, Chicago, 1958, pp. 163-194.

PART 3 PRINCIPLES OF MUSIC EDUCATION

Every music educator has multiple responsibilities and plays varying roles. At different times he is a program developer, a teacher, an administrator, a supervisor, and an evaluator. While his primary responsibility may involve one of these roles, he must be competent to serve in all the others.

The intent of Part Three is to apply the theoretical insights developed in Parts One and Two to the organization and conduct of the music education program. Each of the processes in education—program building, instruction, administration, supervision, and evaluation—is treated in detail. The nature of each process is clarified and the techniques involved are explained and illustrated with numerous examples from day-to-day experience. The principles governing each process are developed.

Objectives
for Music Education

6 Purpose is prerequisite to learning and progress. Music educators as a group exhibit this characteristic to a marked degree. They are generally resolved to enrich the musicianship of their pupils, to extend music's force in American life, and to strengthen their own profession.

These ends are not likely to be achieved, however, unless effort is concentrated upon more specific goals. What characterizes musicianship? What kinds of musical activity occur in a healthful musical climate? Too often the music educator works primarily at the obvious and promotional level, forgetting that expanding musical organizations and public approbation are only signs of more basic accomplishment.

Truly, objectives *should* be matters of strong personal conviction, but they must also be a product of wide understanding and investigation. This chapter will deal with the nature of objectives and their uses. Attempting to avoid generalities, we shall discuss methods of forming and establishing objectives and shall suggest patterns appropriate to general music and the musical specialties.

THE FUNCTION OF OBJECTIVES
IN MUSIC EDUCATION

Objectives are often conceived as highly idealistic statements, for use as front material in catalogs and brochures directed toward gullible parents, school boards, and superintendents. On the contrary, honestly held objectives are the most practical tools of the music teacher. They are the foundation of a strong and consistent music program and serve as reference points for every professional decision and action. More specifically, they serve to (1) assure positive relation of musical instruction to the broader aims of the school, (2) form the basis for planning educative experiences, (3) control the daily adjustment of methods and materials, and (4) provide criteria for evaluation of instruction.

Consistency with Broad Educational Aims

Broadly stated, the mission of the schools is to assist the individual to live in and deal wisely with his environment and, by this means, to strengthen and improve the useful institutions of society. In attempting to interpret this mission, educators have evolved conflicting philosophies. It must be understood that American schools and colleges are not united in pursuit of any particular group of objectives.

Some educators contend that the primary ends of education are social: the individual should be equipped with the abilities valuable to society. Others believe education should be conceived in terms of growth in individual capacity. Between these two extremes lies the *interactive* position. Its advocates point out that education can begin with individual needs and interests, but that these are naturally shaped by one's social participation.

While presenting many difficulties in application, this last position holds the center of the educational scene. It holds that a person needs to be mentally and physically alert to his environment and its lessons and to possess the necessary tools to cope with it. He needs skills and understanding in basic human relationships and he must be prepared to meet vocational and civic responsibilities.

It is immediately apparent that musical activity can help him achieve these ends. To name the most obvious factors, musicianship is vitally important to one's aesthetic growth, emotional feelings, and leisure-time activities.

This, however, represents a roundabout method of identifying the objectives of music education. Chapter Four developed the thesis that music is a basic phenomenon of man's life, that it is embedded in our culture. If music educators can develop in their pupils a greater responsiveness to this medium, they have at once discharged their obligation to the individual, to society, and to the schools. Those objectives which may be associated with a heightened musicianship will best serve in the curriculum.

Musicianship is not reserved to the professional musician. There are many common musical abilities which are derived from universal human nature and which are socially important. Everyone hears and reacts to music. The layman establishes aesthetic values and develops powers of musical discrimination. Because music is so pervasive, society expects of the individual some degree of musical understanding and active participation. It is the primary function of objectives to define such musicianship.

Planning Educative Experience

Another basic use of objectives is to provide clues to the educative experiences which should form the music program. When the teacher fails to understand this connection, his objectives become inert. He merely "sets up shop" and proceeds to appy his notions to the operation of the music program. He develops the usual musical organizations and activities, schedules concerts and musical productions, and uses musical materials and methods of procedure familiar to him.

There is no guarantee that the objectives will be reached by virtue of a well-rounded series of musical activities competently handled. The music program does not actually consist of singing, playing, listening, and so on. Neither does it consist of the music used or the subject matter covered. The music program is the body of *individual experiences* which the student actually undergoes in connection with his active participation, and only these affect his behavior. The point is that certain kinds of experience are conducive to the production of specific behaviors. Only when objectives are known is it possible to arrange the program realistically and efficiently.

For example, if the teacher believes a student should know music of all styles and periods, this student should be (1) surveying the varieties of compositions within the field of music, (2) establishing thorough familiarity with individual works, and (3) applying the resulting acquaintance with such music. These experiences can be sought for him in each music class and organization.

Ordering Instruction

It follows that objectives also provide the basis for the selection of subject matter, materials, and methods. In connection with the above-named experiences the pupil will find use for considerable information about music's historical development, structural patterns, idiomatic usages, and technical problems. He will profit from a tasteful and contrasting selection of musical materials. The teacher will probably find it necessary to deal quite broadly with the music and the student, giving him opportunity to experiment, absorb, and perfect his understanding. Such is the procedure if the student is to know music of all styles and periods.

Basis for Evaluation

Evaluation involves gathering data and interpreting it in the light of certain criteria, and the only criteria applicable to the music program are its objectives. A music program simply cannot be judged in terms of the educational qualifications of teachers, the excellence of its facilities, or the types of activities it sponsors. Instead, it is judged in relation to the objectives, that is, in relation to its effect upon the habits and attitudes and skills of the students.

In order to make the evaluation, the active responses of students must be investigated. In relation to their knowledge of music of all styles and periods, again, do they show any interest or understanding when new compositions are introduced? Do they show any initiative in attending recitals or concerts and in discussing the numbers? What kinds of recordings and radio programs do they select?

Even more definitive are the activities of graduates, as well as any notable changes in the musical habits of the community or area served by the school. If a program is to be judged effective, a school's graduates must be markedly more advanced than the entrants in relation to the objectives. These gains should eventually be reflected in society.

It should be mentioned here that objectives also affect evaluation on a different plane. When marks must be given, it is common to forget objectives and simply test the student's recall of what the teacher has said and done. Who then can blame the student for assuming that assimilation of this material is the true objective? Monroe put it quite bluntly over thirty years ago and his statement is just as relevant, if not more so, in the 1970s as it was in the 1930s:

> There has been much discussion of the importance of teachers formulating their objectives, and, in response to the pressure of authority, they have spent many hours in formulating lists of immediate objectives, that is, the goals toward which the students are expected to direct their efforts. Many of these lists merit commendation, but their influence upon students is practically nil in comparison with the influence of tests administered. Students direct their efforts toward becoming able to respond to the tests they anticipate.[1]

---

[1] Walter S. Monroe, "Some Trends in Educational Measurement," *Twenty-fourth Annual Conference on Educational Measurements*, Bulletin of the School of Education, Indiana University, 13 (4):32, Bureau of Cooperative Research, Bloomington, Ind., 1937.

The fact that students react more directly to tests than to the instructor's stated objectives means only that students are quite practical. They desire grades as high as possible and realize that test results are highly influential to that end. The implication for the instructor is that test items must always be constructed with objectives strictly in mind.

It must also be remembered that tests are not the only means of gathering data. In determining the student's understanding of musical interpretation, for example, a great deal can be learned from observation. Does the student show any independent conception of interpretation as he performs alone or in groups? Do the musical markings mean nothing to him, does he follow them strictly, or can he truly interpret them with taste? There is little point in asking him for the definitions of common musical terms. More reasonable situations can be devised, calling for sight reading, conducting, or a critique upon some amateur performance.

It is impossible to escape the necessity for objectives. Unless the music program is centered upon them, there is no adequate means for determining how and what to teach or how well the job is being accomplished. Actually, such a formless program is unlikely because music teachers usually will fall back on their unconsciously formed assumptions as guides for instruction. Objectives formed as the result of active and enlightened search, however, provide the only sound basis for a truly powerful music program.

FORMULATING OBJECTIVES OF MUSIC EDUCATION

As the central factor in establishing and operating the music program, objectives should be the concern of every music educator. Each teacher needs to understand the process of formulation, for objectives affect every level of the program. The best way to ensure their effectiveness is for each teacher to help in the definition. He may agree in principle with lists that are prepared for him, but these are not so likely to form the actual basis for his teaching. As a general principle, objectives should be formulated by those individuals or groups which will be directly concerned with their application. That is, society and the teaching profession establish the broad social objectives. Specific goals should be determined locally for each educational institution, and the music staff should formulate the objectives of their own music program. Instructor and students should be responsible for fixing the attainments toward which they will work in each music class or organization.

Sincere expressions from parents and students regarding objectives should be sought. Insofar as these people represent society at large, and since they are most directly affected by the school program, they have every right to influence it. The key to this is effective communication—through questionnaires, information bulletins, forums, and casual discussion—whereby the music teachers and their constituents may present their points of view to one another. But of course it is the teacher's professional duty to go on from there to create a working pattern for the music program.

Sources of Objectives

Objectives have their source in human need, the social structure, and the nature of the subject. What musical information can people use, and what skills would improve their command of the art? To what extent is their musical taste subject to development, and what direction should it take? What opportunities for participation in the musical life of the community are open to the student? How can he exert his influence toward more flourishing musical activity in our society?

Answers to such questions are found through direct study and observation of students, as well as by close examination of psychological and sociological evidence. For instance, it is known that people are steadily earning more and working fewer hours. They find it no longer necessary to attend local concerts, but are increasingly exposed to a wide selection of music on radio, television, and records. Individuals today are faced with the need for keen powers of discrimination. And "live" music on the local scene becomes more and more the responsibility of the layman, since the professionals are naturally drawn to the larger centers of population and to the radio, television, and recording studios.

Thus we find that students need an attitude of musical objectivity. They should be able to compare musical styles ranging from serious masterworks to jazz classics to current hits. They should also prize quality renditions of music, since they have the choice, and should purchase radios, recordings, and musical instruments which do justice to the music. They need skills of performance which naturally transfer to their homes and community. They should be able to organize and sing and play in local musical groups. This is the real crux of the matter: to discover what competencies a student needs and can achieve in his quest for personal fulfillment and social usefulness.

This tailor-made quality of education cannot be achieved unless the curriculum makers truly understand the implications supporting their objectives. For example, ordinary social occasions call for the ability to sing many common melodies, and it can be assumed that singing is for the human being an inherently enjoyable, meaningful activity. Therefore, all students need to be taught a certain body of commonly used songs and hymns and should be able to sing these with comfort, understanding, and enjoyment. But is this enough? Many happy and successful people can do no more. Does one *really* need to sing by note and read parts, or indeed, to sing accurately and beautifully some of the great examples of choral art?

Yes, these accomplishments are useful to the individual and to society. If a student can accomplish so much, a greater measure of music's aesthetic qualities will be his, as well as expanded opportunities for social participation. There is a point, however, at which pursuit of complex techniques and knowledge becomes impractical. An extensive vocal range and knowledge of principles of voice production are undoubtedly special needs of the vocal performer or teacher, but pursuit of these ends could easily distort the education of the general student.

It becomes apparent that the identification of objectives is no simple task. One does not concoct them out of thin air. It is necessary to utilize the best of scientific data and expert opinion and to weigh all this in terms of broad educational aims.

The Setting of Objectives

As we have just indicated, all useful musical behaviors are not suited to every type of music program. Each school has a somewhat different function. There are large metropolitan public schools, rural school districts, private and parochial schools and colleges, state universities, teachers colleges, music conservatories, and so on. Manifestly, each type of educational institution caters to certain types of students and attempts to fulfill particular functions in our society. A school may emphasize general musicianship or preparation for teaching, performance, composition, musical scholarship, or any special aspect or combination of these. The general outline of these programs is taken up later in this chapter.

Those who formulate objectives for the music program must keep those distinctions in mind. Let us consider these statements:

1. The musically educated person performs music with facility and taste.
2. He demonstrates and explains the principles of tone production and techniques on various instruments.
3. He plays and sings from memory the standard repertoire in his particular field.

Although these three items are closely related, they are incorrectly stated, for they differ in scope and application. The first pertains alike to the professional and the layman. But the general student, and even the professional, need not know the technical principles pertaining to all the instru ments; only the music teacher finds this imperative. Full maintenance of repertoire is necessary only to the profession- al performer. These objectives should read:

1. *The musically educated person* performs music with facility and taste.
2. *The qualified music teacher* demonstrates and explains the principles of tone production and technique on various instruments.
3. *The performing artist* plays or sings from memory the standard repertoire in his particular field.

Classification of Objectives

It is easy to confuse objectives with other elements of the teaching process. The following statements are often (and falsely) regarded as objectives: (1) origin of the classical forms; (2) to integrate music with the other school subjects; (3) the student should be able to perform Bach's *Two-part Inventions.*

The first item is simply a statement of a topic to be covered, while the second only indicates that the teacher intends to introduce music in connection with the other subjects. Neither of these tells anything about the results to be expected. The third statement is more concrete; it tells us exactly what pieces the student must play, but it says noth- ing regarding the rendition itself nor what qualities of musi- cianship should be displayed. In actual fact, there are good pianists who have not studied these particular compositions.

True objectives relate to certain varieties of behavior. This classification has been used:[2]

The cognitive domain ... includes those objectives which deal with the recall or recognition of knowledge and the development of intellectual abilities or

---

[2] Benjamin S. Bloom, ed., *Taxonomy of Educational Objectives, Hand- book I: Cognitive Domain*, David McKay Co., Inc., New York, 1956, p. 7.

skills. . . . A second part of the taxonomy is the affective domain. It includes objectives which describe changes in interests, attitudes, and values, and the development of appreciations. . . . A third domain is the manipulative or motor-skill area.
Let us consider each form of behavior separately.

Knowledge. Among the outcomes of any musical activity should be knowledge of terminology, facts, beliefs, trends, and categories. For example, the musically educated person (1) is acquainted with a variety of musical compositions, (2) recognizes basic musical patterns and usages, and (3) recalls essential facts in music's development as an art. Since behavior of this type is relatively concrete, a little thought will produce the essential items of knowledge suited to any particular musical activity or level of schooling. Indeed, it is difficult to avoid overemphasis upon information at the expense of other outcomes equally important.

Understanding. The student's comprehension and application of facts is a higher form of behavior, and goals in this area merit careful consideration. It is of slight value to know the principles of diaphragmatic breathing unless this knowledge is accompanied by an understanding of the problems of application in performance. Likewise, knowledge of any musical form should be accompanied by comprehension of subtle variations and alterations of the standard pattern.
Understanding implies the ability to analyze and to generalize. For instance, we should expect from the musically educated person (1) perception of the technical problems of performance, (2) insight into the elements of musical interpretation, and (3) comprehension of the structural factors in a musical composition.

Skills. The need for basic musical skills is quite clear. These will include (1) factors of aural awareness and discrimination and (2) tne ability to solve technical problems associated with musical performance and composition. Illustrative of these skills would be (1) the ability to perceive and follow a melody, (2) the ability to perform with good intonation, and (3) the ability to produce a pleasing tone.

By way of preliminary drill, some teachers promote many unnecessary skills. Many students become highly skilled in reading by syllables, performing scales and vocalises, and in baton twirling. Only skills which are of intrinsic value to the student should qualify as objectives.

Attitudes.   In the common preoccupation with musical knowledge and skill, the emotional reactions of students are easily forgotten. We have all known students who make "straight A's" on tests and win all manner of contests, and yet develop a distaste for music and the musical vocations. It is definitely important that the student develop positive attitudes, such as (1) respect for the musical preferences of other people, (2) recognition of the musical efforts of his associates, and (3) desire to improve his musical competence

Appreciations.   The perception of music's aesthetic content is often thought to be an incidental outcome of instruction. The teacher too easily assumes that more acquaintance with music should result in appreciation of it. Instead, experiences must serve to highlight the differences in musical content and device. Criteria for judging musical quality need to be established. Such instruction tends to produce a student who (1) responds to the expressive quality in music, (2) differentiates among musical styles and idioms, and (3) judges the degree of skill and taste exhibited in musical performance.

Initiatives.   A number of desirable musical initiatives instantly come to mind. For example, the musically educated person (1) seeks to play and sing with others, (2) supports school and community musical activities, and (3) listens selectively to radio and TV broadcasts.

These forms of musical behavior are primary goals and do not necessarily accrue from a wide background of musical knowledge and skill. Indeed, many professional musicians and music teachers fail to qualify in these respects. Such criteria are implicit in any evaluation. They should be formulated so that instruction can be organized to produce them.

Levels of Objectives

Much confusion exists in grouping and applying objectives because the operation of different levels is so often misunderstood. Some primary aims are constantly applicable throughout the schools, while others are more specific objectives appropriate to certain situations and not to others. Many other desirable behaviors are naturally associated with particular music classes or activities and cannot be readily approached in other settings. Thus, unless objectives can be properly classified and aligned, they are likely to confuse instruction rather than to strengthen it. The following outline of objectives, by level, is intended to illustrate the way in which objectives are interrelated:

1. *Broad aim* of school music:
   A society whose members use music more fully in daily living.
   As a means to the above aim—

2. *Concrete social objectives*, defining basic musical behaviors sought of all citizens:
   a. familiarity with a body of standard musical works
   b. broad but discriminating musical tastes
   c. awareness of basic musical design and the general outline of its evolution
   d. ability to perform by rote and by note
   e. initiative in musical activity appropriate to one's interests and talents[3]
   As a means to the above—

[3] National Association of Schools of Music, *Proceedings of the 43rd Annual Meeting*, Washington, D.C., 1968, p. 70.

3. *Program objectives*, defining the musical behaviors desired in a particular institution's graduates:
   Knowledge of:
   a.   musical literature from all periods and idioms
   b.   basic musical patterns and usages
   c.   musical vocabulary and meanings
   d.   music's development as an art
   e.   the principal forms and composers
   Understanding of:
   a.   problems in performing and learning to perform
   b.   the elements of good musical interpretation
   c.   the general methods by which music is constructed
   Skill in:
   a.   producing a rich tone with acceptable intonation
   b.   playing with reasonable facility and accuracy
   c.   performing by ear
   d.   reading music of appropriate difficulty
   e.   performing with others, independently, yet in pro-
         per relation to the ensemble
   f.   hearing and following the main elements of musical
         compositions
   Attitudes of:
   a.   musical broadmindedness and the necessary dis-
         crimination of quality
   b.   respect for music as an art and a profession
   c.   intention to improve one's musicianship
   Appreciation of:
   a.   skilled and tasteful performance
   b.   good music in any medium, style, or period
   Initiatives:
   a.   frequent and efficient individual practice
   b.   proper selection and care of instruments
   c.   participating wholeheartedly in musical groups
   d.   proper rehearsal attendance, deportment, and
         attention
   e.   selecting good recordings, searching for more musi-

cally satisfying radio and TV programs, and attending worthwhile concerts[4]
As a means to the above—

4. *Instructional objectives*, defining specific competencies to be developed in each music class or activity, over a limited time span, such as the following:
A student after completing fourth-grade music class:
   a.   will repeat any simple and brief melodic pattern just heard
   b.   will sing alone a recognizable version of any song that has once been learned by his class and occasionally reviewed
   c.   will play at least three of the standard classroom instruments in proper and characteristic fashion, and use any one of these to accompany singing
   d.   after standard listening examples are presented live or recorded, will identify the meter, two- and three-part song forms, and the principal themes and their return
   e.   after having learned to use the syllables (movable *do*) in singing simple songs and tonal patterns, will sing alone any set of three basic intervals (four tones) from the given syllables
   f.   will repeat any ordinary rhythmic pattern and maintain it with a steady beat and accurate subdivision
   g.   after having been introduced to the basic elements of notation, will identify lines and spaces in the treble clef and find *do* from a given key signature
A student after completing beginning clarinet class, fifth grade:

[4] Robert W. House, *Instrumental Music for Today's Schools*, Prentice-Hall, Inc., Englewood Cliffs, N.J., 1965, pp. 22-23

a.   will assemble and disassemble the clarinet properly
     and without damage, within two minutes
b.   if he possesses an adequate instrument, will pro-
     duce a reliable and characteristic tone, with accept-
     able intonation, on any passage within his technical
     powers
c.   after adequate group rehearsal of any suitable pas-
     sage, will perform it alone at a practical tempo
     with reasonable tonal and rhythmic accuracy
d.   when properly conducted or prompted and using
     an appropriate grade of music, will produce the
     marked dynamics and natural phrasings, and will
     perform with the proper style (legato, staccato ·
     marcato)
e.   when new material has been definitely assigned,
     will demonstrate his practice of it at the next
     lesson by his familiarity with the essential patterns
     and problems within it
f.   as a regular matter during rehearsals and lessons,
     will normally maintain alertness and avoid distrac-
     tion; he will respond positively to the teacher's
     directions and promptings; and he will strive to
     improve his own quality of performance
g.   after completing the first year of clarinet instruc-
     tion, will freely elect to continue his participation
     in the instrumental music program

It should be noted that the instructional objectives just
used in illustration are of the type often called *behavioral
objectives*. Although all objectives are properly concerned
with the behavior expected of students, true instructional
objectives must specify *observable* behavior which the student will be asked to use in demonstration of what he has
learned. Secondly, since instructional objectives are for a
particular class and group of students, the *conditions* under
which the student is expected to demonstrate achievement
are to be indicated; that is, the grade of music, type of
equipment, time limits, number of examples, etc., need to be

specified. Finally, the *criterion of evaluation* needs to be roughly established, consisting of the percentage of correct trials, the comparative quality of response, and so forth.

One of the great advantages of properly formulated instructional objectives is the ease with which they are translated into test items or check lists. A quick look at the lists given just above will show how this can be so. Another advantage in the use of instructional objectives lies in the ease with which they can be modified en route to fit the class—by allowing additional trials, reducing the time limits, etc. They are also easily understood by the student, who may well be allowed to assist in formulating and modifying them.

It may be seen in the above examples that each higher level is more general and comprehensive and depends upon the kind of job done with the next lower level. In this hypothetical situation, the teachers of the beginning clarinet class and of the fourth-grade music class would teach and evaluate their students in terms of the stated instructional objectives. Concurrently, the teachers of other classes and musical activities would be pursuing the instructional objectives especially appropriate to their own situations, all being calculated as steps to the kind of graduate defined by the program objectives. Graduates of that school, in turn, would join those from other schools and colleges whose musical behavior is likewise conceived in terms of the concrete social objectives, and thus help create "a society whose members use music more fully in daily living."

Validation of Objectives

Any objective formulated on the basis outlined should be legitimate in itself, yet it may fail to fit into an integrated pattern. If there is any indication that this is so, objectives should be validated by checking them against the principles upon which they were formulated.

The analysis and review of individual objectives requires the services of expert personnel. State supervisors, college teachers, and representatives of professional associations are often helpful. Sustained study is usually accomplished by a group consisting of the teachers themselves, local supervisors and administrators, and qualified graduates or local musicians interested in the school music program. Each objective should be studied in relation to the criteria and may be altered or rejected.

PRINCIPLES OF OBJECTIVES

The following principles have provided the basis for our discussion and hence serve as criteria for final judgment of our objectives:

1. *Objectives should reflect the aims of democratic society.* Every individual is entitled to the kind of music education from which he can profit. This implies the opportunity to share and understand the common musical heritage and the freedom to extend one's musical powers in accordance with his interests.
2. *Objectives should relate to actual social circumstances.* One case in point exists with the fact that current popular music (rock music) is a considerable force in our society. Many feel that anything of such magnitude and effect must be dealt with in the curriculum. Opponents argue that such music has insufficient merit to justify its study and, anyway, little can be added to what the youngsters already know about it. There are also a great number of pianos in America, along with a common regard for pianistic ability. Not only does the current music program fail to provide sufficient piano instruction, but it also fails to produce the necessary private teachers. On the other hand, there is not room for all the professional performers and composers which the schools actually produce. Objectives must be pointed toward building an army of skilled musical amateurs.
3. *Objectives should promote desirable social change.* Mu

sic educators must not be content to educate their students in terms of today's system but rather to promote abilities which they can use in enhancing and enlarging music's function in society.

In the first place, it would appear that the crown and scepter in composition and performance are passing from Europe to America. Today's students will need more understanding of musical techniques and more tolerance for new forms and idioms. Americans must become skilled critics, for their tastes will determine the direction of new paths in music.

The large number of community symphonies, "barbershoppers," and special church-choir presentations is evidence of healthful musical ferment. Unfortunately, school music has contributed to the idea that music should always be presented by large groups for large audiences. But the mass media may have taken over this market. School music should place more emphasis upon skills and appreciation in chamber music.

4. *Objectives should lead to the fulfillment of human needs.* Musical objectives must be in line with normative patterns for the particular age group, as well as the physical, social, and psychological development of the individual student. Needs are also influenced by the socioeconomic environment, parents, and peer group, and all other educative influences.

Most students have acquired the needs for personal achievement, status, and group approval. Music education can, of course, go far in meeting such needs, although the process will take many different forms. For instance, a third grader may acquire more status from merely owning a violin and being considered worth the cost of music lessons than from any ability to play the instrument. This fact can lead, however, to the satisfaction of the student's fundamental need for responsiveness to music. It can gradually produce an acquaintance with many types of music, the habit of seeking to hear good music, and abilities to perform and create music.

5. *Objectives should permit the utmost development of*

individual capacity. Although all people are inherently responsive to tone, there are undeniable variations in perception, muscular control, and intelligence. Some students can never really develop fine vocal accuracy or a decent facility on an instrument. Many are slow to grasp the finer points of musical structure or even to read music with ease. It has already been said that such students are equally a concern of the music educator along with his brightest, quickest students. Hence, the teacher's objectives must be realistically broad.

For instance, a teacher should be able to work toward the objective that students should sing beautifully and accurately. What is beautiful and accurate for one is not so for another; it is a matter of degree. Unfortunately, many teachers set a rigid standard for singing and rate as failures those pupils who do not reach it.

It is a fact that people of the same age have many common interests and experiences and behave similarly in many ways. This is particularly true at the earliest stages of growth. Individual differences and distinctly personal experiences lead people into increasingly diverging paths. Is it not possible, for example, that a high school freshman could exhibit readiness for serious musical composition? Fortunately, this kind of student usually goes right ahead and composes and accidentally discovers for himself the main theoretical principles. Such occurrences should not be extracurricular, but should be definitely included within the realm of the music program.

The vast majority of the school population will become musical amateurs. A very small percentage will turn to the musical professions as teachers and performers. Since these specializations grow out of general music training, the first duty of school music is clear: to produce the musical competence needed by the general public.

It is commonly assumed that the elementary

schools are the stronghold of general education, while the universities are places for specialization. This assumption is basically correct, yet specialization begins very early and general education never stops. Thus the elementary teacher should not thwart the growth of future music teachers and performers, and neither should college music departments exist only for the vocational education of the few.

6. *Objectives should be consistent with one another.* Music educators should never become snobbish about the outcomes in music and promote an exclusive musical taste for the "classics." This would rule out the band, the stage band, rock and modern folk groups, and a vast literature in light opera and Broadway musicals. Are these things inherently so unmusical, or are they just not the realm of the musically elite? Then again, can students become cooperative, working members of a group at the same time they are developing a fiercely competitive spirit? Does sound educational practice permit keeping pupils in a continual state of nervous tension over their place in the trumpet section or the rating a judge is going to give them?

7. *Objectives should be attainable by the means available.* Some very desirable qualities are not directly a concern of the schools, since schools were set up only to transmit cultural elements which have become too complex for society at large to handle. One would indeed learn a great many things if there were no schools at all. Popular entertainment, for instance, is really sustained independently of the schools. Having no means to control the outcomes, the schools have no business in this field.

On the other hand, the final stages of preparation for professional performance and composition are usually approached through private study. These high-level skills demand a form of on-the-job training. Even the finest conservatory cannot claim that musical learning in its entirety can be achieved within its walls. The really strong music program is limited to those ends which can be achieved by its particular students, staff, and facilities.

8. *Objectives should be readily interpretable into the program.* Valid objectives are concretely stated in terms of specific kinds of pupil behavior so that they may be used to determine the kinds of educative experience which should be sought and to serve as the stable criteria for the purpose of evaluation. Program objectives should picture the ideal graduate of a school, whose competencies result from pursuit of the avowed instructional objectives on each level and phase of the program. Objectives which fail to provide a clear-cut focus and direction to the organization and conduct of the music program are useless and insupportable.

OBJECTIVES IN GENERAL MUSIC

The most universal and stable segment of music education should be the area of general music instruction. Its manifest function is to provide every citizen with the key to his musical heritage. This task represents one phase of general education pursued throughout the period of formal schooling and beyond.

Obviously the objectives of general music must encompass those musical competencies which have broad application to the enrichment of living and which are not readily acquired through ordinary social intercourse. This rules out all forms of specialized vocational skill, as well as elemental musical awareness gained at mother's knee.

There is no firm agreement on the particular objectives which should be sought. In the belief that every person needs music, because of its appeal to man's aesthetic sense, we have suggested that the primary consideration of general music is heightened musical responsiveness. This implies several discrete qualities of musical behavior. The individual will need to know a variety of music and to understand many things about it. He will need the ability to participate in making music and should develop musical habits and appreciations to sustain him musically throughout his life. Precisely what things might a person do which would contribute to his musical responsiveness?

From this standpoint, objectives should include knowledge of musical compositions and styles, acquaintance with musical patterns and usages, and understanding of how music is composed, performed, and interpreted. Objectives must cover such necessary skills in singing and playing and listening as reading and improvisation, rhythmic and intervallic accuracy, and so on. It is also necessary to define the standard of musical taste needed by the common citizen, his feeling for the music itself, and his attitudes toward musicians and musical study. Finally, how should the musically educated person react to musical programs, practicing, invitations to sing or play, and so on? In other words, what consumer habits will be useful to him and to society?

The following list, developed by the National Assessment of Educational Progress, represents a broad but practical definition of skills to be developed by the musical layman:

1. Perform a piece of music.
    a. Sing (technical proficiency not required).
        Age 9
        Sing a familiar song with others.
        Sing it alone.
        Sing it in a new key.
        Maintain a part in a familiar round.
        Age 13
        (in addition to age 9)
        Maintain a harmonizing melodic line to a given melody.
        Age 17 and adult
        (as for age 13)

b. Play or sing (technical proficiency required).
Age 9
Sight-read.
Play a prepared piece.
Age 13
(as for age 9)
Age 17 and adult
(in addition to age 9)
Sing a prepared piece

c. Invent and improvise (technical proficiency not required).
Age 9
Add a rhythm accompaniment to a given melody. Sing a second phrase to complete beginnings of melodies.
Age 13
(as for age 9)
Age 17 and adult
(in addition to age 9)
Add a melodic-harmonic line to a given melody to provide a harmonic accompaniment or a descant.

2. Read standard musical notation.
a. Identify the elements of notation, such as clefs, letter names of notes, duration symbols, key signatures, and dynamic markings.
All ages
Distinguish isolated music notation symbols from other kinds of symbols.
Identify music notation symbols in context, i.e., in a given line of music.

b. Identify the correct notation for familiar pieces.
All ages

c. Follow notation while listening to music.
All ages
Identify place in score where music stops

Identify place in score where there is a discrepancy between the performance and the notation.

d.   Sight-singing.
     All ages

3. Listen to music with understanding.
    a.   Perceive the various elements of music, such as timbre, rhythm, melody and harmony, and texture.

    1. Identify timbres.
       Age 9
       Identify by categories the manner in which the instrument is played (e.g., struck, bowed).
       Identify individual instrumental timbres—unaccompanied.
       Identify individual instrumental timbres—with accompaniment.
       Age 13
       (in addition to age 9)
       Identify individual vocal timbres—with accompaniment.
       Identify ensemble timbres, instrumental and vocal.
       Age 17 and adult
       Identify by categories families of related timbres (e.g., woodwinds, plucked strings).
       Identify individual instrumental timbres—unaccompanied.
       Identify individual instrumental and vocal timbres—with accompaniment.
       Identify ensemble timbres, instrumental and vocal.

    2. Perceive features of rhythm and meter.
       Age 9
       Repeat rhythmic patterns just previously heard.
       Distinguish duple and triple meters when they are prominent.

Age 13
(in addition to age 9)
Distinguish syncopated from other rhythmic versions of the same piece.
Be aware of changes of rhythm in successive performances of a piece of music.
Identify where the change occurs (beginning, middle, or end).
Distinguish rhythmic from other kinds of changes (e.g., melodic and harmonic).
Age 17 and adult
(as for age 13)

3. Perceive features of melody.
   Age 9
   Repeat melodic patterns just previously heard.
   Distinguish melodic movement by steps or skips.
   Distinguish melodic direction (e.g., up, down, up then down).
   Age 13
   Repeat melodic patterns just previously heard.
   Distinguish melodic movement by steps or skips.
   Be aware of changes of melody in successive performances of a piece of music.
   Identify where the change occurs (beginning, middle, or end).
   Distinguish melodic from other kinds of changes, such as rhythmic and harmonic.
   Age 17 and adult
   (as for age 13)

4. Identify differing textures in the music heard by means of pictorial patterns representing the textures.
   All ages

5. Be aware of changes of harmony in successive performances of a piece of music.
   Age 9
   None

Ages 13, 17, and adult
Identify where the change occurs (beginning, middle, or end).
Distinguish harmonic from other kinds of changes, such as rhythmic and melodic.

b.   Perceive structure in music.
Age 9
Recognize repetition in two adjacent sections delineated by dynamic levels.
Recognize the phrase as a section in music.
Distinguish the return of an opening motive, phrase, or period, from different musical material.
Identify small forms (2-4 phrases long), such as A-A-B-A.
Identify familiar melodies in varied versions.
Age 13
(as for age 9)
Age 17 and adult
(in addition to age 9)
Identify larger forms (more than 4 phrases long), such as binary and ternary.

c.   Distinguish some differing types and functions of music.
Age 9
Associate musical rhythms with body movements.
Ages 13, 17, and adult
Distinguish musical structures by distinctive performing forces and/or manner of performance.
Distinguish distinctive manners of performance within the same performing forces.
Identify pieces by their regional characteristics.

d.   Be aware of (and recognize) some features of historical styles in music.
Age 9
None

Age 13

Recognize in a group of three selections the one which is in a different style.

Age 17 and adult

(in addition to age 13)

Identify specific historical styles:

—"classical" music: Renaissance to modern.

—Jazz piano styles: ragtime to modern.

4. Be knowledgeable about some musical instruments, some of the terminology of music, methods of performance and forms, some of the standard literature of music, and some aspects of the history of music.

 a. Know the meanings of common musical terms used in connection with the performance of music, and identify musical instruments and performing ensembles in illustrations.

  Age 9

  Identify pictures of instruments:

  —individual instruments.

  —families of instruments in a standard symphony orchestra.

  Identify pictures of performing ensembles.

  Identify terms denoting methods of performance.

  Identify musical instruments by name and manner in which they are played.

  Age 13

  (in addition to age 9)

  Identify the terms for musical forms.

  Age 17 and adult

  (in addition to age 13)

  Identify the terms for, and constitution of, standard performing ensembles.

 b. Know standard pieces of music by title, or composer, or brief descriptions of the music, or of literary-pictorial materials associated with the music from its inception.

Age 9
Identify pieces when distinctive excerpts are played, both classical and familiar (folk, patriotic, etc.).

Ages 13, 17, and adult
(in addition to age 9)
Know classical pieces with distinctive titles by composer and title.

   c.   Know prominent composers and performers by name and chief accomplishment.

Ages 13, 17, and adult

   d.   Know something of the history of music.

Age 9
None

Age 13
Know the approximate chronology of the historical eras from the Renaissance to the present and of representative forms and composers of these eras.

Age 17 and adult
(in addition to age 13)
Know something of the typical stylistic features of these eras.

5. Know about the musical resources of the community and seek musical experiences by performing music.

   a.   Know whether or not there are music libraries and stores in the community, and know where concerts are given.

Age 17 and adult

   b.   Seek to perform music by playing, singing, taking lessons, joining performing groups, etc.

All ages

6. Make judgments about music, and value the personal worth of music.

   a.   Distinguish parodies from their models.

All ages

b.   Be able to describe an important personal "musical" experience.
Ages 13, 17 and adult[5]

We have tried to show that the *instructional* goals must vary from level to level in order to contribute meaningfully to the final product. In the elementary school the idea is to build basic musical competence which will flower into more complex and subtle forms. One should work for clear singing tone, solid rhythmic feeling, accurate singing, expressive phrasing, clean enunciation, acquaintance with the musical score, a sense of harmonic tendencies, enthusiasm for new songs, and stylistic discrimination. There should be some knowledge and facility with the keyboard and with other instruments. The student should complete elementary school with the feeling that music is a rewarding activity, and he should actively seek further development of his musicianship.

Since instruction is more compartmentalized in the secondary school, general education in music is often neglected. The general music class is the logical answer to this situation. Objectives for this course should include the extension, clarification, and refinement of the broad musical competencies which have grown out of previous general music instruction in the elementary school.

Furthermore, secondary school performing groups and special music classes should extend the student's general musicianship. The band or orchestra member's experience need not be limited to a particular type of literature and specialized performing techniques; he should also develop greater accuracy in sight reading, wider musical tastes, theoretical understanding, finesse in interpretation, and other such general abilities. In addition, he should understand the value of a good musical instrument and how to take care of it, realize the effect of his playing on the ensemble, and acquire the habit of deliberate practice. These are patently objectives of general music.

[5] Eleanor L. Morris and John E. Bowes, eds., *Music Objectives*, National Assessment of Educational Progress, 1970.

The ultimate stage in general music is represented by the college liberal arts major, who deliberately takes care to avoid overspecialization. Objectives for such students have been stated as follows:

Musicianship
  a. Functional knowledge of the language and grammar of music.
  b. Ability to hear, identify, and relate esthetically the elements of music—rhythmic, melodic, harmonic, and formal.
  c. An understanding of the methods by which music is composed, the esthetic requirements of a given style, and the way by which those requirements are shaped by the cultural milieu.
  d. Intimate acquaintance with a wide selection of musical literature, the principal eras and genres.
  e. Maturing of musical taste and discrimination.

Musical performance
  a. Functional ability in those performing areas appropriate to the student's needs and interests.
  b. Fluency in sight reading.
  c. Understanding of performance procedures in realizing an appropriate musical style.[6]

THE MUSICAL SPECIALTIES

There are four fundamental branches of specialized music education: performance, composition and theory, musicology, and music teaching. Some students continue in one or more of these areas to a point as musical amateurs; others remain in them with vocational intentions. Furthermore, there are many side areas and special combinations within these fields; one may become a symphony player, a professional conductor, a public school music supervisor, an organ-

[6] National Association of Schools of Music, *Bulletin*, February 1967, pp. 100-101.

ist and private teacher, a music arranger, and so on. Since any professional program in music involves to an extent all the branches of music, people are frequently able to make shifts in their nominal specialization. Nevertheless, these constitute truly specialized forms of music education to the extent that they require competencies not needed by the layman.

Performance

Specialization in performance is the first item to consider, because the student so often starts sooner on this road than the others. Furthermore, it is the most immediately evident of the specializations, owing to the widespread popularity of instrumental and choral organizations as well as private instruction.

Students learn to sing and play as part of their general musical training; specialization begins when goals become associated with extra accomplishment in a particular species of performance. This may happen very early—even at the preschool level—and may extend to and beyond the graduate level.

Objectives center around the student's technical facility and command of the important musical literature in his chosen medium. The trumpet player, for instance, must have a good embouchure and range, an expressive tone, and the ability to read and play with speed and accuracy. He should be able to play the major trumpet solos artistically, and he should also be acquainted with important band and orchestral material. He should be able to transpose and to lead a section and should have good stage presence. He should possess the qualities essential to improvement, such as an understanding of technical problems, ambition, and good habits of practice.

Equivalent objectives are easily developed for the pianist, the singer, or the violinist. Objectives of this type should be considered in planning any of the ordinary performing activities—private and class instruction, large and small ensembles. Such objectives might be regarded as "electives" for those who have achieved considerable general musical competence.

Theory and Composition

Specialization in composition or theory attends a creative and practical interest in music's structure and organization. This interest, too, can develop quite early in a student. The particular needs of such a student include an appreciation of the creative possibilities in music and a realization of music's structural beauty and complexity. He needs an understanding of past developments in composition along with a knowledge of the ingredients of the principal musical idioms. In translating his ideas into reality, he needs an intimate knowledge of the inherent possibilities of the various performing media.

Such a person must be able to analyze the musical ideas and techniques of the music he hears. By some means, either from the keyboard or by acute visual and aural imagery, he must be able to translate musical scores with ease. He must have the ability to set his musical intentions on paper and to rehearse and perform his own works effectively. He closely observes the progress of his contemporaries and works constantly to improve his own techniques. His constant goal must be sincere individuality of expression.

Musicology

Specialization in musicology is associated with interest in research and historical knowledge of music. In this area, one is concerned with the systematization of knowledge pertaining to the entire field of music. The student solicits basic meanings; he investigates the theory of music theory; he wants to know why and how music is what it is.

This, again, is a more common type of specialization than one would imagine. In connection with the ordinary musical activities of the school, teachers find it necessary and educationally sound to provide some background for whatever they expect the student to learn; musical insight requires extensive information. The serious-minded student thus acquires a taste for inquiry; he becomes curious concerning the nature of the musical art. If he is to progress in this area, he must learn to work objectively and to build a true understanding of music's acoustical and psychophysiological effects. He needs to know the musical practices in the various cultures and in previous eras. He must be able to investigate carefully and to interpret his discoveries accurately. Such a student keeps informed of new findings about music and constantly seeks to discover useful knowledge.

Full-blown specialization in musicology is reserved for the upper levels of the educational system since it is here that research acquires its full meaning. To build the necessary competencies for that task is nevertheless a long process, and one that music educators must not suppress.

Music Teaching

Preparation for music teaching is a massive undertaking; it should include the essential factors in all areas of music education as they have been outlined, plus special competencies which are necessary in order to carry music's values to the student. These are all in addition to general education in the basic fields of knowledge, which are as important to the teacher as to anyone else.

For specific objectives, the reader is referred to the listing which forms part of the Music Education Curriculum as recommended by the National Association of Schools of Music.[7] This mentions competencies within the areas of general education, basic musicianship, performance, and professional education.

Specific preparation for teaching is strongly vocational and should only be undertaken after a wide musical background has been developed. A number of students, however, show marked interest and promise in this field before reaching college age; for example, some high school students have

[7] National Association of Schools of Music, *By-Laws and Regulations*, The Association, Washington, D.C., 1965, pp. 26-30.

picked up the ability to manage and rehearse large and small organizations. These students can be entrusted with student ensembles, pep bands, stage bands, marching drill, and so on, thus developing not only their musicianship but also some of the desired teaching and social competencies.

Indeed, it is difficult to say when and where any individual undergoes the crucial experiences which will largely set his course in the field of music. Music educators must be alert that no phase or segment of the music program becomes a separate discipline to the extent that the student's range of development is forceably restricted. Certainly the objectives that have been outlined here are not so narrowly conceived.

This does not rule out **the** necessity for membership restrictions in many phases of music. For instance, some students who want to join the high school orchestra or become music teachers or doctoral candidates are simply not eligible—at least, in terms of particular conditions of time and place. Such students have not acquired the necessary competence. It is only tragic when the music program has not given them every opportunity to do so.

The necessity for objectives should be clear; it is equally true that they must be intelligently formulated. Without objectives, the music program is rudderless on the educational seas. It is therefore a prime responsibility of each teacher to see that his sector of the program is not found wanting in this regard. The objectives that have been stated herein are only illustrative. No one set of objectives can be universally valid. The individual must face up to the task of carrying out his objectives if music education is to have its full impact on American society.

SUMMARY

When based upon music's value to the individual and to society, objectives assure the proper relation of the music program to the broader aims of the school. They are the foundation upon which one sets up the needed educative experiences, and thus they finally determine the teacher's choice of music, subject matter, and methods. The effectiveness of the program is evaluated on the basis of its objectives.

Objectives are best formulated by the people who must use them. They are identified through investigation of the needs of students and their roles in society, and the pattern of objectives logically varies from school to school. The several forms of behavior should be carefully considered What knowledge and understanding, attitudes and appreciations, skills and habits should the student acquire? A pattern must be established wherein the program objectives defining the graduating student are carefully distinguished from the supporting instructional objectives.

Objectives are ju'~ ¹ valid in relation to the principles upon which they have been founded. Are the objectives rooted in our way of life and do they tend toward its improvement? Will they truly satisfy human needs and will they cover wide differences in interests and capacities? Are they consistent and practical?

The function of the program in general music is to foster a heightened musical responsiveness in all citizens. This involves broad acquaintance with music and its techniques, skills in listening and performance, musical tastes, and habits of participation. General musical competence must be promoted in every phase and segment of the music program

Specialization in music takes several forms and is not reserved to the upper levels of schooling. The school musical groups easily lend themselves to production of special forms of competence in musical performance. Likewise, added abilities associated with music theory and composition can be fostered at any level of music education. Many students will establish a scholarly concern with all forms of musical knowledge. A complex form of specialization occurs in the preparation for music teaching. Here, the student must acquire all the essential ingredients of musicianship, plus teaching and social competencies which are vital to his task.

QUESTIONS FOR DISCUSSION

1. What basic error does the establishment of real objectives help avoid? How can they help music instruction to achieve its proper role within the curriculum? In what ways do they assist in planning and conducting musical instruction?
2. Who should be involved in formulating the objectives for any music program? Why is active participation in this process important?
3. Where do the ideas for particular objectives come from? Illustrate how certain facts can provide clues to the necessary objectives.
4. Why will objectives vary from school to school?
5. What kinds of musical behavior are included among legitimate objectives? Create some examples of each type.
6. Indicate several objectives for a single music course or activity which might relate to a single program objective. Can you think of other activities which might also help achieve the same objective?
7. Why is it necessary to consider our objectives in context with social conditions and aims? What criteria must be met?
8. For whom are the objectives of general music conceived? How would you describe general musicianship? What aspects of musicianship would not be legitimate goals of general music?
9. What are the primary forms of musical specialization? How do the objectives in each area differ from those of general music?
10. At what point does specialization occur? How can we know that a student is developing special interest in any one phase of music? In what circumstances should this be encouraged?
11. Appreciation has traditionally been an objective of im-

portance to music educators. In view of the current emphasis on behavioral definition of objectives, what specific behaviors would you accept as valid evidence of the presence of appreciation?

SELECTED REFERENCES

Aronoff, Frances Webber. *Music and Young Children*, Holt, Rinehart and Winston, Inc., New York, 1969.

Bloom, Benjamin S., ed. *Taxonomy of Educational Objectives, Handbook I: Cognitive Domain*, David McKay Co., Inc., New York, 1956.

Bruner, Jerome, S. *The Processes of Education*, Vintage Books, New York, 1960.

Burmeister, C. A. "The Role of Music in General Education," *Basic Concepts in Music Education*, National Society for the Study of Education Fifty-seventh Yearbook, Chicago, 1958, Part I, pp. 215-235.

Gagné, Robert M. "The Analysis of Instructional Objectives for the Design of Instruction," R. Glaser, ed., *Teaching Machines and Programmed Learning, II*, National Education Association, Washington, D.C., 1965, pp. 21-65.

Gronlund, Norman E. *Stating Behavioral Objectives for Classroom Instruction*, The Macmillan Company Collier-McMillan, Limited, London, 1970.

Kaplan, Max. *Foundations and Frontiers of Music Education*, Holt, Rinehart and Winston, New York, 1966.

Krathwohl, David R., Benjamin S. Bloom, and Bertram B. Masig. *Taxonomy of Educational Objectives, Handbook II: Affective Domain*, David McKay Co., Inc., New York, 1964.

Leonhard, Charles. "Evaluation in Music Education," *Basic Concepts in Music Education*, National Society for the Study of Education Fifty-seventh Yearbook, Chicago, 1958, Part I, pp. 310-338.

Lindvall, C. M., ed. *Defining Educational Objectives*, University of Pennsylvania Press, Pittsburgh, Pa., 1964.

Mager, Ralph F. *Preparing Instructional Objectives* The Fearon Press, Palo Alto, Calif., 1962.

Mursell, James L. *Music Education Principles and Programs*, Silver Burdett Company, Morristown, N.J., 1956, pp. 5-70.

Thompson, Merritt M. "The Levels of Objectives in Education," *Harvard Education Review*, 13:196-211,1943.

"Teacher Education in Music, an Interim Report of the MENC Commission on Teacher Education," *Music Educators Journal*, October 1970, pp. 33-48.

The Music
Education Program

Bert is soon to graduate from high school. He has found great value in his musical experiences and is planning a career in music. As a young child he liked music, and there was no question in his mind when the band director announced in his elementary school class that beginning instrumental groups were being formed. Although Bert had not done exceptional work in regular classroom music, he quickly showed promise on the cornet. The director encouraged Bert and never appeared to worry whether he learned much *about* music; however, when a certain item of information was necessary, the director could supply it.

Bert was glad to join the orchestra also, when the director needed another trumpet player. He noticed that the strings had more responsibility and therefore acquired a cello and began study with a private teacher. Before long he was at the top of the section. He began to enter contests in both his instruments and to extend his technique and style. His curiosity made him examine the musical scores, and he was thus led to try his hand at composing a few marches. These were only adequate, but the director allowed him to rehearse these numbers with the band and to conduct them at public concerts. By now, Bert is helping to lead and coach some of the small ensembles and has been elected by his fellow students to an office in one of the large organizations.

There are other students in the school whose development closely parallels Bert's; they are good students in general, but music seems to them the most rewarding activity in the school. Others have not found such a special interest, but are nevertheless enthusiastic about musical activities. It is not surprising that this school's musical groups tend to dominate state competitions, and their activities are strongly supported by the community.

There is a familiar ring to this hypothetical case. Music educators will recognize this as a normal preliminary to the musical professions and to rich musical life within a community. Why and how do such things occur? Many schools have bands and orchestras and choirs yet produce no such results. The difference lies not only in the natural aptitudes of students but also in the kinds of educative programs which music educators are able to construct. Unless they can assay the students' needs and interests and set up the musical activities so that students will become actively engaged in musical learning, the positive outcomes of schooling will be negligible.

This chapter describes what the music program is and how it is used. It considers the planning and organization of musical instruction and the manner in which better programs can be developed. A general picture is given of the various musical activities as they might be handled at the elementary, secondary, and collegiate levels.

THE SUBSTANCE OF THE MUSIC PROGRAM

Any music program is a conscious attempt to prescribe the musical experiences of students; it serves to control the educative environment in the interest of particular outcomes of schooling. The program is *not* the pattern of courses in which students enroll or the musical organizations in which the music program is pursued and takes shape.

As a matter of fact, the student's transcript gives only

the barest outline of the program followed. It indicates, for instance, that he sang in the school chorus for three years and took a course in music theory. From this, one can figure the number of hours during which the student was exposed to various kinds of musical literature, but there is no clue concerning his reactions or the changes which occurred in his musical behavior.

The real music program defines the environmental encounters, or experiences, which students must have in order to acquire desirable traits of musical behavior. It establishes a pattern of musical activity, a selection of musical materials and musical information, and a mode of procedure in which context the necessary learning should occur.

No specific course or educational activity will automatically supply the needed experiences within that area. The member of the beginning string class, for example, may learn to play his instrument, but will he also develop an appreciation of its possibilities and good habits of practice? To do this, he needs the following kinds of experience: (1) observing the expressive power of the instrument, (2) noting technical problems which arise in performance, (3) estimating personal success in meeting the demands of the music, (4) establishing alternate patterns of execution and interpretation, and (5) perceiving the differing quality of musical effects produced.

Such experiences are not produced by ordinary drill upon finger and bowing exercises. This string class needs real music to play, demonstrations by the teacher or by advanced students, and many opportunities to hear and observe one another. Students need not be given long technical indoctrination, but they do need simple answers to their questions, explaining why a given method of execution is better or worse than another.

RELATION TO CURRICULUM

One may speak of the string program, the choral program, or the music program itself. These are segments of the school curriculum. The curriculum includes all influences which the school brings to bear upon its students. Actually, musical experiences are inextricably combined with many other phases of schooling. Regular classroom activity frequently includes folk dancing, rhythmic activity, and dramatic productions; musical examples are often found useful in the study of various peoples; it is possible to make and play toy instruments, combining handicrafts and music. Indeed, students who never enroll in a music course per se may undergo many musical experiences in a school. These experiences and consequent outcomes must not be regarded as incidental; they are part of the music program.

There are three basic styles of curriculum, and the pattern followed by each school will have its influence upon its music program. The *activity curriculum* is an expression of Deweyan, progressive educational theory. Activities are supposed to develop from the "felt needs" of the students and classroom atmosphere is likely to be relatively improvised. The students and teachers plan activities and projects which may be more or less musical, but the progression of musical study may be abruptly terminated or turned into other channels, depending upon the developing interests of the students. In effect, the music program is contingent upon music's function in larger enterprises.

The *core curriculum* is an attempt to cross subject lines in a different way, by setting up topics or areas of study which will draw upon subject matter from several disciplines. In these situations, music will not be separated from its ordinary setting in social activities but taught as the occasion arises. Typically, music is introduced in the study of transportation, war, religion, and during recreational activities.

The activity and core concepts have been influential but difficult to apply and sustain. They have succeeded in modifying strict subject lines in many schools which are still operating basically as conventional subject curriculums. Even in the modern non-graded elementary school, therefore, music is still regarded as a separate discipline, and the development of musicianship is carried on more or less independently of the other school subjects.

It is indeed more practical to consider the music program as an entity within any curriculum. Otherwise, the musical outcomes may become incidental and haphazard. Wherever music is employed in several phases of the curriculum on a loose and informal basis, therefore, music teachers and supervisors should be especially careful to assume responsibility for coordinating all these activities so as to produce an effective experimental sequence. That is, a unit on Far Eastern Cultures, employing music of the same, should give more than the flavor of the East. Enough study of exotic instruments, scales, and forms should be included to produce illuminating comparisons with the students' understanding of equivalent factors in Western music.

FORMS OF PROGRAM PLANNING

There are several concepts upon which music programs are based. One very prevalent practice is to build around a progression of musical skills. Since it is known that children develop more and more precision and insight through learning, it is deceptively easy to assign skills by level, as it were, and to surround each phase with the necessary musical materials and content. In the field of performance, the pattern may be something like this:

1. Singing by rote
   a. Simple songs and folk melodies
   b. Basic rhythmic patterns

2. Singing and playing by note
   a. Musical rudiments
   b. Factors in instrument care and tone production
   c. Progressively more difficult melodies and exercises

3. Performing with taste and dexterity
   a. Music in parts and in complex forms
   b. Principles of style and interpretation

It must be understood that the above sequence is overlapping. Rote learning continues as one begins to establish basic reading skills. Similarly, the grasp of musical rudiments is extended as one progresses to more demanding and complex literature.

The point is that this will happen anyway. One will likely learn to perform if given progressively graded tasks and materials, but what of his powers of musical discrimination and his attitudes toward musical study?

In the attempt to meet this objection, musical instruction has sometimes been tied to an unfolding pattern of subject matter. Since there is a certain body of musical facts and beliefs with which musicians must deal, these are introduced as logically and progressively as possible. The student learns note names, time values, phrase patterns, and harmonic values. Technical problems are explained and mastered. Historical facts are introduced, and the finer points of musicianship are gradually brought out. Again, such a process is usual in any good music program, but it cannot in itself guarantee the experiences which will produce the desired outcomes.

Recognizing this fact, some teachers believe the music program should evolve on a day-to-day basis. A loosely-conceived, improvised program develops in response to the immediate needs and interests of the students. It is quite possible to do this, discovering at one point, for instance, that the children wish to create a more complete musical setting for some melody they have learned. Various harmonic and formal principles are introduced, and much skill is developed in singing and writing music. Such freedom is often a good thing in musical activities, but there is still no reason to believe that the essential outcomes of instruction will be reached by this method.

The music program is most logically built around the experiences of which it consists. These can never be predetermined in detail; but the general types of experience can be outlined, and all elements of instruction can then be arranged to fit those requirements. For example, the objective of active participation in forms of amateur performance implies these kinds of experience: (1) discovering the particular appropriateness of music in various situations, (2) observing technical and stylistic problems to be met, (3) adjusting to the performance standards of the musical ensemble, and (4) noting satisfactory reception of one's musical efforts.

These kinds of experience clearly demand several school musical groups, each making suitable public appearances. Not only must the music be worthwhile in itself, but the students should also be able to master its difficulties readily and to judge their degree of success. It is not the exact quality of performance, but rather the effect upon the students that is at issue. Having these experiences in mind, the teacher can organize and conduct appropriate musical activities deliberately aimed at producing them.

MEETING LOCAL NEEDS

Some broad aims and methods in musical study are almost universal. For example, there is a typical sequence of musical activity in the elementary school, and most secondary schools have large choral and instrumental groups. College music programs contain a stable core, consisting of private instruction, music theory, and music history. National and regional groups have tried to stabilize these arrangements by indicating content, hours of instruction, and standards to be met.[1]

It is a mistake, however, to attempt the transplant of a music program *in detail* from any such plan or from another school. Each music program is unique and evolutionary. In previous chapters it has been shown how objectives have changed with a changing society and how the type of school and immediate circumstances dictate a singular pattern of objectives. What happens in each school must be in accord with its particular goals and clientèle.

Music educators work to create a newer and better music program within the ordinary educational framework.

---

[1] See National Association of Schools of Music, *By-Laws and Regulations*, The Association, Washington, 1965.

They try to determine what elements of musicianship students should possess and how these are to be attained and then revamp the instructional process to meet these demands.

Seldom does the opportunity arise to collect students and staff, move into a new building, and establish an independent music program from the ground up. Program building is thus accomplished en route, through cooperative experimentation.

The usual mistake is to adopt some simple formula which completely overturns existing patterns of instruction. Since the faculty will have limited understanding and interest in the formula, the action will produce chaos and eventual reaction in favor of the original system. A music supervisor would be unwise, therefore, to simply "install" the Kodály method, for instance, in an elementary school system, by rewriting the courses of study and calling workshops to train classroom teachers in the necessary techniques. Instead, the supervisor must work to create forces for change in that direction. Several teachers might be sent to conferences or summer clinics where the Kodály principles are to be discussed and demonstrated. Or, an "expert" might be brought to the local schools for a few demonstrations. Then, parents, students, and alumni could be brought together with teachers to discuss and examine the likely outcomes and possible difficulties in introducing such new methods. Individual teachers would need to attempt certain phases of the plan, thus offering a model for general scrutiny and emulation. Finally, the courses of study would be amended to include such new practices as prove valuable and practical. The result should be the progressive modification of the type and relationship among the musical experiences of students.

DETERMINING THE EXPERIENCES

The Nature of Experience

We have necessarily referred many times to experiences, because they are the heart of the educational process. They determine what one learns and what his future actions will be. Before one can build the music program, he must have an adequate conception of the role of experiences.

An experience consists of the interaction between an individual and his environment. We speak of an experienced musician or teacher as one who has met and dealt with many situations within those spheres. Every moment of our lives is occupied with this process of noting the circumstances in which we are placed and reacting accordingly. Our reactions are partially dependent upon our past experience, enabling us to perceive the causes and effects of our actions.

This chain of experience is not altogether efficient. That is to say, many experiences are abortive, since they are not supported by ensuing experiences which would bring out and strengthen their effect. This is the real justification for formal schooling, which represents an attempt at an efficient organization of experiences toward specific changes in the individual's behavior.

Thus we see that the usual prescriptions for musical instruction are entirely superficial. We are asked to provide experiences in singing, experiences with different rhythms, experiences with the orchestral instruments, etc. Of course, we can do this, but we have not produced an integrated series of definitive reactions. What *kinds* of experience can singing bring about?

Singing together is simply an activity in which infinite experiences are possible. At any particular instant, one choir member might be:

1. comparing various modes of interpretation
2. analyzing aural effects
3. adapting to technical demands of the music
4. discovering the interdependence of the separate musical lines
5. applying specific principles of voice production
6. analyzing the role of the teacher
7. evaluating the effectiveness of conducting techniques
8. noting the application of scoring techniques
9. following the lead of his neighbor
10. associating music with tedious drill

Students vary greatly in their readiness for particular experiences. One who has never felt deeply the power of music or noted the ways in which performers may heighten the effect is not yet able to compare various modes of interpretation (item 1 above). For this reason, the teacher must know the student and must keep him under continuous observation. When the student *is* ready to compare musical interpretations the teacher must give him the chance, by freeing him from technical problems, experimenting with tempos and dynamics, and pointing out the effect produced.

Experiences are not simple, overt actions such as tapping the foot or asking a question; they may or may not be manifest to the teachers. One has many experiences while quietly reading a book or listening to a piece of music. The experience arises from (1) the actual circumstances of the moment, (2) the individual's perception of the situation, and (3) his possible lines of action in the fact of the situation. Knowing the background of a student and having carefully prepared for the moment, it is theoretically possible to forecast his reactions to a rendition of Debussy's "Clair de lune." In actuality, of course, the teacher has no such exact means of control; he can only arrange conditions which would seem to favor the kind of experience he has in mind.

The verbal statement of an experience is easy to confuse with an activity on the one hand and with an objective on the other. Experiences result from or lead toward activities. It may be noted that there is a cognitive element in the ten experiences just listed. The subject is reacting to the situation and gross activity (singing) in which he is engaged, *in terms of consequent mental or physical activity*. It is these reactions which are precious, fleeting, and educative and are termed experiences.

These reactions, in their turn, do constitute behaviors of a sort, and it is thus possible to confuse them with objectives. In actuality they are *fragmentary*, *latent behaviors* which, with proper cultivation, may gradually combine and assemble themselves into various concrete behavioral changes—our objectives.

One further thing should be noted: that there is not a one to one relationship between experiences and objectives. Experiences are so fleeting that it may take an infinite number of them to produce any noticeable swerve in behavior. This being the case, it is wise to evoke the experiences in a natural psychological sequence: (1) exploration and investigation, (2) conceptualization and generalization, and (3) application and evaluation.

Verbal description of experience is bound to be incomplete and artificial, because we here approach so closely the roots of human existence. When verbal description is necessary, however, the statements should be as concrete as possible. They must convey the sense of instant contact and recoil with life situations. For instance, in hearing a piece of music one does not instantly establish its form and stylistic consequence; this follows from his minute observations of rhythmic pulse, melodic contour, harmonic progression, tonal color, dynamic contrast, and so on. Neither does one *experience* sonata form as an immediate whole, but rather, he experiences the process of tracing its thematic formula from beginning to end through direct perception of discrete but interrelated tonal materials.

If a student is to acquire a concept of musical forms or to acquire any other species of musical behavior, therefore, the teacher must have some idea of the proper experiences. He should not blankly expose the student to music. It is too often believed that more and better music, the latest teaching methods, and the best in equipment and facilities will automatically produce better musicianship. This is not so. These tools are haphazard in their effect unless the teacher first outlines the kinds of experience which he wishes to evoke.

The Selection of Experiences

When introducing new material and visualizing the possible problems, teachers are forced to consider the reactions desired of the students; the formal selection of experiences is merely a careful and reasoned extension of that ordinary process. The teacher examines each of his objectives, listing the kinds of experience which he deems necessary to produce it.

Each class is operated in a characteristic fashion which affects the perception of the students. For instance, the study of music literature is approached rather analytically in the theory class, while a freer approach is generally used in the school chorus. Students in music theory might be (1) discovering the techniques employed by composers, (2) analyzing the process of scoring, and (3) testing their ability to express musical ideas. The members of the chorus could be (1) noting the effects of various idiomatic techniques, (2) determining the characteristics of specific forms and styles, and (3) conceiving interpretations in keeping with broad structural ideas.

Note that these are rather obvious things for students to do if they are to understand music's construction. Nevertheless, choral directors commonly repress insights into the effects of music with their insistence upon details of execution; theory teachers easily devote their energies to prescribing rules and methods rather than stimulating true analysis. There is a great advantage in simple outline of desired experiences as a basis for the organization of instruction.

In constructing this list the teacher must rely primarily upon his own experience and best judgment. He must analyze how he and his previous students have traveled the road to musicianship. There is little definitive research to depend upon, though ideas are to be found in courses of study published by the various state departments of education.[2]

ORGANIZATION OF THE MUSIC PROGRAM

The music program is conducted in segments, year by year and class by class. Each level and phase of the program rightfully fulfills a unique function in relation to the entire

---

[2] See the list of curriculum guides at the end of the chapter.

program. It behooves the music educator to plan accordingly, so that the experiences of students are naturally progressive and reinforcing, and not unrelated. A well-planned sequence and a natural division of musical activity are a necessity; instruction must be clearly outlined and yet remain inherently flexible.

Sequence

It is comparatively easy to create a logical sequence for the program based upon one of the more concrete elements of instruction. Broken down into assimilable bits of information or topics, subject matter has served as a convenient framework upon which to build sequence. Likewise, musical skills have been reduced to a developmental pattern which provides an orderly sequence. The only difficulty is that students often overstep these bounds, showing little regard for the supposed prerequisites. Anderson states:[3]

> The content of the curriculum can be divided into (a) skills and knowledge, which are reasonably specific and are acquired by continuing practice under formal conditions, and (b) general complexes of skills, knowledge, attitude and understanding that are gradually acquired through life experience. Research has shown that these complexes are built up gradually rather than suddenly and that emphasis should be thrown, not so much upon a particular or precise location of instructional content, as upon methods and materials adapted to the age and maturity of the child.

As a matter of fact, students are introduced to the concept of dotted notes early in their schooling and are still learning about them when they graduate. It is not the knowledge of dotted notes or skill in performing them which is sequential but rather the *experiences* with this musical concept which

[3] G. Lester Anderson, "Problems of Method in Maturity and Curricular Studies," *Child Development and the Curriculum*, National Society for the Study of Education Thirty-eighth Yearbook, Chicago, 1939, Part I p. 420. Reprinted by permission of the publisher.

are actually progressive. There *is* a natural sequence that can be produced through proper introduction of activities, subject matter, musical materials, and teaching method.

The clue to programmatic sequence lies in human psychology. A child does not learn to speak through identifying nouns, pronouns, and verbs and diagramming sentences; he becomes acquainted with objects and forces in his immediate environment, develops concepts, and applies them, steadily extending his facility to express his thoughts. So it is in music. A student investigates music as it exists and develops an acquaintance with its usage and vocabulary; he arrives at many conclusions about music and tests and refines them. This may appear to be a jumbled process, since investigation in one area proceeds in hand with experimental application in another; the child is investigating note values while he is testing his ability to sing them. Nevertheless, this is the sensible basis upon which to plan instruction.

It is manifestly impossible to outline a rigid series of experiences in music education; such a plan would be as artificial as any sequential system now in use. The real control of sequence lies in the proper use of teaching method and musical materials.

It is pointed out in Chapter 8 that learning activity should be from concrete to abstract. This means, first, that musical materials at the various levels of instruction should be progressively more complex and subtle, demanding ever finer perception and performance. Secondly, the teaching methods must be designed to meet this challenge. The younger child must be caught up in the raw material of sound and music; gradually he must be led to consider what is occurring and how he can best refine and apply his musicianship. Teaching methods should progressively call forth more thinking and independent action from the pupils.

Therefore, the young pupil needs exposure to every possible variety and category of music, singing and playing whatever he can and listening and moving to the rest. There should be more experimentation with classroom keyboard and rhythm instruments and with flutophone and fretted instruments than is usually the case. The emphasis at this stage should be on observation, trial, and familiarization.

During the middle years of schooling, roughly occupying grades four through eight, the pupils' main attention should be directed toward consolidating the information already gained about music. More and more the pupil should deal with the *significance* of a piece of music, and the reason *why* and *how* certain techniques are applied in its composition and its performance.

This middle stage, that of generalization, imperceptibly leads on to the point where the pupil takes more initiative for his own musical development. He applies and evaluates his conclusions. He now has a solid basis for experience involving comparison and judgment among all types and kinds of musical literature. Furthermore, he should be judging how his own musical abilities stack up with others and what he might wish to do about it.

Again, this kind of sequence is not arranged in terms of the orderly presentation of musical facts or skills, but in terms of a procession of experiences—largely controlled by the specific musical literature and teaching methods employed. To put it briefly, as the student becomes more musically mature, he must be fed more demanding musical tasks and approached on a more mature basis.

But the concept of a three stage curriculum is only a rough outline. It should be apparent that some pupils will progress to the top stage much sooner than others. Furthermore, each new phase of music must be undertaken from the beginning. For instance, those students who begin study of a band or stringed instrument in the middle grades, as is usual, will start with mainly *explorative* experiences. They will be facing the same old musical problems in a different context. And it will happen again when the students are initiated into the marching band and again when they begin the deliberate study of music theory.

To the onlooker, of course, the student may appear to be following a static curriculum while he is a member, often for several years, of the same performing organization. Although fresh literature is regularly introduced, and the personnel changes from time to time, the individual is apparently doing about the same thing all the time—namely, rehearsing music for performance. Not so. His daily experiences are altering his musical knowledge and skills. His perception changes. Although he performs the same few tones each day, they are in different patterns and his musical insight and facility grow. His musical initiative and discrimination increasingly flourish. He is really following a spiral curriculum.

Divisions of the Program

The various subjects or titles of courses and the time and credit allotted to them are ordinarily considered of great importance. For many people they actually define the music program. In actuality, however, they only define the type of activity to be pursued. The essential point is that profitable musical experiences can occur within nearly any pattern of courses. Although a student generally expects to sing in a school chorus and to study music's construction in the theory class, there is much overlap in function; the student should be able to gain much theoretical knowledge without taking a course in theory per se.

These categories are a matter of convenience. It happens that an acquaintance with advanced choral literature is not so easily achieved in a general class but is more adequately handled in a group especially organized for that purpose. There are other natural approaches to musical study—such as band, orchestra, music theory, and music history—but no single pattern fits all circumstances.

It has seemed generally useful in the elementary classroom to study and examine music from all angles; the need for specialization is not great and the experiences of the students are essentially investigative. Hence, the structural and historical phases of music can be profitably handled in connection with active listening and performance. Music specialists and musically qualified classroom teachers must usually work together as partners in the enterprise of general musical instruction. But special instructors are usually needed for instrumental music classes in the upper grades which lead the students directly to membership in the school's band and orchestral groups.

The general music class in secondary schools is an extension of the elementary school pattern. Many students never specialize in any particular phase of music but do desire to advance their understanding of the art. Properly, this is not an appreciation class; it should offer a balanced approach to musicianship through an extensive study of a variety of musical literature.

Many high school students, however, also need the opportunities afforded by special performing groups. The high school band, orchestra, and chorus are organized, along with the necessary preparatory groups and supplemental small ensembles. Theoretical and historical understanding is properly developed in this context, although special classes are sometimes offered in these fields.

College music programs, falling heir to both the general and the preprofessional student, are characteristically divided into many forms of activity. The performing groups are continued at this level, and there is a general music class called Introduction to Music or Music Appreciation. Vocational specialization in music leads to intensive private study and branching of the theoretical and historical subjects. For example, one finds harmony, sight singing, keyboard harmony, counterpoint, form and analysis, orchestration, and composition—all being special aspects of music theory. It is immediately apparent that any of these courses must deal with content borrowed from the others.

Seeing this, many institutions offer courses unifying ear training, written harmony, and keyboard into "music theory," and experiments have been made in the further inclusion of music history and form within this basic core.[4] It is

[4] The Juilliard School of Music, *The Juilliard Report on Teaching the Literature and Material of Music*, W. W. Norton & Company, Inc., New York, 1953.

likewise possible to teach conducting and beginning instrumental techniques as integral parts of an expanded course in methods of teaching music.

The actual division of musical subjects at any level of schooling should be determined on the basis of practical considerations. The shape of the daily class schedule and the backgrounds of the teachers themselves will indicate the proper grouping of experiences. But no music course should be considered an individual discipline, complete in itself; the teacher studies the type of activity involved, identifying immediate objectives which can contribute to the central objectives of the program and which may be attained within the time and facilities available.

Differentiation of Instruction

Students vary widely in intelligence, personality, and musical aptitude; furthermore, their individual backgrounds of musical experience are unique and tend to grow more divergent with maturity. These facts demand great flexibility in the music program. The objectives of music education, fortunately, may be attained by different paths. For instance, one person may achieve broad musical taste by the simple expedient of listening and comparing styles; another requires active performance of many works over a period of years.

As a matter of fact, a rigid program wherein all students are exposed to the same factors inevitably produces a wide variation in experiences. This is due to the different perceptions of students and their varying power to react. A flexible program, catering to these differences, should actually produce more consistent outcomes.

Methods of meeting this challenge have included (1) ability groupings (special sectioning), (2) homogeneous groupings (special-interest groups or electives), (3) remedial treatment, (4) extracurricular activities, and (5) use of programmed learning materials.

The widespread use of these methods is notable. We schedule beginning, intermediate, and advanced performing groups; small ensembles are formed; assistance is offered to student-organized projects; individuals are coached on their special difficulties.

Actually, group rehearsals are inherently suited to the flexible approach. While the American history students all hear the same lectures and read the same text, members of an orchestra play different parts. It is true that all must play at the same time and must be under firm control of the conductor, but a near beginner is often found seated beside a polished performer. The talents of both are used and developed. The energy one uses in learning his part is matched by the other's effort in helping fellow players, leading sectional rehearsals, tuning the group, managing the library, or preparing special solos. Most well-run school musical organizations exhibit the properties of a true learning laboratory or workshop.

There are at least three good reasons in support of this idea: (1) concerted action gives added definition to problems, (2) the group helps to discover and avoid individual errors, and (3) group planning and working foster interdependence based upon individual specialties.

This general idea can be profitably extended to the more intellectual phases of musical study. Music theory and history need not be conducted as dry revelation of facts but can be approached through student research projects and informal critiques. Results should include stronger definition of goals, initiative in seeking information, better pacing, and enlightened self-evaluation by the students.

Outlining Instruction

The official courses of study drawn up by state committees or by local music supervisors are only of supplementary value to the instructor. These outlines are best viewed as samples, since the objectives cannot possibly fit each particular instance nor can the detailed procedures cover each specific situation. The individual teacher, having helped plan and organize the entire music program, must carry this process to its logical conclusion: he must plan and execute the instruction in his particular sector.

The teacher's course outline is a practical plan for producing the desired experiences, through setting up the proper educative environment. Without it, one easily reverts to drill and testing of skills and the recall of facts, follows the textbook, or simply prepares his students to perform a series of concerts. It is necessary to plan more creatively if the program is to be consummated.

A good course outline may be quite informal and its style depends upon the one who constructs it. One simply determines the ends to be reached and means to reach them. Plans may take the form shown in Table One (page 238).

Other teachers prefer to organize instruction in terms of units or central problems which are more or less self-contained, each with its distinctive pattern of development. Basically the same design is used, but the periods of study are defined in relation to the topics themselves, such as music and the dance, music and the theatre, music in the church, folk music, chamber music, and symphonic music. Such a plan works well in the highly integrated curriculum, in the general music class, and in the more intellectual phases of musical study. The concerts themselves become the units or nodes of activity for the performing groups.

Instructional objectives in seventh-grade General Music would include the following. Upon completion of each unit, the student:

1. will orally describe the ways in which any of the musical forms studied were and are related to the everyday lives of individuals
2. will produce a paper tracing the development of musical forms and styles treated in the unit
3. will correctly identify the majority of those compositions he has studied and assign them to the proper composer and era
4. on the first hearing of a composition, will give a brief written description of it, identifying at least the per-

forming medium, the type and form of composition, and the era or idiom in which it was composed

See Table One for an outline of procedures which might fulfill these objectives. What matters more than the form of the outline is that the various elements of it be legitimate. Objectives must be true expressions of musical competence, and the experiences named must be natural reactions to specific circumstances. Materials, subject matter, and method must bear an obvious relationship to the experiences desired. For instance, cheap, manufactured tunes, analyzed phrase by phrase, cannot lead to valid experience in observing good melodic contour; neither will the hearing of highly advanced compositions, unattended by the proper background and explanations. Finally, ordinary tests, demanding simple recall of facts and ideas presented, will not sufficiently relate to the objectives. The course outline should serve to ensure that this sort of thing does not happen.

IMPLEMENTING THE PROGRAM

Although the elements in planning and organizing the music program have already been outlined, it is clear that the actual process of engineering the change is another matter. The music program is an integral part of the school curriculum, which is itself an expression of the ideas and practices of the community, the students, school officials, and individual teachers. No one person, therefore, can successfully revamp the music program; it is only possible to initiate moves which will involve other people in the task and to guide these efforts toward eventual improvements in the program.

There are several characteristic forms of curriculum revision. Most often, one or more music teachers undertake to create new patterns of instruction for themselves, automatically influencing the remainder of the program; such proceedings often go unrecognized as curriculum efforts. In other instances the music program is reviewed as a unit,

TABLE ONE

	Unit I	*Unit II*
Topics: (dealing with particular bodies of fact and belief)	Music and the Dance: primitive dance; evolution of jazz and its mutations; court dances and ballet	Music and the Theatre: music in pageantry; minstrel shows; operatic forms, operetta and musicals; music for motion pictures and TV
Kinds of experience to be stressed:	Exploring all dance forms and styles; noting and comparing characteristic rhythms and melodic devices; classifying dance forms and idioms	Reviewing the evolution of theatrical forms; noting music ability to represent appropriate mood and feelings; glimpsing problems inherent in fitting music to story, and observing some solutions
Materials: (books, music)	Recordings: folk dances of Africa, West Indies, and Europe; Dixieland; Swing; progressive jazz; cool jazz; rock and roll; early dance suites; classical and modern ballet	Recordings: Purcell, Gluck, Rossini, Wagner, Verdi, Rodgers, Menotti, etc. Current movie and TV theme music

Procedures: (methods of presentation)	Student discovering similarities and differences in dance forms; record listening and discussion; demonstrations by dance instructor; quizzes	Presentation of examples of film and TV music; discussion of special techniques in writing for films; short excerpts in class from any musical currently in rehearsal locally; student selection or composition of music for a theatrical production
Evaluation: (evidence of progress toward the objectives)	Check their ability to identify correct form and era; check reactions to contrasting styles; check sense of historical perspective	Check concepts of how music and stage action are synchronized; check ability to distinguish inspired from contrived art; check for snobbishness toward music of any era or medium

which process employs the sustained efforts of the entire music staff and the affected classroom teachers. Yet again, full-dress proceedings are inaugurated in the entire school system and cover every subject area and grade level; the influence of the community is sought by means of open forums, opinion polls, and everyday discussion. Sometimes the effort is in response to initiatives by the Parent Teachers Organization or an accrediting organization. In all circumstances, basic responsibility for the music program still rests with the music specialists and classroom teachers.

Techniques for Program Change

Any attempt to improve the music program requires steady investigation and experimentation. Only in this way can conviction and know-how be developed, so that new ideas may be put into effect. Means must be found to involve everyone concerned with the program.

One approach is to initiate a survey of existing practices in other schools and a study of established patterns recommended by accrediting bodies or authoritative commissions. Representatives or experts may be called in to review the local program and recommend changes. Comparisons are made, ideas are tried, and evaluation of results leads to further adjustment. This approach usually results in little more than revision of schedules and addition of facilities and staff. The teachers themselves may not understand what they are trying to accomplish.

It is also possible to depend entirely upon local resources, setting up workshops and committees which do basic research. There may be study of psychological findings, a gathering of data concerning the activities of the school's graduates, and the establishment of objectives. Musical offerings may be realigned and a general course of study created. Such measures work well when there is sincerity and conviction and the need for change has been demonstrated. Materials useful in this kind of approach are often available from state departments of education.

Successful revision of the music program, however, usually proceeds in more indirect fashion. The professional growth of teachers, in itself, creates pressures for instructional revision and improvement. School personnel are interested in the problems at hand, and the solution of these provides the impetus for cumulative changes in the program.

The problems exist ready-made in any school. Students may not be learning to read music properly; there may be difficulty in securing personnel for the performing groups; public apathy toward school music activities may exist. Since teachers can recognize such problems, it is comparatively easy to secure their cooperation in investigating the causes. In essence, this is an evaluative process. Recognition of the problems just mentioned suggests that participation in and support of musical activities are vital objectives; data are therefore gathered concerning the effectiveness of the program in gaining them. Once this is done, the needed changes in instruction are more readily achieved, and there is a better climate for further investigation and change.

For example, public apathy toward musical activities may be traceable to weak development of musicianship in students and in their parents before them. Contest winning, spectacular half-time shows, or high-pressure salesmanship for music cannot, *by themselves*, alter this circumstance. Parents must be able to see evidence of musical development in their children. Do they practice regularly, purchase good recordings, tune in on musical events, and so on? Demonstrable lack of these traits in children builds pressure for a higher quality of musical literature, more inspirational rehearsals and discussions, a wider variety of concerts and public appearances.

Discovery of basic problems, investigation, and development of deliberate corrective measures do not occur spontaneously. Some form of group study must be initiated, perhaps accompanied by intensive observation and testing of students. Combined concerts or projects may stimulate evaluation and comparison. One of the best means of building pressure for change is the demonstration class. One class or musical organization is thrown open to staff scrutiny; objectives are stated, the pattern of instruction is outlined, and data on results are carefully gathered and interpreted. Teachers naturally translate proven concepts to their own situations, and the frame of reference for further investigation is thereby established.

Personnel in Curriculum Change

The traditional roles of school personnel fit admirably into the process of program development; indeed, the various school positions have largely evolved to conform to this process. Personnel on three levels are primarily involved: (1) the titular head of the school unit (superintendent, principal, college president, or dean), (2) the effective leader of the music program (music supervisor, consultant, or department head), and (3) those entrusted with musical instruction (music specialists and classroom teachers).

The head of the school system.   The head of any school system is directly responsible for providing the setting for music instruction, a task which necessarily involves organization and control of the music program, its outline, the materials used, and the facilities employed. He must help foster any moves in the direction of better music program. These matters are more fully discussed in Chapter 9.

The music supervisor.   Because he is closer to the daily problems of instruction, the music supervisor has a crucial role in any healthful development of the program. His task is to provide leadership in improving instruction, largely through program development.

The music supervisor should be constantly engaged in study of the program itself, observing and testing the students, discussing problems with the teachers, and consulting with parents and visitors. He spotlights problems and encourages the evaluation of the program or particular segments of it.

The evaluative process requires careful guidance. Teachers need to be assisted in gathering evidence of their pupils' reactions and in determining what these data mean. If marked weakness in musical discrimination is found, for instance, the staff must be led to define the qualities of good music and the attributes of good taste.

Accompanying this effort, the supervisor stimulates the examination of instruction. He helps judge the musical compositions used and the ways in which they are taught. New materials are recommended and new procedures are suggested. Ideas which show promise are passed around and tested. The changing pattern is consolidated and outlined.

The results of all this effort cannot be put into operation without further aid from the supervisor. An individual teacher may need assistance in devising specific plans for daily classroom activity. He may find it necessary to rearrange schedules and course offerings. If the situation requires new sets of music books, additional recordings, or more classroom space, he must undertake to secure them.

As changes in the program materialize, the supervisor stands ready to help meet unlooked-for problems. He must overcome misconceptions and guard against the misapplication of plans. In this task of steady observation, however, he is already beginning the job of reevaluation, pointing toward further improvements in the program.

The teacher.   The role of the teacher in revision of the music program should by now require only brief explanation. Only the teacher has the fundamental power to change the program by altering the daily use of content, method, and musical materials in his classes. He can do this whether or not the suggestion is made.

A great number of teachers, however, have established a pattern for their own instruction which they consider inviolable. In years past they have experimented and feel they have found the most practical system for their own use. They may actively resist any investigations which threaten to affect them, perhaps fearing that the primary result will be some form of teacher rating. This attitude is a major stumbling block to healthful program revision.

TABLE TWO

Steps in curriculum development	*The music supervisor*	*The music teacher*
Discovery, of the need for an improved program	Carries out testing and research Records student activity and achievement Stimulates staff to recognize major problems and their relation to the music program	Investigates the music program as it stands Weighs data concerning the musical competence achieved by students Makes tentative judgment of the strengths and weaknesses of the music program
Delineation of program objectives	Prepares reference material, bibliographies Encourages staff study and research Outlines proposed objectives	Examines curricular material Investigates philosophical and sociological evidence pertaining to the outcomes of music education Joins in the collective decision about the validity of each objective
Selection of experiences	Spotlights specific classroom activities and their effect upon students Encourages experimentation Organizes worthy practices and suggestions into an ordered pattern	Considers the educative uses of each type of musical activity Defines actual experiences designed to produce specific objectives

Organization of in-struction	Arranges for necessary alterations in offerings and schedule	Develops specific objectives for each of his classes
	Works with teacher in building instructional plans	Isolates the experiences to be promoted therein
	Sees that needed equip-ment and facilities are made available	Creates a consequent plan for the use of particular musical compositions and factual material
		Plans actual classroom procedures
		Determines methods of evaluation
Operation of the re-vised program	Observes changing class-room activity	Carries out instructional plans
	Assists as special problems arise	Observes students' reac-tions and alters pro-cedures as required
		Provides flexibility of activity as needed by students
		Evaluates the progress of students toward declared objectives

The teacher should realize that his job includes more than the skillful presentation of his particular subject. An orchestra director is not simply an orchestra director. He has accepted a responsibility to society and to his pupils which implies the quest for a better and stronger educational impact. He cannot in conscience avoid involvement in program development.

It is therefore a prime responsibility of the teacher to join in the investigation of the music program and the determination of its objectives. He should maintain an experimental attitude and incorporate worthwhile ideas into his own pattern of instruction. He should inform the supervisor of difficulties as they arise. Such action, when the supervisor also fulfills his obligations, ensures the full communication necessary to valid program development.

The Sequence of Program Development

The natural progress of activity toward a better music program has been implicit in our discussion. It may be conceived in terms of the steps shown in Table Two. The outline given must not be interpreted too literally. A music program does not evolve by discrete stages but remains in a complex state of balance. While the program is in operation, it is being evaluated and reorganized. There is no time limit on experimentation and discovery. At the time new patterns are being installed, investigation of older practices may be just commencing. Program development is a cyclical *series* of operations, each proceeding at its own pace.

The person who wishes to set about revising the music program therefore begins at any logically indicated point in the cycle. Perhaps there already exists recognition of certain needs and a pretty fair idea of objectives in one area. For example, desirable performing skills may be rather well defined, and one can go on from there to the consideration of better means to achieve them. On the other hand and at the same time, problems in the creative aspects of music may be lying dormant, requiring much preliminary investigation. The encouraging thing is that as people work with the music program they learn, and succeeding effort becomes more productive

PRINCIPLES OF PROGRAM DEVELOPMENT

The entire task of building and implementing the music program can be summarized in terms of guiding concepts or principles. Ten principles of program development are given below:

1. *The program should be conceived in terms of individual educative experiences.* People learn only by means of experience; at every instant one is responding to his environment and learning by this means new ways of meeting life's situations. The business of the school is to arrange the conditions so that educative experiences will develop which are conducive to desired kinds of behavior. This depends upon knowledge of the students and of the proper use of methods and materials. A student, for example, may be listening to an unaccompanied Bach cello sonata. If he is a cellist who has already studied the work, both he and his environment are quite different from another who has no prior acquaintance with the piece; his actual experiences will be quite different also. Listening to music is involved in either case, but the one student brings a knowledge of technical and stylistic usage, the structural development, and an actual understanding and anticipation of the sounds as they are scored. This person is in a better position to visualize the actual tonal relationships, to judge the quality of interpretation, and to discover the expressive meanings of the music. These are crucial experiences in the development of musical taste and understanding.
2. *The program should be determined on the basis of the objectives.* Although a great many experiences may be desirable, the time allotment for the music program is

insufficient for the attainment of the objectives unless the program is definitely geared to them.

Experiences are related to the objectives by a process of logical inference. Beginning with any specified quality of musical behavior, one plans for the types of experience most clearly related to it.

3. *The program should be developed in terms of the most favorable means of student learning.* The program must be set up in such a way that the pattern of experiences will have the utmost impact upon the student. Dewey has proposed that the program will be most effective when there is continuity and interaction between experiences.[5]

In keeping with this principle, one finds these characteristics in the effective music program:

    a. Instruction is planned to stimulate new needs, interests, and useful problems.

    b. The student is assisted in defining his own goals and in choosing the means to attain them.

    c. The student is given access to rich and varied resources in solving his problems; he is shown *how* such facts are used, *when* certain usages apply, the relative merits of various techniques, and *why* particular generalizations hold true.

    d. Activities are focused upon a clear purpose.

    e. Evaluation is stimulating and continuous.

    f. There is opportunity to extend and perfect the meaning of experience through practice.

4. *Program development is based upon continuous evaluation.* Is the program accomplishing all that is intended? To what extent is the actual program fulfilling its theoretical promise? How nearly are the objectives being attained? What improvements are indicated?

A great mistake is made in assuming that a program is fairly evaluated in terms of hours required, subject matter introduced, materials provided, qualifications of

---

[5] John Dewey, *Experience and Education*, The Macmillan Company, New York, 1938, Chap. 3.

teachers, available equipment, practice facilities, budget, and so on. These matters may be beautifully arranged and yet fail to produce adequate outcomes. A music education program is judged in terms of its objectives; then, as factors in creating those outcomes, the actions undertaken by staff and administration, the provision and use of course time, materials, facilities, and money may be considered. Only through the realization that the students are not reaching certain specific objectives may intelligent provision be made for revising and strengthening certain areas of experience, so that the program may indeed develop progressively.

5. *Program development should involve everyone rightfully concerned with that program.* Arbitrary change in the music program by a supervisor or director is utterly futile. Real change is effected only through altering the purposes and actions of the teachers and their students; these in turn are somewhat dependent upon the attitudes of the administration, fellow students, parents, and the community. Hence, it is important that all these people be drawn into the effort to improve the program. The problem can be approached in the spirit of general investigation and inquiry; this can be done by very informal means.

6. *Program development should be evolutionary, rather than revolutionary.* An entire music program, currently operating, should not be discarded simply on the theory that it is outmoded, for it is evidently a result of much previous experimentation and has at least partially accomplished its mission. There are many features in any music program which require only a few specific alterations; this will create better results than wholesale revision.

In the long run, program development depends upon teacher improvement. Unless there is to be wholesale hiring and firing, an improving music program means reeducation of the teaching staff. This is partly accomplished through teacher participation in program construction. Improvements should be put into use immediately so that their effect may be evaluated and thus exert pressure for further change.

7. *The music program should consist of an orderly sequence of experiences.* Since the various musical activities, subject matter, and materials are only elements of the program, they should not be used for the primary determination of sequence. One must plan for the kinds of experience which the student can achieve at a particular stage in his musical education. The natural progression is from general investigation toward formation of specific generalizations and concludes with deliberate action or testing of the acquired beliefs. This cycle occurs with the introduction of new material at any level of the program.

8. *The music program should be divided into series of related forms of activity.* The usual pattern of courses has been found satisfactory for the teacher and student in carrying out their purposes and tasks. If there is any persistent error in this regard, it occurs in the professional programs, in which specialized courses proper to the various curricula are often transposed to an unsuitable role in other professional programs.

There are only a few fundamental approaches to the art of music. If one wants to deal with a piece of music he must either listen to it, investigate the historical and cultural facts which may be connected with it, study the way it is constructed and scored, or perform it.

The public school music program thus falls naturally into three areas—the study of musical performance, music's construction and organization, and its historical and cultural background—and listening to music is an integral function in each of these areas.

At the collegiate and graduate levels there is a further breakdown of the activities. Future musical theorists and composers can gain from the special study of musical form, orchestration, and harmonic and contrapuntal techniques; they will also find it valuable to burrow and delve into certain aspects of musical performance and history. An analogous procedure is indicated for the future performer, conductor, teacher, or musicologist. It must only be stressed that undue proliferation of courses produces artificiality.

For instance, the topic of instrument care and repair may be much more intelligently and efficiently handled as the problem arises in connection with actual performance, than as a theoretical course based on mock problems. It is likewise difficult to study harmony without reference to ear training and even harder to keep counterpoint strictly separate from harmony and musical form. Subdivision of the music program should occur at the point where new and valuable qualities of experience can thus be made available to the student.

9. *The music program should allow ample scope for the unique and individual pattern of experience.* The variables in the make-up of each individual—physique, intelligence, experience, personality, attitudes, purposes, etc.—are closely akin to the factors which determine readiness. These differences create real differentiation in the program. It is far better if instruction is deliberately geared to such flexibility.

10. *Each segment of the music program should be outlined in terms of the practical elements of daily instruction.* Definitive instructional plans are essential unless the teacher foresees a sort of free-activity atmosphere or intends to follow and expand upon textbook materials. Without some practical outline for daily reference the most beautifully thought-out program can relapse to a simple exposition of whatever the individual teacher happens to know and believe.

When the teacher personally creates this instrument he can then understand it, use it, and adjust to the actual circumstances of instruction. He needs to develop specific objectives for the particular course; the activities, subject matter, and materials need to be considered in relation to the necessary experiences; teaching procedure needs definition; and evaluative techniques must be chosen.

OPERATIONAL LEVELS OF THE MUSIC PROGRAM

Each level and phase of the music program is, of course, a study in itself. A tremendous volume of useful information and applied experience has grown up in each of these areas. This material is available from many sources. All that can be done here is to indicate the shape of the music program in terms of some general conclusions which follow from the principles that have been discussed.

The Music Program in the Elementary School

Music in the elementary school is essentially a program of general music. That is, its proper objectives are the musical competencies needed by any citizen—whether music becomes a career or an avocation. These are outlined in Chapter 6.

In keeping with the principles of programmatic sequence, the students' efforts at this level should be largely investigative of all the aspects of music as it affects the individual and makes its appearance in society. This broad approach is achieved most effectively by pursuing in combination all the legitimate musical activities. The student sings, plays, responds rhythmically and creatively, and listens to music—and in each instance he should be noting various features of musical organization and stylistic content.

This basic orientation in music must not be upset by early insistence upon rules and beliefs about music. Gradually the student does acquire certain technical controls and music reading ability. These, however, are outcomes of maturation and earlier experience—not evidence that the student has launched a professional career or should necessarily be exhibiting an intellectual grasp of the art.

The usual music program lays great emphasis upon outcomes in performance. These ends are often conceived only in terms of the student's level of proficiency. He also needs an understanding of ways and means to better performance, useful attitudes toward the performance of himself and others, and the habits which will sustain his musical progress.

Thus, before the young violinist can acquire fluent bowing and fingering technique, he needs to achieve an appreciation of the instrument's beauty of tone and an active desire to become a good violinist. The kindergarten child must learn to anticipate singing as a pleasurable activity. Such objectives are not only prerequisites to technical development but are also continuing goals of schooling.

The objectives of performance in school music are not the same as those of the private studio. The idea is not to emphasize performance per se but to view singing and playing as a means to developing broad musicianship.

If the proper musical development is to be ensured for each child, it is not enough to sing joyously, clap and dance, and listen, any more than it is profitable to beat musical facts into children's heads. Instead, the various musical activities need to be examined carefully in order to see what useful experiences they might yield; this must be followed by a deliberate attempt to foster such experiences by means of the actual music to be used, the mode of presentation, and the needful information which can be brought to bear.

Singing has been the staple fare of elementary school music for a number of reasons. Not least among these is the fact that rather artistic results can be obtained with a minimum of technical training. That is to say, we can take a meaningful text and beautiful melody and breathe life into them with very young children. We should stress rhythmic impulse and fine tonal perception; the effect should be expressively plastic, warm, and rich.

Real music of lasting value can be found to replace those synthetic creations which are so often supplied the child. Songs should never be difficult in the sense that they are labored over, although it is sometimes surprising how difficulty melts away when members of the class bring real purpose to their performance. Good vocal habits and tone quality must be promoted without a great deal of conscious attention by the pupils, and song presentation must not become ritualized but fitted to the requirements of each song.

Playing activities are particularly good in establishing concepts of musical ensemble and offer special advantages in developing reading skill. Instrumental work becomes the primary road to musicianship for many pupils.

Ideally, all students should have full opportunity to attempt any and all instruments. Because of a lack of time and money, however, we are forced to supply a general background in the preorchestral instruments and then to offer a *choice* of the standard instruments. It is tragic that even this much is often not achieved. If there is such a thing as musical talent, it is probably best manifested in the unusual affinity of certain individuals for particular instruments, yet an appalling number of children are given no opportunity to work with the string and keyboard instruments.

Instrumental instruction should be conceived as a continuous process from nursery school and kindergarten on to the completion of schooling. It begins with rhythmic activity, record listening, keyboard exploration, and experimentation with the classroom-type instruments.

Elective beginning classes in piano, strings, and band instruments should be open to students of the middle and upper elementary grades. Teachers should not recruit, in the sense that they select students on the basis of some test and prescribe the instruments which will later assure the proper instrumentation of the high school groups. The choice of instruments should be on the basis of student preference, qualified by obvious handicaps; then, those whose progress is unsatisfactory should be allowed to transfer to another and perhaps more needed instrument.

Rhythm is, of course, a primary element in music, but special rhythmic activities are devised in the elementary program in order to ensure a sensitivity and freedom of rhythmic response. These activities may take many forms, so long as the attention is not unduly focused upon mathematical abstractions. When properly handled, rhythmic expression becomes one form of the so-called "creative activities."

The musical creativity of students is seldom done justice. Although most elementary schools sponsor certain creative activities, outcomes are often vague and poorly defined. Often, these attempts consist of recitation of poetic lines while, phrase by phrase, the children suggest certain tunes. This is "composition by consensus." Such sterile activity is happily forgotten at the secondary level but with little to take its place.

It is no wonder that musical creativity is largely practiced *sub rosa*. The schools literally force students into out-of-school jazz groups where creative freedom holds greater sway.

Creativity is generally misunderstood. It is manifested both in the ability to create music in formal fashion and in the ability to improvise and embellish. Few products of our schools can do either thing. Music history tells us this has not always been so, but it is a natural result of the increasing complexity of our lives and of our music. We emphasize the perfect rendition of music and the intellectual rather than the emotional and exuberant aspects of performance. Consequently, we deliberately suppress the natural desire to sing and play by ear; we frown on the embellishments which trumpet players like to add upon occasion; we smile patronizingly at student efforts to emulate the professional composer. Wherever such judgments can be avoided, we tend to strengthen the student's self-confidence, his willingness to make mistakes and fail, and his valuing of unconventional responses.[6]

It has been well said that musical creativity is not taught; it is allowed to happen. One of music's primary attributes is its ability to stimulate the imagination. Hence, a creative approach to it is quite natural. It is quite true that "the fine arts can be more easily taught in a playful manner, and research continually shows a relationship between playfulness and creative behavior."[7] Young children take delight

---

[6] Educational Policies Commission, "The Role of the Fine Arts in Education," National Education Association, Washington, 1968. (Reprinted in *Music Educators Journal*, October 1968, p. 29.)

[7] Loc. cit.

in embellishing melodies and improvising harmony parts and accompaniments. Unless this tendency is bred out of them, they will compose when they acquire the necessary understanding and facility with music. Musical creativity is not taken up as an independent topic but is dependent upon the presentation of the songs and rhythms and recordings.

Nearly all phases of musical activity, of course, involve listening to music. Elementary school music is definitely not a theoretical, intellectual discipline, and children must be pretty well surrounded by "live" music. Constantly they are listening.

The methods outlined in Carl Orff's *Schulwerk* constitute one attempt to heighten and emphasize the development of children's musical creativity. It is essentially an active, unrestrained approach. A variety of responses—singing, playing, dancing—are simultaneously employed. Improvisation is encouraged. There is a minimum of technical explanation.

A broad range of skills, attitudes, and habits is associated with listening. After all, music is an aural phenomenon, and the most fundamental approach to it is through listening. It is easy to forget that the performer also listens and that the amateur performance is partly justified on this basis. Likewise, the study of music's history and its internal organization can serve to sharpen aural comprehension.

It has been said there are three levels of listening—the sensual, the perceptual, and the imaginative.[8] Whatever the case, the student should be equipped with a wide repertoire of listening experiences. He should be able to perceive the sheer beauty of tone and should be sensitive to the constant interplay of pitch, intensity, and color. He should apprehend the rhythmic pulse, melodic line, and harmonic texture. There should be a critical awareness of formal, technical, and interpretative patterns and an ability to appreciate the total effect of a composition.

The use of musical recordings in instruction is chiefly of

[8] Max Schoen, *The Understanding of Music*, Harper & Brothers, New York, 1945, Chap. 3.

value in supplementing the musical diet with examples which are beyond the capability of direct production locally. There is an inherent danger here that examples may be used not only which are beyond the performing capabilities of the children but which also offer little within range of their musical comprehension. Revealing facts about the music should be introduced *as a means to greater comprehension of the music*. But care should be employed in using music strictly for *illustration* of certain forms or merely to accompany some story concocted by the teacher or by the composer himself. The teacher can give the legend of *The Sorcerer's Apprentice*, but he does not need to point out where one broomstick becomes two bassoons!

Performing, listening, moving, and creating are things which the children can do with music and are properly discussed one at a time as we have done. In the classroom, however, it is most natural and effective to engage the children in several types of activity simultaneously. It must be stressed that "elementary music instruction has often been splintered into separate activities that are unsystematic and lacking in cohesiveness."[9] General music at any level of schooling should be conceived as *the study of music literature*, to be approached by means of:

1. understanding many types of music through guided listening or performance,
2. studying music through singing, playing instruments, moving to music, or a combination of these,
3. arranging and composing music for instruments and voices,
4. understanding and using music notation.[10]

It is also true that music is an inseparable part of the child's life both within and outside the school and need not be

[9] Committee on Implications for the Curriculum, "The Tanglewood Symposium," *Music Educators Journal*, November 1967, p. 77.

[10] Loc. cit.

artificially fused or correlated with other subjects. Instead, ordinary classroom activity, the approaching seasons, and special school projects all provide functional occasions for the use of music. Music study is always more meaningful when thus related to the content and rhythm of the school year.

The Music Program in the Secondary School

General music.   The music program at the secondary level is characterized by gradual partitioning, in accommodation to the divergent paths of student needs and interests. A general music class in the secondary schools, however, is a necessity for those students who have developed no particular concern for any one phase of music. It is equally important for those who might tend to overspecialize in any one field of the art. Members of this class, therefore, should represent a cross section of the student population rather than cases of arrested music development.

Continuity between elementary and secondary levels of the program is maintained because the central objectives are the same; there should be a considerable difference of approach to these goals, however. Not only are the musical materials and subject matter a good deal more advanced, but the teacher's handling of the class must also allow for considerably more initiative by the students. Above all, the general music class must not become a watered-down version of the school chorus nor simply a listening class. The students should be studying good musical literature from all angles— singing and playing it, listening to it, and examining its organization and derivations—and this process can become quite intensive. It is generally wise to organize this course in definite segments or units which will favor attention to all phases of music and each type of musical literature.

Typically, the general music course is scheduled daily throughout the seventh grade, or during one semester of both the seventh and eighth grades, or on alternate days throughout both years. It is usually required only of those who are not enrolled in a performing organization. Actually, the requirement should *not* be waived when the student elects band or chorus, but rather when he shows promise of adequate general musicianship. In practice, this means periodic reevaluation of each student and, consequently, smaller classes at each succeeding grade level.

General music is now being handled in different fashion by some schools. Instead of, or in addition to, the junior high school course, a one semester advanced course is offered for high school seniors. In essence, it is the music appreciation course ordinarily taken by college freshmen and is felt to be equally appropriate at the high school level.

The same reasoning is being applied in the case of the Humanities course, which is typically for college sophomores. A slightly less abstract version is now being offered in a number of high schools. The art of music and its literature is, of course, a major concern in such a course, in concert with the graphic arts, literature, and the cultural history of Western man. Thus, if competently taught, the Humanities course serves to accomplish a great deal of the job in general music. The danger is that the teacher may treat music so academically that the students' experiences are essentially cognitive and never aesthetic.

Vocal music.   Choral organizations—the choir, the glee clubs, and the various small ensembles—offer an unusual opportunity for effective musical development. Few schools are too small to have worthwhile choral groups. Many factors which plague the instrumental program are not present here; these include costly equipment, the long training period for the student, securing correct instrumentation, required outdoor appearances, more limited literature, missing parts, uniform fitting, and so on—to say nothing of the almost insurmountable problems in intonation and technical facility. Even more fundamentally, the choir director escapes the inherent competition with the instruments themselves for the students' undivided attention and hence can exert his personality and musicianship to the fullest extent. With all these advantages it is surprising that high school choirs are not better than they are.

Admittedly, many problems counterbalance these advantages. Voices mature slowly and bad habits of voice production and enunciation occur; students are sometimes overly attracted by the glamour and pageantry of a band, and boys sometimes consider singing rather effeminate. Nevertheless, the choral program remains quite direct; it is a most personalized medium of expression and can contribute greatly to the student's musical responsiveness and to his later musical participation in adult life.

The rich choral program certainly involves the use of an extensive literature and many opportunities for performance. The inherent versatility of choirs should be exploited; they can take part in large productions, theatrical or purely musical; they can always mount a complete Christmas or Easter program unsupported by instruments. Good and great music of all types and eras is available for choral use, and every student in the school can be given the chance to participate.

The mixed chorus.   The mixed chorus is an almost universal organization in secondary schools, but because of limited scheduling or entrance requirements, many students are still denied the opportunity to sing in such a group. On the other hand, some students discontinue singing in the chorus because the experiences provided lack sequence and progression from year to year. It is desirable to have at least two choruses, and more if possible, including a beginning chorus for singers with limited proficiency and experience and one or more choruses whose members are selected on the basis of vocal quality and musicianship.

Every effort should be made to maintain balance among parts in the selective groups, even if it means reducing the total number of singers. Artistic results cannot be achieved when sopranos in a choral group outnumber tenors by four to one, a not infrequent situation in high school choruses.

The mixed chorus should sing a variety of music of a difficulty consistent with the proficiency of the singers.

Some choral directors limit their repertoires unduly. As a result, the incongruous spectacle of a richly robed chorus singing only folk, novelty, and popular music is not uncommon. At the other end of the scale, a repertoire consisting exclusively of compositions sung a cappella is too highly specialized and difficult to justify unless the singers have previously had a more varied singing experience and the group has been organized for the specific purpose of singing one style of music. It is essential that mixed choruses provide students with progressive sequential experience singing and learning to understand a generous sample of the magnificent heritage of choral music with all periods and styles represented.

Glee clubs.   Glee clubs make a unique contribution to the secondary school music program. The boys' glee club has a rich, virile tone quality which appeals both to adolescent boy singers and to most listeners. Furthermore, the traditional repertoire is attractive and zestful. Many boys who would not consider singing in a mixed group readily join a glee club, and, as a result, later become interested in singing in a mixed chorus or church choir. The boys' glee club, with its provision of comradeship for members and its incomparable value in attracting and developing boy singers, is an essential part of the secondary school vocal program. Every school should have one or more.

The girls' glee club has a charm and value all its own. Although the tonal and dynamic resources of such a group are limited, a skillful director can obtain a strikingly beautiful and delicate result. Furthermore, because of the early maturation of girls' voices, such a group can be trained to sing with a level of finesse and artistry all but impossible when immature boys' voices are involved. Girls' glee clubs are indispensable in the secondary school, both for the quality of musical experience they afford and for their value in providing an opportunity for all girls in the school to sing.

Vocal ensembles.   Vocal ensembles represent an excellent means to the individualization of instruction and to the development of musical independence. Every school should have a variety of such groups operating throughout the school year. They should include trios, quartets, sextets, and double quartets of boys', girls', and mixed voices, and a madrigal group. The madrigal group may properly be composed of the most proficient singers in the school and represent the height of selectivity. It is desirable, however, for small ensemble experience to be available for singers of all levels of experience and proficiency. The music teacher should coordinate the organization and rehearsals of the ensembles and should be available to give supervision and assistance when necessary, but he should not actively rehearse each group. Not only would doing so make too great demands on his time, but the students learn more and develop musical independence when they are called on to recognize and solve their own problems of selecting and interpreting music. The practice of using advanced students to coach beginning ensembles produces excellent results in terms of the musical learning of both singers and coaches. It is essential that vocal ensembles be considered an integral part of the secondary school music program rather than as selective specialized groups organized to entertain the public and enter contests.

Voice classes.   Students with mature voices and special interest in singing can profit greatly from participation in voice classes. Primary emphasis should be placed on providing acquaintance with and experience in singing literature for the solo voice rather than vocal development as such. The classes may range in size from six to fifteen or so students. It is desirable to place students with high voices, both boys and girls, in one class and those with low voices in another. With this kind of grouping students can learn and sing songs together without vocal strain brought about by extreme ranges.

Instrumental music.   The instrumental program, as has been indicated, is perhaps more specialized than the choral. Not only do proficiency standards rule out advanced work for some students and enhance it for others, but one's instrumental activity is also usually confined to a specific instrument or instruments. That is, while some shifting can always be done, the student eventually must settle down to a concentrated effort in one or two fields; if he does not do so, he will remain a beginner. Beyond this, financial considerations have the effect of limiting the number of trials upon the different instruments.

These facts are reflected in the relatively limited number of students who participate fully in the specialized instrumental program as well as in the sense of exclusiveness and dedication which many develop in this field. While encouraging this seriousness of study, the instrumental teacher must take care to avoid the tendency toward extremely narrow specialization. The program must be set up so that the student is not forced to choose among the major organizations. If he wishes to and is able, he should be allowed to play the trumpet in the band and the violin in the orchestra and sing in one of the choral groups. There is an unfortunate practice in some schools of scheduling all these groups during the same school period. Several reasons are advanced for this, including the theory that some students must be prevented from electing music at the expense of other subjects. In practice, however, this only prevents the student from taking advantage of wider forms of musical experience.

We have mentioned the need for beginning instrumental classes in the elementary schools, in piano, string, and band instruments. Such instruction must also be offered at the secondary level for those who do not begin so soon. The teacher must not become involved in a high-pressure campaign for tangible results and needed replacements for the advanced organizations. Beginning classes should be considered not only as a preliminary step to advanced instruction but also as legitimate musical ensembles where real music can be played and appreciated.

Graduates of the piano class are recommended to good private teachers and are given opportunity to accompany other students and to appear as soloists on school programs. The beginning band and string classes become intermediate groups, whose members are carefully introduced into the advanced organizations as they become qualified and as vacancies occur.

In some situations this is all done by age grouping, so that junior high band members automatically become senior high band members at the appropriate time. Laudable as this educational policy may be, the musical requirements of the individual and of the group would seem to dictate considerable latitude in the application of such a procedure.

The gravest danger in the instrumental program is that the student will be exploited in the interests of school public relations or the aggrandizement of the director. There are obvious possibilities here that some directors cannot resist, and it is but one step until the students are actually regarded as employees. This stage is reached when the director begins to think, "What can he (the student) do for me?" rather than, "What should I be doing for him?" The wise instrumental director realizes that, as in the case of Solomon, his search for wisdom to meet the needs of his students will eventually be rewarded by satisfaction, prestige, advancement, and public esteem.

The band.   The school band is a powerful and useful institution in the American school music program, but there is one basic problem which merits consideration. It lies in the fact that the band is a multipurpose organization. The main trunk of instrumental musical development has long been orchestral, and the band was originally assigned an outdoor military function. Playable orchestral transcriptions were soon added to the band's repertoire in order to make possible its appearance as a concert group. When the band program became fully established in the schools, the light and popular style also became attached to its domain, since the orchestra never acquired prominence in this area and the dance band has been generally ruled out of the schools. Only recently has concert music of high caliber been produced solely for band use. Consequently, the band is many things to many people One knows what the orchestral or choral groups should be doing, but the band director must walk a tightrope among several possibilities. On the one hand, a pure marching organization offers few educational possibilities, while from the standpoint of both serious concert work and the light and popular idiom the band is logically in no position to compete with the other instrumental and choral groups.

In spite of this difficulty bands thrive because people like to hear them and to participate in them; they have become universal in the American schools. Band work inherently offers some of the advantages ascribed to team play. Here, perhaps more than in any other area of the music program, the twin factors of competition and cooperation may operate to their best advantage. Good bands are charged with an atmosphere at once keenly competitive and yet of tremendous unity.

In keeping with these characteristics of bands, the director must establish a program that is quite broad and truly forceful. He must keep things moving and progressing, he must promote a very wide and tasteful repertoire, and he must use every means to develop the initiative and responsibility of the players. Above all, he must recognize that the band, like all school musical organizations, should be a *means* to the musical education of the students and not an end in itself.

The orchestra. In spite of its longer tradition and larger selection of fine literature, the school orchestra is to be found only in ten to fifteen percent of the schools. It cannot compete with the band and choral groups in popularity nor in producing and exploiting the values of team spirit. Membership in an orchestra usually requires many previous years of study, and therefore the number of available players is normally quite limited. In view of all this, many directors attempt to popularize their groups, adding wind players for more volume of tone, filling up the string section with beginners in order to restore the instrumentation, and programming simplified or bombastic misarrangements wherever necessary. Such a program cannot succeed in developing the qualities of experience which should flow from orchestral work; it cannot even maintain a hold upon the players or the public. The school orchestra program must be created with a long-term view, and instruction must remain patient and musically imaginative. By patience, however, is not meant that method of instruction which causes the players to drill endlessly on fingering and bowing patterns for the day when they may be admitted to some professional symphony. The time for music is always *now*; the orchestral literature is certainly extensive enough, so that good material can be found for a group of any size or level of proficiency.

Small instrumental ensembles.   Neglect of small-ensemble work in many schools is attributed to the director's lack of time. This is extremely unfortunate, for few activities can be so educationally productive. Not only is there a rich and rewarding literature for these groups, but they can be organized quickly and maintained with a minimum of effort. Students react well to ensemble playing because it naturally contributes to the fulfillment of their individual needs and interests and offers great scope for the exercise of individual initiative and leadership.

The way to develop the program is to organize a series of groups in which students of equal proficiency work together. This means that the ensemble combinations must vary from year to year as some players graduate or lose interest and others develop. From year to year, one should try to maintain basic groups such as the woodwind quintet, string, clarinet and brass quartets. Dozens of other groupings may be employed as the players become available.

Such operation demands a large ensemble library containing music for all types of ensembles. Rehearsal schedules must be coordinated; public appearances must be well planned; and student responsibilities must be clearly outlined. The teacher assumes the role of coordinator and coach rather than that of conductor.

Special mention must be made of larger groupings which often require regular supervision of the director. These include the woodwind, brass, and string choirs, large percussion ensemble, pep band and stage band. The stage band is increasingly popular as a vehicle for exploring all types of dance band literature and developing proper style and facility.

Private instruction.   Private study is a necessary preliminary to the musical professions. It is really a type of conservatory training aimed at the attainment of (1) advanced knowledge of a particular literature, (2) highly specialized musical tastes, and (3) artistic performance skill.

These goals are not incompatible with those of the public schools, but it is doubtful whether private instruction in the normal sense of the term is actually a legitimate part of the public school music program. True, many teachers employed by schools teach privately on a full-time or part-time basis, and their work clearly contributes to the outcome of the program. Whether the teacher does this on his own or "school time" and whether he is compensated by the school or directly by the student is incidental; such a teacher must recognize that he is fulfilling a dual role.

The distinction needs to be made between individual *coaching*, which is a function of any teacher, and private *tutoring*, which is part and parcel of preprofessional education. A student has the right to individual attention and guidance when the normal group activities of the school fail to produce sufficient momentum on the road to the central objectives of that program. But this arrangement is supplemental and remedial in nature. Those students who may later enter one of the musical professions should be led to secure intensive private instruction outside the school.

Music theory and literature.   If the proper kind of instruction were given in the regular school music courses, with theoretical content introduced wisely in connection with the musical literature being studied, there would be no justification for a special course in music theory. This area is of such a nature that the prevocational student can be given the necessary guidance and references on an individual basis, along with ample opportunity to evaluate his creative efforts.

But when it is found that the regular activities develop little more than sight-reading ability and a few critical standards, it may be helpful to institute special courses in music theory and literature. Study should not be a dry prerequisite to college work; it must succeed in doing what the other activities have failed to do in bringing out the organizational patterns of the important musical idioms. Music should be examined first-hand in terms of why and how it is written, and these lessons should be applied as creatively as possible.

The Music Program in Higher Education

The objectives of the college general music program retain continuity with the public school program. Those courses and activities open to the general student—band, chorus, Introduction to Music—must not become highly specialized but should be advanced forms of the same activities found in the secondary schools. They should be operated in such a way as to advance the students' common musical competencies.

A student who is majoring in performance, composition, or musicology, however, should be given the full preprofessional treatment. These are *new* programs for the student in which he begins on a new plane and works toward new objectives. This student must be given a thorough background in his field, and he must eventually acquire the technical sureness and polish which will be necessary in meeting the requirements of his profession. Inefficient prerequisites are no help in this regard. If a student is to understand music theory and composition, he must soon begin to write music; if he is to become a professional violinist, he must commence quickly to master the advanced literature. In effect, he has elected conservatory training.

Many of the problems encountered in college music programs stem from the fact that facilities are not extensive enough. The students are usually carried right along with the much larger group of future music teachers; and, of course, the huge majority of music majors will one day find themselves to be music teachers.

The teacher-preparation program should be quite distinctive from other types of music programs. As has been mentioned in Chapter 6, the music teacher not only must possess balanced musicianship but also needs special teaching and social competencies. Thus, the musical subjects should not be taught to the future teacher as ends in themselves; that is, performance is not to be taught for performance sake, nor should music theory be presented as if the student were to become a theorist or composer. This is sometimes difficult for specialists in these fields to perceive. Even the area of pedagogy should not be regarded as a distinct discipline; all learning here must have practical application in actual teaching situations. That this is not always so is precisely why instruction in this area is so often bitterly attacked.

A constant plague in music-teacher preparation is the tendency to clutter and extend the program. Because of the necessarily broad coverage, the staff often recognizes gaps in the students' preparation and proceeds to design new courses to fill them. Basically, however, music-teaching programs should be no longer or more complex than any other program.

Designing instruction strictly in terms of the music teacher's qualifications makes it possible to avoid much wasted motion. For instance, students can be taught instrumental techniques and the appropriate teaching methods *at the same time*; they can participate directly in the business affairs of the musical organizations rather than in courses devoted to those problems. In such ways the education of music teachers can become quite practical and streamlined.

SUMMARY

Some students progress well in school music and others do not; this circumstance is largely due to the kind of music program provided. The program does not consist of the subjects taken but of the experiences undergone by the student; these may be scattered throughout the school curriculum, but they actually form the music program. Planning is based upon the experiences themselves. No music program is successfully transposed in detail from one locality to another, for each school must serve unique purposes.

The individual experiences of students are established through control of circumstances—the kind of music, the facts brought to bear, teaching methods, etc. These conditions, in combination with the student's background, produce reactions which affect subsequent behavior. Experiences are selected on the basis of the objectives.

Much depends on the organization of the program. Experiences must be planned in a natural series and the program must be divided into related forms of activity. The entire structure must be flexible in order to adjust to the different needs and capacities of the students. Practical plans must be devised for daily instruction.

The elementary school music program is designed to promote over-all musical growth and provides general experience with a wide variety of music. Since music is dealt with so directly at this period, singing, playing, listening, and rhythmic and creative activities actually merge into one comprehensive activity.

General music continues into the secondary schools, but this class should not substitute for other musical activities. The choral program has many advantages and these should be fully exploited in terms of wide extension of participation, a rich and varied repertoire, and versatility in performance.

Instrumental activities are more specialized by reason of technical problems and the need for concentration of study. Beginning classes in winds, strings, and piano should be offered where the student may develop technical prowess through the agency of legitimate musical experiences. The high school band should offer a wide kind of musical background and many advantages of vigorous group action. The orchestra should offer musical experience of the highest and purest type. Many educational opportunities will be lost unless these major groups are supplemented with active small musical ensembles.

The college has responsibilities for both general and preprofessional music students. The music majors actually begin anew, following a path toward new objectives. Often, the future performers, composers, musicologists, and music teachers are put through very similar courses, and this fact creates many problems. The teaching program is actually the broadest, and no branch of it can well be taught for its own sake; if it is properly developed in terms of needed professional competencies, this program can be much simplified.

QUESTIONS FOR DISCUSSION

1. Why is the well-considered music program so important? Do course offerings define the music program? What *is* the music program and what does it accomplish?
2. How does the music program relate to the curriculum? Describe various systems for planning music programs. Why should the music program be locally designed?
3. Define the educative experience. What factors bring it about? How may the teacher control experience?
4. Why does the sequence of instruction depend primarily upon the students' experiences? Describe how sequence can be arranged.
5. Upon what basis do we divide the music program into specific subjects or activities? Are there any dangers to avoid in such a division?
6. Why does instruction affect individual students so differently? Are there any ways to accommodate this situation?
7. What is the value of a course outline? Who should construct it?
8. Describe the various methods of instituting changes in the music program. How can concentration upon ordinary school problems result in program change?
9. How is the teaching staff brought into the task of

program development? How does the music supervisor stimulate and guide program change?

10. What general type of experience should be sought in the elementary school music program? What kinds of musical activity does this entail? How are these properly conducted?

11. Why is the general music class in the secondary schools so important? What kind of a class should it be?

12. Why are the high school choral groups particularly vital to the music program? What are some of the advantages and problems to be faced?

13. How may beginning instrumental instruction be organized? What dangers are to be avoided?

14. What problem does the school band have in connection with its literature? What is the peculiar strength of this organization?

15. What kind of an organization should the school orchestra be? How can legitimate training be achieved?

16. What special advantages are inherent in small-ensemble work? How are such groups organized?

17. What is the relation of private instruction to the school music program? To what extent do students deserve individual coaching?

18. Why are special classes in music theory and literature often needed? How should these be taught?

19. What should the college music department offer to the general student? What kind of program should be designed for the music major? In what ways is preparation for music teaching different from preparation for other musical specialties?

SELECTED REFERENCES

Andrews, Frances M., and Clara E. Cockerill. *Your School Music Program*, Prentice-Hall, Inc., Englewood Cliffs, N.J., 1958.

Aronoff, Frances Webber. *Music and Young Children*, Holt, Rinehart and Winston, Inc., New York, 1969.

Goodlad, John S. "Schooling and Education," *The Great Ideas of Today, 1969*, Robert M. Hutchins and Mortimer J. Adler, eds., Praeger Publishers, Inc., New York, 1969.

House, Robert W. "Curriculum Construction in Music Education,"*Basic Concepts in Music Education*, National Society for the Study of Education Fifty-seventh Yearbook, Chicago, 1958, Part I, pp. 236-260.

Juilliard School of Music. *The Juilliard Report on Teaching the Literature and Materials of Music*, W. W. Norton & Company, Inc., New York, 1953.

Krug, Edward A. *Curriculum Planning*, Harper and Brothers, New York, 1957.

Leeder, Joseph A., and William S. Haynie. *Music Education in the High School*, Prentice-Hall, Inc., Englewood Cliffs, N.J., 1958.

Mix, J. "Orff-Schulwerke; A Means or An End?", *American Music Teacher* 17, February 1968, p. 37.

Music Educators National Conference, *Changing Emphases in Elementary School Music*, Gladys Tipton, ed., The Conference, Philadelphia, 1964.

——: *The Study of Music in the Elementary School*, Charles L. Gary, ed., The Conference, Washington, 1967.

Nye, Robert, and Vernice T. Nye. *Music in Elementary Schools*, 3d ed.,Prentice-Hall, Inc., Englewood Cliffs, N.J., 1970.

Sheely, Emma D. *Children Discover Music and Dance*, Teachers College Press, New York, 1968.

Smith, G. Russell. "Introducing Kodály Principles into Elementary teaching," *Music Educators Journal 54, November 1967, pp. 43-45.*

Sur, William R., and Charles F. Schuller. *Music Education for Teen-Agers*, 2d ed., Harper & Row, New York, 1966.

U.S. Office of Education. *Music In Our Schools: A Search for Improvement*, Report of the Yale Seminar on Music Education, Claude V. Palisca, ed., OE-33033, Bulletin, 1964, No. 28, Government Printing Office, Washington, 1964.

CURRICULUM GUIDES

A Teaching Guide for Public School Music in Oklahoma,
    Grades K-12, Oklahoma State Department of Educa-
    tion, Oklahoma City, 1967.
Music in Vermont Schools, Vermont State Department of
    Education, Instructional Services, Montpelier, 1965.
Teaching Music in the Elementary Grades, Curriculum Bulle-
    tin, 1959-60, No. 5, Board of Education of the City of
    New York.
Music Education in Indiana: A Curriculum Guide, The In-
    diana Music Educators Association and the Department
    of Public Instruction, State of Indiana, Indianapolis,
    1963.
Music: A Basic Program for the Classroom Teacher, Publica-
    tion No. 341 of the State Superintendent of Public
    Instruction, Raleigh, N.C., 1961.
*Music in Your Classroom: An Elementary Music Curriculum
    Guide,* Bureau of Instruction and Curriculum, West
    Virginia Department of Education, Charleston, 1963.
Music Guide for Arizona Elementary Schools, State Depart-
    ment of Public Instruction, Phoenix, 1964.
*Music for the Schools of Missouri: A Curriculum Guide for
    Grades Seven, Eight and Nine,* Publication No. 116G of
    the State Board of Education, Jefferson City, 1959.
*Music for the Schools of Missouri: A Curriculum Guide for
    Grades Ten, Eleven and Twelve,* State Board of Educa-
    tion, Jefferson City, 1964.
Music in the Secondary Schools, Illinois Curriculum Program
    Bulletin No. D-Eight, Office of the Superintendent of
    Public Instruction, Springfield, 1966.
U.S. Department of Health, Education and Welfare, *Music
    Curriculum Guides,* Office of Education, Government
    Printing Office, Washington, 1964.

Methods
of Teaching Music

8 This chapter has as its purpose the development of valid concepts of teaching methods in music education. It begins with definitions of teaching and teaching methods, describes successful music teaching, and explores the bases of methods of teaching. It continues with a discussion of basic patterns for teaching performance skills, appreciation, knowledge and understanding, and attitudes. The chapter closes with the presentation of eleven principles of method which are applied to the teaching of music.

TEACHING AND TEACHING METHODS DEFINED

Learning was defined in Chapter Five as the process by which meaning is apprehended, clarified, and applied. Chapters Six and Seven emphasized the central role of objectives in program planning and the function of experiences in reaching the stated objectives. Teaching has a logical relationship to both learning and program planning.

Teaching is defined as the organization and conduct of learning experiences. The purpose of teaching is to facilitate learning. Fundamentally, there can be no teaching unless learning takes place, but it must be recognized that learning often takes place without the formal guidance of a teacher.

Teaching is the activity of a person who stimulates and guides learning by organizing and conducting the learning experiences of his students. A crucial point in understanding the relationship between teaching and learning is that it is the student who learns and that every student must do his own learning. Teaching merely serves to arrange the learning environment for the student and to increase the efficiency of his learning.

The procedures used by a teacher to organize the learning experiences of his students are called *teaching methods.* Since students learn from all contacts with the school environment, it should be recognized that teaching methods include more than the techniques used by a teacher in conducting a class or a musical activity. For example, students may learn from listening to music before and after classes, by experimenting on their own with musical instruments, by participating in the selection of recordings for the school library, by supervising the record library, and by assisting in the planning of a public program. Procedures which involve students in these kinds of experiences likewise represent teaching methods.

Chapter One pointed out that the work of the school consists of a sequential but interrelated series of processes, including curriculum, instruction, supervision, administration, and evaluation. Students may participate at times in all these processes. For example, they may participate in curriculum building by serving on a committee to plan a series of musical activities or to develop a unit in the general music class. When advanced students help beginners learn to play an instrument, they are participating in instruction. A student committee setting policies for the use of the music library or for the organization of the band is taking part in administration. Likewise, students may be called on to evaluate the music program or some phase of music instruction. All these experiences result in student learning, and the procedures used by the teacher to arrange these kinds of student participation also constitute methods of teaching.

The professional literature of education identifies several different types of methods, including lecture, recitation, project, laboratory, dramatic, socialized recitation, and group discussion. These methods of teaching fall into two broad categories, teacher-centered methods and student-centered methods. Lecture and recitation methods are patently teacher-centered. Both are characterized by teacher domination in instructional planning, in the conduct of classroom activities, and in the evaluation of results. The other types of methods were developed because of the desirability of involving students more directly in all phases of instruction. In student-centered instruction the students assist in the selection of objectives, in the choice of subject matter, and in the evaluation of results. In short, they exercise the optimum amount of control of the total learning situation

It must be recognized that no one method of teaching provides the solution for all music-teaching problems. Each teaching situation dictates the most appropriate method to be used, and all methods of teaching or variations and combinations of methods may be used at different times.

Even though it is impossible to prescribe teaching methods for a particular situation, there seems little doubt that music education lends itself admirably to student-centered instructional methods. Lecture and recitation methods have little or no place at the lower levels of the music program and undoubtedly are used excessively at the higher levels.

The use of the lecture method is justified in three circumstances: (1) when the lecturer can provide information not conveniently available to students, (2) when the lecturer is able to present a unique synthesis of information which will contribute to student understanding, and (3) when the lecturer is able to establish an inspirational attitude or mood essential to student learning. Under other circumstances the use of the lecture method is open to serious question.

General music lends itself especially well to student-centered instruction. In fact, the success of the general music program at all levels depends to a great extent upon the amount of consideration given to student interests and the amount of student participation in determining objectives, selecting subject matter, planning experiences, structuring assignments, and evaluating outcomes.

Performance groups often exhibit a regrettable and largely unjustified degree of teacher domination. This condition undoubtedly results from a transference of attitudes and procedures from professional performing organizations to school organizations, but it is not tenable in performance groups with an educational purpose. Means must always be consistent with ends. The means to optimum student learning and musical and personal development are essentially different from the means to high-quality professional performance. In the former, the performance of music is a means to student development; in the latter, the performers are a means to the performance of music. The difference is obvious.

The following factors derived from the preceding discussion are paramount in any consideration of methods of teaching music: (1) it is the students who learn, and they must be the center of consideration; (2) methods of teaching music must be compatible with the objectives sought; and (3) students learn from all influences surrounding the learning situation.

WHAT IS SUCCESSFUL MUSIC TEACHING?

Music teaching can be considered successful only if it produces authentic musical achievement by students. Student progress toward valid objectives is the measure of successful music teaching. This means that the music teacher from the outset must assure himself that he is teaching for worthwhile objectives and that his students are making significant progress toward those objectives.

What do these statements mean in terms of music instruction? They imply generally that successful musical instruction results in broad and lasting musical learning which will eventuate in musical independence. Successful teaching in general music results in student attainment of musical understanding, musical skills, appreciation, and other musical learnings which are associated with a musically educated person. Successful piano teaching produces people who can play the piano expressively, who can read music readily, who can play by ear, and who have musical understanding. Successful teaching in music theory leads to a functional understanding of the structure of music which the learner can continue to apply in all his musical endeavors. Successful teaching in music history results in stylistic understanding and comprehension of the broad sweep of stylistic development.

These results stand in sharp contrast to those sometimes attained in musical instruction. Products of the music education program who cannot sing, read music, or play an instrument and who have developed no lasting interest in or appreciation for music are not uncommon. Countless people have had private instrumental or vocal instruction and have appeared in recitals but, after a few years, have no residue of musical skill or understanding. Such results indicate unsuccessful teaching. The lack of success is due either to invalid objectives or to poor teaching practices.

Some music educators minimize the importance of musical achievement and excuse the lack of it by emphasizing concomitant values of musical participation such as personality development, social development, and physical development. Many have taken refuge in slogans such as "We don't teach music; we teach children" and "A singing school is a happy school."

Music education can indeed contribute to social and personal development, but only through solid musical achievement. A person does not develop an attractive personality and social competence without having skills, qualifications, knowledge, and understanding. Attempting to develop the personality through music without musical achievement subverts the music education program, fleeces the student, and often results in music's being labeled a frill subject without substance and value.

THE BASES OF TEACHING METHODS

The bases of teaching methods include the nature of the subject matter, the objectives of instruction, the nature of the learning process, the maturational level, experiential background and present needs of students, teacher competencies, and such physical conditions as materials available, time available, and class size.

The close relationship between subject matter and methods of teaching has been well established. Dewey stressed the fact that the nature of the subject matter dictates the method of instruction and that a search for a method of instruction applicable to all kinds of teaching is doomed to failure. "Apart from effort to control the course which the process takes, there is no distinction of subject and method. There is simply an activity which includes both what the individual does and what the environment does."[1]

Methods of teaching music can never be rightly considered except in relation to the nature of music as an expressive art. The best methods are those that involve students in meaningful musical experiences. As a consequence of their involvement and their engagement in musical experiences they learn. Teaching musical techniques, notation, history, or theory outside a musical and expressive context is never justified.

A method of teaching can be considered successful only in so far as it results in progress toward the objectives of a course. The fact that music education has a variety of objectives indicates the necessity for flexible and varied methods of teaching. Development in one area of objectives must not be allowed to have an abortive effect on progress in another area. For example, too highly specific emphasis on technique often results in a lack of musical responsiveness, and undue emphasis on the intellectual aspects of musical meaning may

---

[1] John Dewey, *Democracy and Education*, The Macmillan Company, New York, 1916, p. 195. Reprinted by permission of the publisher.

lessen the affective appeal of music. Methods of teaching music, regardless of the level of specialization, should exhibit breadth and consistency of organization and should be conceived with the realization that in any given situation learnings are multiple and that more than one objective is involved.

The basic principles of and guides to successful teaching method have emerged from two sources, the psychology of learning and analysis of successful practices. Efficient teaching requires an intimate knowledge of the learning process. While disagreements exist among psychologists as to how learning takes place, the disagreements generally represent differences in emphasis and approach:

> Psychology has never presented in one place a complete, unified, coherent and universally agreed upon account of the nature of learning. The science of psychology has not yet reached the stage of maturity which would make such a pronouncement possible. Despite this fact, much is known about learning and a number of valid principles of great importance to curriculum builders has been established as the result of the efforts of psychological workers.[2]

The issue of logical versus psychological organization relates directly to methods of teaching. The former emphasizes the orderly presentation of subject matter; the latter implies that what is logical to the teacher may not be so to the learner and that the experiential background of the learner must be taken into account. The most carefully planned lesson fails when the learner finds no meaning or value in it. It should be recognized that both logical and psychological organization function in good teaching methods. A strictly logical organization ignores the student as a person with needs, likes,

[2] Glenn M. Blair, "How Learning Theory Is Related to Curriculum Development," in Arthur Coladarci, ed., *Educational Psychology: A Book of Reading*, The Dryden Press, Inc., New York, 1955, p. 12. Reprinted by permission of Henry Holt and Company, Inc., New York.

dislikes, readiness, and mental set. Psychological organization functions more realistically in the sense that it takes into account the desirability of the learner's being able to select those aspects of the lesson which have meaning for him. The method has additional strength when the material presented has some logical organization.

There has been much effort made to systematize musical knowledge. Most authors of music books give attention to presenting the material in a logical order. Music history is treated chronologically; music theory moves from the simple to the complex; listening begins with easy compositions and progresses to difficult material. The wise music teacher welcomes this wealth of logically organized information as source material but does not follow it slavishly, because he knows that logical organization cannot replace musical experience and that the accumulation of musical information does not constitute musical understanding. He also is aware that students learn with more lasting and more authentic results when they use their own minds in organizing material and arriving at generalizations than when they simply memorize the organization and generalizations accomplished by others.[3]

Teachers should exercise great care in using methods of teaching which have proved successful for other teachers. The unique complexities of each teaching situation provide many chances for error in selecting and adapting teaching methods. Imitating teaching methods used by others rarely proves successful. A far better approach is to analyze successful teaching practices one discovers or observes and arrive at

[3] See George Katona, *Organizing and Memorizing*, Columbia University Press, New York, 1940. This classic experiment showed the decisive superiority of teaching methods which emphasized pupil understanding of the nature of problems. Among his conclusions is the following: "Pupils should learn to learn—that is the best the school can do for them. They should not merely learn to memorize—they should learn to learn by understanding" (p.260)

generalizations which can be applied to teaching problems one encounters.

The realities inherent in specific situations always condition methods. Since teacher competencies vary, methods must also vary. For example, a fine pianist with a wide repertoire at his fingertips may teach very effectively from the keyboard. Another teacher, with less piano facility, must rely on recordings and student accompanists. The wise music teacher takes into account his strengths and weaknesses and plans his teaching methods accordingly.

Physical conditions such as materials available, time available, and class size affect teaching methods directly. Some desirable teaching procedures may be impossible because of lack of equipment. The class which meets daily has time for rewarding but time-consuming activities which cannot be worked into a class meeting once a week. When class time is scarce, class work must be more tightly and efficiently organized; and more out-of-class assignments are often necessary.

The maturational level, experiential background, and present needs of students represent highly important factors in the selection of teaching methods. Teaching without regard for these factors is not uncommon in music education. For example, teaching methods appropriate for advanced applied music students are sometimes used with beginners. Teachers should recognize that, while the adult well advanced in applied music may profit from careful and intensive practice on technical exercises and scales, the adult or child beginner may receive little or no benefit from such work.

It should be apparent that many varied and complex factors affect teaching methods. The teacher must take all the variables into account and devise methods in terms of his own unique situation. This fact does not vitiate the concepts and principles of method contained in this chapter, but it does mean that their application will be affected by existing conditions.

BASIC PATTERN FOR TEACHING PROCEDURES

The discussion of learning in Chapter Five emphasizes the importance of concept formation in the learning process and provides the major clues to understanding the basic pattern for teaching procedures. Teaching centers broadly on establishing concepts, clarifying them by providing meaningful practice situations, and analyzing the results of the practice. This, in turn, leads to further practice to fix the correct responses. The following discussion describes teaching procedures useful in teaching performance skills, appreciation, knowledge and understanding, and attitudes.

We have emphasized that students learn as a result of musical instruction only if they are directly involved in meaningful experiences with music. Analysis of musical experiences has resulted in the identification of five avenues to musical learning: (1) performing, (2) hearing, (3) feeling, (4) discriminating, and (5) knowing. These avenues are distinguished from the products of musical learning (see pp. 132-142) in that the avenues are viewed as *means* to musical learning while the products represent the ends or results of musical learning.

Performing.   Performing includes playing, singing, reading music, writing music, and composing music. Performing provides experience in projecting musical meaning, and such experience is essential to the development of a deep responsiveness to music and of musical understanding. It generates a unique level of involvement with music and enthusiasm for it, both of which are basic to successful learning of music. In addition, it serves as a valuable means to the clarification and refinement of musical meaning for students.

Hearing.   The word *hearing* is used in this context, rather than "listening," to imply a deeper level of involvement on the part of the student than is often associated with listening as a musical activity. The avenue of hearing leads to the development of precise listening skills, the primary basis for all musical achievement. The avenue of hearing embraces such experiences as hearing one's own part in relation to other parts, hearing repetition and contrast in melodic, harmonic, and rhythmic motion in music, relating tonal movement to the tonality, identifying the characteristic sounds of instruments and voices, and recognizing the elaboration and development of thematic material.

Discriminating. Discriminating means making judgments about music. Relevant topics for experiences in discriminating include the quality, expressive purpose, style, and form of music the student performs and hears and how one composition is related stylistically to another. Such topics serve as foci for organizing experiences for students in making discriminations about music.

Feeling. The avenue of feeling involves the aesthetic dimension of musical experience and leads directly to appreciation. It provides the means by which music education becomes aesthetic education.

Music education as aesthetic education is education in the affective domain. It takes place when students have experiences with music that enliven their spirits and touch their hearts. Such experience frees the human spirit and allows it to soar when students project the expressive import of music as performers and composers and when they react in a feelingful way to the import of music as listeners.

The avenue of feeling involves responding to line and phrasing in music, to changes in the level of intensity generated by music, to the movement of the rhythm, and to the unfolding of the expressive import of music.

Knowing. The avenue of knowing involves the cognitive domain. Cognition in connection with musical experience enables the student to gain and use significant information *from* and *about* the music he is experiencing. As a result of cognitive experience associated directly with musical experience, he forms musical concepts and develops musical insight.

The cognitive learning is cyclical and the learning pattern includes these elements: experiencing music; forming concepts as a result of organizing experience with music; labeling concepts; gaining information; formulating generalizations; developing insight.

The avenue of knowing includes such experiences for the student as (1) differentiating the stylistic characteristics of different compositions he hears or performs, (2) relating each composition he hears or performs to the broad sweep of stylistic development, (3) discovering, recalling, and putting to use the factors involved in expressive performance, (4) learning and using appropriate terms in thinking and talking about music.

Using the Avenues in Instruction

While the degree of emphasis on these five avenues properly varies in different classes and activities which constitute the framework of the music program, all of the avenues should be incorporated into the experiences organized for students in every music class and every musical activity including large and small performing groups, instrumental and vocal instruction, and music classes of all kinds and at all levels.

In performing groups, for example, primary emphasis is properly placed on performance itself, but the avenues of knowing, feeling, hearing, and discriminating must also be brought to bear on the students' learning experiences if their musical learning is to be other than one-sided. On the other hand, a class in music literature properly emphasizes hearing and knowing, but the avenues of performing, feeling, and discriminating must also be included.

A useful measure of the effectiveness of music teaching lies in applying this criterion after each class period: To what extent have I involved students in all five avenues to musical learning? If a music teacher discovers, on analysis of his teaching, that he is consistently emphasizing one or two avenues to the neglect or exclusion of the others, he has a strong cue to the need for broadening his view of musical learning and restructuring his teaching methods to involve his students in all five avenues.

The Three-Phase Pattern

The process of teaching music has been analyzed as a three-phase pattern of (1) synthesis, (2) analysis, (3) synthesis.

Synthesis.   In this phase the teacher provides the students with an overview of the composition under study through the avenue of hearing or performing or, under many circumstances, both. Activities involved in the synthesis phase may include listening, singing, playing instruments, moving to music, and reading music. The essential characteristic of the synthesis phase is that students have an opportunity to perceive and react to the expressive effect of a composition and conceive it as a whole before the beginning of the analysis phase.

Analysis.   The purpose of the analysis phase is the revelation to students of musical detail in the composition they have experienced—detail that is significant to its expressive effect. The teacher's role in this phase is to structure the learning situation and guide the students' thinking in such a way that they are enabled to explore the composition and discover significant detail in it. The detail may be related to the mood, melody, rhythm, harmony, form, style, text, or tone quality of the composition under study.

    Discovering significant detail in music implies such experiences as:

1. Feeling and describing the mood of a composition.
2. Identifying the musical devices used by the composer to obtain the expressive effect he desired.
3. Analyzing and describing the melody, rhythm, harmony, and form of a composition.
4. Discovering repetition and contrast in tone patterns,

rhythm patterns, harmonic patterns and phrases through analysis.

5. Identifying musical characteristics that are important in determining the style of a composition.
6. Comparing compositions in different styles.
7. Making and substantiating value judgments concerning quality in performance.

Synthesis.   In this phase the teacher provides the students with the opportunity to experience again the music they have studied. As they reexperience the music, their response to it is heightened and refined as a result of their increased awareness of the music, its expressive effect, and the details of its structure and style.

Repetition of this three-phase cycle from day to day throughout the year with a variety of music leads to the development of appreciation, the refinement of musical competencies and the clarification of musical concepts. These learnings enable the student to perceive music more clearly, hear it more precisely, perform it more expressively, and to think and talk about it in terms that are meaningful to him.

Teaching Performance Skills

Learning performance skills requires the formation of both aural and movement concepts. The task of teaching performance skills centers on helping the learner develop both types of concepts, on directing and leading practice, and on assisting the learner in analyzing the results. Teaching is largely a matter of demonstrating, explaining, and providing for practice. Analysis of the results of practice provides the clues for further demonstration, further explanation, and further practice.

The teaching of performance skills should be carried on in a rich musical context. Since teaching movement patterns in isolation from musical results has little meaning or relevance, the instruction should begin with the establishment of an aural concept of what is to be achieved. Once the learner has an aural concept to guide his efforts, he needs to develop a concept of the movements required. In developing both kinds of concepts the teacher provides a model by demonstration and presents verbal explanations. He supplements the demonstration and explanation with pictures, recordings, diagrams, movies, and other means.

The teacher should introduce practice very early and should not expect the learner to conceive a perfect pattern before he engages in practice. Rather, practice should follow perception of the "big idea." The best pattern for teaching performance skills is brief demonstration, brief explanation, and a large amount of practice. A detailed illustrative example of the steps in teaching a beginning instrument class follows.

Establish concepts.   The instructor plays a short solo on the instrument or plays an excellent recording which demonstrates the instrument's tone quality and expressive possibilities. He plays single tones and short scalewise passages to demonstrate good and poor tone and demonstrates how the instrument is held and how the tone is produced. He explains to the pupils how to hold the instrument and how to produce the tone, making use of pictures, diagrams, slides, or movies.

Pupils take up the instruments and experiment with producing single tones and scalewise passages. The instructor puts the notation and fingering diagrams for the scalewise passages on the board. Pupils practice to establish basic control. The instructor plays a short, simple melody familiar to the students. They sing the melody until it is well in mind.

This phase of instruction will vary in length depending upon the background of the students and the complexity of the instrument.

Provide experience with the whole.   Students next have tryout experience playing the song they have heard and sung. The tryout experience has several important results. Movement concepts are clarified and enlarged; the learner finds out what he can and cannot do, thus preparing himself for part practice in a meaningful context; the teacher discovers what the different students in the class can do; motivation is enhanced; and, finally, valuable self-teaching takes place.

This phase of teaching enables the student to understand and recognize key points in the playing process and to develop a clear focus for his further practice. He verifies the correct portions of his concepts and modifies wrong ones. Since feelings and attitudes are involved, it is important that there be no pressure, anxiety, or embarrassment connected with this tryout phase.

Analyze the performance.   Once practice begins, teaching should concentrate on diagnostic procedures, detecting and eliminating difficulties which are blocking progress.

Provide for practice of parts as necessary.   Teacher and students single out parts causing difficulty. For example, string students may need to have specific practice with the bow arm to gain more freedom and control of movement, and wind instrument students may need special attention to the embouchure, again blowing single tones.

Reanalyze the performance.   Cooperative analysis by members of the class is highly effective at this point.

Reestablish the whole performance.   Parts singled out for practice should now be put back together through performance of the melody.

Students repeat this pattern in their own individual practice. As a result concepts are gradually clarified and movement pattern gradually refined.

It is common practice in teaching instrumental music for teachers to attempt to establish a perfect form before actual playing begins. The teacher of strings, for example, may give detailed and highly specific instruction for the position of the bow arm, the way the instrument is held, the exact angle of the elbow, and so on. Such practice assumes that a best form exists for playing an instrument which is applicable to all players of that instrument.

Such an assumption is open to grave question. Observation of artist players reveals great variation in form. In fact, no two instrumentalists can possibly use the same form. To ignore all the other factors making for variation, simple differences in physical conformation obviate the possibility of identical form among different players. Ragsdale makes this point succinctly:

> Motor skills have style, form, internal organization and coordination with external objects or events in greater or lesser degree. They are not fixed, stereotyped or invariable. . . .There are good and bad forms of an activity even though there is not usually one best form. This means that the human body as a biophysical organism acts within certain limits of force, range, speed, and other human functioning. Within these limits there may be a large number of equally good "forms" and the effort to find and teach the *one best form* for a given motor activity is futile.[4]

The applicability of his statement to the motor aspects of performance skills appears obvious.

Beginning instruction in performance skills should seek to establish concepts of good form and to start the student off within the limits of good form. It is useless to attempt to establish correct details at once. Beginning student trials in this type of learning are inevitably generalized and mass in character, but they are essential to the thinking and reflection which lead to efficient movement.

In teaching beginning instrumental performance skills, the first step is to bring about a general acquaintance with the instrument, provide a simple demonstration, and provide for beginning trials. Detailed and specific demonstrations and explanations are useless at this stage. The teacher should direct attention to the essential features of good playing form

---

[4] C. E. Ragsdale, "How Children Learn the Motor Types of Activity," *Learning and Instruction*, National Society for the Study of Education Forty-ninth Yearbook, University of Chicago Press, Chicago, 1950, Part I, pp. 71-72.

and efficient movement and introduce the details gradually as the learner gains more precise control of his body and the instrument.

Teaching Music Reading

In order to read music well, a person must gain the ability for tonal thinking and precise control of notation. The ability for tonal thinking results from continuing ' emphasis on conceiving the tonal and rhythmic movement in music through hearing, sight, and kinesthetic sense. Control of notation is attained through varied meaningful experience with the score.

Concepts essential to the development of skill in music reading include:

1. Concepts of tonality and tonal relationships. The formation of these concepts results from emphasis on hearing the tendencies of scale tones and the relationship between tones. Syllables or numbers may clarify tonality and tonal relationships for some students, but experience with the space frame of an instrument is essential for most people. Experience with the Autoharp, recorder, and the piano keyboard is especially valuable.
2. Concepts of the meaning of notation. To establish this concept teachers should help students relate their tonal and rhythmic experience to notational symbols, beginning with the general characteristics of notation and moving gradually to specifics.
3. Concepts of the beat and of rhythmic movement through the measure. Students form these concepts by moving to the rhythm of music, swinging the beat, creating rhythmic accompaniments, differentiating various meters and rhythmic patterns, and other activities of this type.
4. Concepts of the shape of phrases and of structural organization. The teacher continuously calls to the at-

tention of the students the structure of the music they perform and hear. As a result the students develop expectations of repetition and contrast, of harmonic and melodic tendencies, and of relationship between antecedent and consequent motifs and phrases.

Experiences important in the formation of these musical concepts include (a) singing and playing a wide variety of appealing music expressively, (b) using rhythm instruments and informal instruments to increase the expressive value of songs, (c) rhythmic and melodic improvisation which leads to freedom and control of musical expression, (d) bodily movement in response to the beat and to the motion of rhythmic patterns in music, (e) creative experiences such as playing and singing parts by ear and spontaneous musical expression, (f) listening to a variety of music and relating tonal and rhythmic patterns heard to those encountered in other musical experience, (g) exemplifying the movement of the phrase line through expressive movement, and (h) relating tonal and rhythmic patterns to the notation.

In the early years of the music program the teacher's primary concern should be to help pupils experience and conceive musical sounds through the ear and the kinesthetic sense, with special emphasis on spontaneous musical expression. After the children have learned to read language well and can express musical ideas with freedom and control, the notation should be introduced in connection with singing, playing, and creative experiences.

In teaching music reading, teachers should work toward overall musical understanding, upon which the ability to read depends. They should realize that the notation can have meaning only when pupils have learned to use their ears, have developed acute awareness of the movement of tonal and rhythmic patterns, and can discriminate among differing patterns.

There follow twenty suggestions to teachers which are applicable to the teaching of music reading:

1. Introduce pupils to notation through songs with which they are familiar.
2. Help pupils sing and play parts by ear and relate the result to the score.
3. Help them move to the beat of music and relate the movement to the score.
4. Help them conceive of music they hear and perform as a series of related tonal patterns or configurations rather than as a succession of separate tones.
5. Use instruments such as the recorder, tone bells, and piano as means both to musical expression and to the understanding of tonal relationships.
6. Place increased emphasis on spontaneous musical expression and improvisation.
7. Use vocal chording to develop a sense of tonal relationships and tonality.
8. Have your pupils set up the tonality for every song they sing or read by singing the chord progression I-IV-V7-I.
9. Be concerned with the specifics of notation only when their musical meaning has been clarified through musical experience.
10. Base all learning on actual music which the pupils have experienced and enjoyed. Begin with music, draw the specifics out of the music, and return to the music.
11. Be sure your pupils understand what you and they are trying to accomplish.
12. Utilize all the musical experiences your pupils have both in and out of school.
13. Enhance motivation by emphasizing the advantages of being able to read music.
14. Make increased use of the score in listening in the upper grades.
15. Provide for copious practice in reading a variety of easy music. Always make sure the beat and the tonality are clearly established before the pupils begin reading. When tonal problems arise, help the pupils solve them by clarifying the relationship of the problem passage to the tonality. When rhythmic problems occur, help the pu-

pils solve them by clarifying the relationship of the rhythmic pattern to the beat.

16. For beginning readers supply a chordal accompaniment to assist them in maintaining the tonality and the beat.

17. Teach your pupils to grasp tonal configurations rather than separate tones.

18. Help them analyze the music they are reading for familiar tonal and rhythmic patterns and for repetitions, similarities, and contrasts.

19. Recognize that pupils vary widely in their musical capacity and musical experience and that they will learn to read at different rates of speed. Encourage each pupil to develop his own approach to music reading. The teacher's role is to guide and motivate him to learn to read and to organize a learning situation which provides the most stimulating and meaningful musical experiences possible.

20. Recognize the importance of music reading, but do not become obsessed with it to the detriment of the overall musical learning of your pupils.

Teaching Appreciation, Knowledge, and Understanding

All kinds of learning include affective and cognitive responses in some degree. In learning motor skills, for example, motor responses are predominant, but these are reinforced and clarified by affective and cognitive responses. Appreciation, knowledge, and understanding develop through meaningful affective and cognitive experience. In learning appreciation affective experience predominates, but cognitive experience clarifies the affective. In learning knowledge and understanding, cognitive experience receives primary emphasis, but affective experience illuminates the cognitive.

The sequence of teaching does not vary greatly from one type of learning to another. The steps outlined in relation to teaching performance skills generally hold in teaching appreciation, knowledge, and understanding. That is, the teacher must give first attention to the development of concepts and then make provision for experience, trials, practice, and fixation of correct responses.

The first requisite for teaching appreciation is the development of awareness of and responsiveness to the affective power of intensity and release embodied in the tonal movement of expressive music. To bring this about the teacher should provide varied experience with good and great music well performed. This includes musical experience through performance and through listening. Once the concept of musical expressiveness is formed, it, like all concepts, should be named. The terms *line* or *phrasing* may be used, the former probably being preferable. Young children understand and react favorably to the term *shape* as a name for this concept.

Teaching devices useful in clarifying the concept of line include having students exemplify the movement of line in expressive bodily movement, drawing curves on the blackboard which rise as intensity increases and fall as release takes place, performing the same composition both with and without good expressive contour, and playing recordings of different performances of the same composition, one with expressive line, the other without.

As a result of this type of experience, pupils learn to expect music to progress from intensity to release, and this is the basis for appreciation. Once the basic concept of musical expressiveness has been developed, the teacher seeks to refine and clarify it by constantly drawing the pupils' attention to the expressive quality of all the music they experience. As musical experience continues, the teacher brings pupils in contact with music of different styles and helps them become aware of stylistic differences and develop expectations appropriate to the various styles. As a result the pupils learn a different set of expectations for folk music, classic music, romantic music, and contemporary music, but all music is bound together by their basic expectation of alternations between intensity and release through tonal movement. As stylistic concepts are formed, the teacher assists pupils in naming them, clarifying them through experience, and applying them to all their musical pursuits, whether listening, performing, or composing.

It would seem to be obvious that teaching appreciation must be carried on in connection with affective musical experience, but teachers sometimes attempt to teach musical knowledge and understanding in isolation from musical experience. This is a gross error and can never lead to successful results. Examples frequently encountered include teaching rhythm and meter on a strictly mathematical basis, teaching intervals in isolation, teaching harmony without regard to hearing, and so on.

Successful teaching of musical knowledge and understanding begins by providing affective experience with music. The teacher helps the pupil develop basic musical concepts by singling out from compositions heard and performed general musical elements such as melody, harmony, and rhythm and giving him the word symbols that serve as labels for these elements. After the pupil has had affective experience with a composition, the teacher points out the basic rhythm, the different melodies, and the structure of the composition, including repetitions of melodies and contrasting sections. He helps the pupil orient himself to the basic tonality and to changes from it and apprehend the meter, the tone quality of the instrument playing, and so on. The pupil learns the word symbols which represent these concepts. Further teaching is focused on assisting the pupil in gaining further musical experience and in clarifying his concepts, forming new and more specific concepts, and, finally, in generalizing his concepts. The teacher causes the pupil to contrast the meter from one composition to another, the tone quality of different instruments, the structural organization of different compositions, the difference in expressive intention and stylistic characteristics, and so on.

The essential point is that successful music teaching emphasizes vital affective experiences with music. The teacher's task is to use real music as a means to pupil learning. Every piece of music heard, performed, or composed serves as a project for musical learning. Every musical experience provides a laboratory, as it were, for the pupil to develop appreciation and understanding and to acquire knowledge.

The teacher raises questions about the music experienced, encourages the pupil to raise questions, and assists him in answering the questions and in applying his learning to the musical task at hand, whether it be more artistic performance, more perceptive listening, or mastering some musical technique. Finally, the teacher, as a guide to the pupil in his exploration and discovery of musical meanings, assists the pupil in developing a method of attacking musical problems.

Many teachers proceed on the assumption that applied music instruction and performance groups should be limited to developing skills of performance and that musical knowledge and understanding are gained exclusively in general music classes, theory classes, and so on. For example, a choral director or voice teacher may deplore the fact that his pupils cannot read music but refuse to accept any responsibility for teaching them to read. This kind of segmented approach to music teaching has no justification. Every type of musical activity should result in integrated musical experience. While each type of activity properly has its own principal focus, all teachers should be concerned with the overall musical learning of their pupils. For example, applied music instruction has as its principal focus the development of performance skill, but the teacher should also aim toward appreciation, knowledge, and understanding of the music used in performance and should assist the pupil in integrating the learning he gains elsewhere and applying it to his performance.

Teaching Attitudes

Attitudes toward music are learned. They result from experience both within and outside the music program. They also affect musical learning directly. The music teacher cannot assume responsibility for all the attitudes pupils acquire, but he must take all possible steps to ensure that pupils learn sound constructive attitudes toward music and toward their own music making as a result of their school music experience.

Chapter Five indicated that attitudes may be acquired as a result of (1) cumulative experience over a period of time, (2) a single vivid experience, (3) emulation of person or organization, and (4) association of a total situation with one factor in the situation. These ways of acquiring attitudes provide valuable clues to appropriate procedures for teaching attitudes.

Music teachers should seek to provide continuity and consistency of favorable experience with music throughout the music program. This can be achieved by heeding the musical interests of pupils, emphasizing success in music learning, and by doing the best possible job of teaching musical skills, knowledge, understanding, and appreciation. When the music used appeals to pupils, when success and confidence attend their musical learning, attitudes are inevitably favorable. Thus successful teaching itself is the most potent force in the formation of desirable attitudes toward music.

The music teacher must constantly be on the alert to anticipate critical points in musical development when negative attitudes are likely to develop. Any time a pupil fails in a musical experience, the teacher should provide sympathetic guidance in helping the pupil understand the reasons for his failure and should provide assistance in overcoming the difficulty causing the failure. A highly critical point often occurs when boys' voices begin to change. If understanding by fellow students and the music teacher is lacking at this time, many boys develop highly damaging negative attitudes toward music as a result of embarrassment arising from the difficulty in controlling their voices.

Music teachers should avoid placing pupils in situations where failure is likely to occur. For example, pupils should not be forced to play in public a piece about which they are not confident. Likewise, an inexperienced performing group should rarely be placed in competition with a highly superior group.

The teacher can also influence favorable attitudes by providing from time to time musical experiences of unusual inspirational value. For example, arranging for pupils to hear a performance by a renowned artist or musical organization frequently transforms their attitudes. Other procedures of value in this regard include making it possible for pupils to perform in a festival under an inspiring conductor, to take an excursion to a fine musical event in a neighboring city, or simply to hear an especially moving recording.

Making provision for a large measure of pupil participation in planning musical instruction and the music program tends to develop favorable attitudes. Such procedures as permitting pupils to select compositions for instruction and public performance, involving pupils in the administration of musical activities, and encouraging pupil-planned social events for pupils participating in the music program point toward the development of favorable attitudes.

The music teacher should seek to personify the attitudes and the ideals he seeks in his pupils. If he has narrow musical tastes and disparages one or more types of music, or is scornful or unappreciative of the musical efforts of others, many of his pupils are likely to reflect his attitudes. On the other hand, if he demonstrates cosmopolitan musical tastes and values the musical contributions of other people, his pupils are prone to emulate him. At least some of the lack of acceptance of contemporary music on the part of the general public is due to the negative attitudes of overly conservative and ill-informed music teachers.

A powerful factor in the development of attitudes lies in the amount of prestige associated with the different phases of the school music program. In some secondary schools the general music program is considered principally as a catchall for musical misfits; the orchestra or chorus has much less prestige than the band; and so on. Pupils are sensitive to discrepancies such as this and adopt attitudes consistent with the condition. The solution is to develop a balanced, cooperatively planned program in which every type of activity is recognized as making its own unique contribution to the overall musical development of all the pupils in the school.

Psychologists recognize that practicing outward acts of a desired attitude frequently results in the formation of that attitude. Teachers should encourage good concert deportment at all school concerts and should insist upon acceptable behavior in music classes, rehearsals, and assembly sings.

It is of utmost importance that teachers recognize that attitudes are learned and can be taught. Desired attitudes should be listed specifically and concretely as part of the objectives of music instruction along with the teaching procedures and other factors which are likely to influence attitudes in the desired direction.

PRINCIPLES OF METHOD

There follow the statement and discussion of eleven principles of method. These principles have resulted from a careful analysis of the psychology of learning and of many examples of successful teaching experienced and observed over a period of years. Each principle is stated, discussed in some detail, and applied to the teaching of music. To gain benefit from the principles the reader should not merely memorize them but should consider each carefully and thoughtfully and derive implications for his own area of music teaching.

1. *Formulate sound teaching objectives in terms of student behavior.* The objectives of learning influence greatly the selection of methods of teaching to be used in a particular situation. Using program objectives as a basis, each teacher should determine where his particular phase of instruction fits and should formulate instructional objectives stated in terms of pupil behavior. One of the first jobs of the teacher is to assist pupils in defining and understanding the objectives of a course and to arouse in them the motivation to achieve the objectives.

   Pupil-teacher planning is essential in formulating instructional objectives. The teacher should discover early what objectives his pupils have for studying music.

He may find that their objectives are ill defined, but, even so, focusing attention on objectives is worthwhile. Pupil objectives usually consist of the immediate things they would like to do with music such as learning to sing a particular song or learning to sing parts by ear Using their objectives as a starting point, the teacher can lead pupils to understand and accept most of his objectives if he shows that he is sympathetic with their points of view and interests and if he demonstrates his willingness to help them in attaining their immediate objectives.

The use of an inventory of pupil musical interests at the beginning of a course of instruction proves highly successful in helping the teacher become quickly acquainted with pupils and in focusing pupil attention on objectives. Other valuable techniques include asking pupils to put in writing what they would like to accomplish in a music class and having periodic group discussions of the question.

The teacher's role in formulating objectives is properly one of leading and coordinating. He does not assume the role of dictator, neither does he serve passively as just another member of the group. His maturity, experience, and insight should qualify him to inspire the pupils and direct their thinking toward worthwhile objectives.

2. *Select valid subject matter and learning experiences which are likely to lead to the desired behaviors.* There should always be a direct relationship between classroom experiences and the objectives of instruction. Furthermore, for efficient results the pupils should be aware of the relationship. For example, if the objectives of a general music class include developing appreciation for all kinds of music, the use of a variety of music in the classroom is essential and experiences such as the following are indicated:

   a. hearing and performing a wide range of musical styles

    b. finding meaning in many types of music

    c. comparing and contrasting different musical styles

    d. discussing with classmates their varying reactions to compositions

If one of the objectives is to develop in pupils an appreciation of quality in music and musical performance, the following experiences seem pertinent:

    a. hearing and performing many different types of music

    b. hearing performances of varying degrees of excellence and identifying the factors that make for excellence

    c. participating in the refinement and perfection of a musical performance

    d. enjoying the satisfaction that comes from highly developed expressive performance

    e. becoming bored with the repetition of trite music

    f. finding increasing enjoyment through repeated contact with great music

The clue to the selection of subject matter and learning experiences is the constant use of actual music of high quality and helping students do things with and about it.

3. *Provide for active participation by the pupils.* Learning takes place only as the learner has meaningful experience; mere exposure and passive reception are not sufficient. The teacher must structure a situation in which the learner, having identified and accepted a problem, is able to release energy in the solution of the problem. For example, in developing fine tone quality in playing or singing, the teacher first brings about awareness of differences in tone quality by presenting examples of good and poor tone quality and demonstrates the superior expressive effect attained with fine tone quality. The pupil develops a concept of good tone quality and evaluates his own playing or singing in relation to his concept. This is, however, not enough. The essential next step is for the pupil, with the guidance of the

teacher, to experiment in producing tone and gradually to discover the controls required for the most beautiful possible tone. The problem is identified when the pupil develops sound concepts of tone and evaluates his own tone. The problem is solved through his active efforts to achieve his musical and expressive intentions.

4. *Utilize a variety of devices to increase perception.* Musical learning requires the development of many kinds of concepts, and the teacher must use appropriate means to establish them. Recordings and personal demonstrations provide the best means of establishing aural concepts and should be used in abundance. Talking about tone, for example, can never be as effective as recordings of both inferior and excellent tone quality.

Insight into expressive interpretation of music can be developed by playing both good and poor performances of the same composition and identifying the factors essential to expressive, stylistically sound performance. The use of the tape recorder to enable individual pupils or performance groups to hear themselves and to contrast a beginning performance with a highly developed performance is likewise effective.

Visual supports also improve the efficiency with which musical concepts are developed. For example, teachers should constantly provide notation to focus pupils' hearing. The practices of writing themes on the blackboard and providing scores are highly recommended for pupils of all ages.

Many excellent movies and film strips on several phases of music are available and have value in music teaching. Movies are especially effective in establishing motivation and good attitudes. Film strips have value in teaching good position for playing instruments. Teachers should bear in mind, however, that films and filmstrips are not substitutes for the teacher. They should be used only when they fulfill a clear-cut purpose of which both teacher and pupils are aware.

5. *Arrange a learning sequence which moves from the concrete to the abstract.* Musical learning entails the development of many abstract concepts, but concrete experience should precede the abstractions. Musical notation, for example, represents a highly developed abstraction and lacks meaning without prior concrete tonal experience. Rich tonal experience gained through singing and playing appealing music should precede and accompany study of the notation. The best sequence moves from aural experience with tonal and rhythmic patterns to the notation which represents those patterns.

Experience with the space frame of an instrument is essential for most people in specific comprehension of tonal relationships and the understanding of notation. Work with simple melody instruments, the Autoharp, and the piano keyboard helps the student to comprehend notational and tonal abstractions and should be an integral part of general music instruction. The value of work of this kind has been established by two studies by Nelson designed to determine the relative value of a music course in the fourth and fifth grades including both vocal and instrumental participation compared with the course including only vocal music. The initial study and a follow-up of the same children conducted after one year showed that instrumental instruction enriches the child's musical background, so that skills are more readily retained and the effect of instrumental study continues to accumulate even after its discontinuance. The study also indicated that the fifth grade is better than the fourth to introduce specialized instrumental instruction.[5]

[5] Carl B. Nelson, "An Experimental Evaluation of Two Methods of Teaching Music in the Fourth and Fifth Grades," *Journal of Experimental Education* 23:231-238, March 1955; and "Follow-up of an Experimental Teaching Method in Music at the Fourth and Fifth Grade Levels," *Journal of Experimental Education* 24:283-289, June 1956.

Other procedures which tend to make musical meanings clear include the use of bodily movement to rhythm, moving the hand up and down to parallel melodic movement (sometimes called melodic conducting), and the use of bodily movement to show line or phrasing.

6. *Secure a high level of motivation.* Managing the learning environment so that optimal motivation is present represents one of the most complex but most important of the teacher's tasks. Motivation is closely associated with interests, setting reasonable and rewarding goals, and experiencing success in attaining goals. Because of the many variables in learning situations it is impossible to describe standard devices for securing motivation, but an understanding of the important factors in motivation enables the teacher to evolve teaching methods which result in a high level of motivation.

Motives are learned. People are not born with interests or motives except those essential to survival, nor do other motives develop spontaneously. All except the most basic survival motives are learned, and all motives are shaped and refined through experience in living.

Failure to understand this fact has led some music teachers to a false notion of what it means to base instruction on pupil interests. They rightly begin instruction on the basis of present interests but fail to take the steps necessary to aid the pupils in developing new and progressively better interests and motives. Musical instruction should indeed be based initially on interests and motives that pupils bring to the instruction, but successful teaching will result in the development of motives that are more complex, more sophisticated, and, most important, motives that are intrinsic to music and the musical experience.

Many pupils are, for example, motivated to play in the band by the prospect of a uniform, the advantages of membership in a prestige group, the opportunity to take trips, and so on. These motives have been learned; they are powerful and legitimate. They are not, however, intrinsic to musical experience.

The proper course for the band director is not only to capitalize initially on these motives but also to exert his best efforts to help pupils learn through musical experience motives that are intrinsic to music, such as the desire for excellence in performance and the desire for the satisfaction that comes with expressive musical experience.

The learning of motives intrinsic to music and musical experience frequently results in the much sought carry-over of school music experience to out-of-school living. Continued reliance on extrinsic motivation almost ensures that the pupil will remain little affected by his school music experience and that he will not continue musical participation once the motivating trappings of the school music program no longer influence him.

The level of aspiration in motivation. Hilgard and Russell have defined level of aspiration as "a goal that an individual sets for himself which he expects to reach or wishes very much to reach."[6] One of the music teacher's most important tasks is assisting pupils in setting a reasonable level of aspiration and in achieving success in attaining it.

Sears's study of the level of aspiration in successful and unsuccessful school children has important implications for music teaching. She found that pupils with prior experience of success tend to be realistic in goal setting. They generally expect improvement but do not expect accomplishment out of line with reality. Pupils who have failed, on the other hand, either are beaten down and expect nothing of themselves or ignore their previous failure and set too high goals.[7]

Goal setting must be learned, and music teachers

[6] Ernest R. Hilgard and David H. Russell, "Motivation in School Learning," *Learning and Instruction*, National Society for the Study of Education Forty-ninth Yearbook, Chicago, 1950, Part I, p. 39.

[7] Pauline S. Sears, "Levels of Aspiration in Academically Successful and Unsuccessful School Children," *Journal of Abnormal and Social Psychology* 25:498-536, 1940.

must assist pupils in learning to set realistic goals. For example, if the teacher does not provide experience that will help the applied music pupil develop a sound concept of accurate and expressive performance, the pupil is likely to set his goals too low and be satisfied with sloppy, inaccurate, and mechanical playing. On the other hand, if he allows the pupil to select a piece too far above his facility, the pupil may experience failure and a feeling of futility about his progress in music.

The best learning takes place when the pupil sets for himself realistic, attainable goals, identifies the problems implicit in the goals he has set, and achieves success in reaching the goals. An important facet of successful music teaching lies in helping the pupil in these tasks and organizing his experiences, so that he sets progressively higher goals as the instruction proceeds.

Administrative factors in motivation. Administrative factors in motivation include marking and grouping practices. Teachers frequently attempt to stimulate achievement through awarding or withholding good grades. Some music teachers, for example, give all pupils A's with the notion that the symbol of success will encourage them to increased accomplishment and will result in good attitudes. Other teachers tend to grade low and to hold out the prospect of higher grades as a spur to learning. Research indicates that marking may not stimulate pupil achievement one way or the other.[8] Other considerations may make a marking system necessary in music education, but it cannot be supported on the basis of its contribution to pupil achievement. A much sounder basis for motivating learning is teacher-pupil diagnosis of difficulties encountered in learning.

[8] Hilgard and Russell, op. cit., p. 58.

Grouping practices do have a direct influence on motivation and pupil achievement, and homogeneous grouping for musical instruction has many advantages. For example, pupils in secondary school general music classes frequently have such a wide range of music experience and musical interests that the teacher has difficulty planning experiences that are rewarding and stimulating to all of them. This problem can be lessened by grouping the pupils according to the extent and quality of prior musical experience.

The use of small-group work influences motivation and is frequently advisable in music education programs. Working with others who have similar interests and comparable ability helps students set reasonable levels of aspiration and encourages the development of musical initiative leading to musical independence. For example, performers in large instrumental organizations frequently exhibit a great range of playing proficiency. Those with high levels of skill usually play the lead parts and gain little acquaintance with harmonizing parts. Those with less skill are usually assigned to second or third parts which provide little challenge or musical nourishment. These lacks can be minimized and motivation enhanced by organizing small ensembles in which players of comparable ability play and study music together. When advanced pupils are assigned to help the less proficient groups, rewarding results accrue for both pupils and pupil-teachers.

7. *Make provision for the individualization of instruction.* We have stressed that each pupil must do his own learning and that each pupil has a unique combination of capacity, experience, incentives, and objectives. This means that the teacher must make definite plans for the individualization of instruction within the framework of the music class. Individualization of instruction may be secured by adapting objectives and standards to individ-

ual needs and by making provision for individual and small-group work.

The key to adapting objectives and standards to individual needs is flexibility in the learning situation. The teacher should organize a common body of learning experiences with sufficient variety and range of difficulty to interest all pupils but should, in addition, make provision for individualization by establishing flexibility of objectives and standards, so that each pupil can find and work at rewarding tasks in which he is especially interested and with which he is likely to be successful. For example, a child in the first or second grade who has not gained control of his voice should not be harassed by efforts to bring him up to the level of the group in this respect. The teacher can gain his wholehearted participation in music by encouraging him to sing with the group, but, at the same time, emphasizing his playing rhythm instruments or tone bells to accompany the singing. Most children gradually gain control of their voices with this kind of experience and treatment. If, on the other hand, he is singled out, embarrassed, and labeled as a failure, he is likely to withdraw completely from musical activities, develop damaging negative attitudes, and avoid musical participation in the future. At the other end of the scale, a child with unusual proficiency in music should be given extra challenges. If he can play the piano or an instrument, for example, the teacher may ask him to prepare and play accompaniments for some of the songs the class is singing.

A child in the upper grades who has had difficulty singing and is just gaining control of his voice should not be expected to sing a part simply because the other children are doing so and the course of study calls for part singing. The teacher should allow him to sing melody until he has a feeling of confidence in his ability and challenge him with singing a part when he is likely to have success.

All musical instruction should provide for the students to initiate and develop individualized assignments. In general music, for example, students should have the opportunity to explore on their own whatever type of music holds particular interest for them. If a student wishes to work out guitar accompaniments for a group of classroom songs or make a study of prominent jazz musicians, he should be encouraged and assisted by the teacher. Work of this kind is a far cry from that required by the typical assignment to keep a notebook of information presented in class, to complete a workbook, or to write a paper on a specified composer, but the resulting musical learning is likely to be far superior.

Teachers of instrumental classes should encourage pupils to play pieces of their own choice, to develop practice materials directly pertinent to their own playing problems, and to explore music outside the instruction book being used. These individualizing procedures stand in sharp contrast to teaching in which the entire group proceeds at the same pace on identical material selected by the teacher.

Another type of individualizing procedure has to do with dividing the class into small groups. For example, instrumental classes and performing groups profit from the formation of small ensembles composed of players of similar interest and level of competency. This type of activity has many advantages. The opportunity for students to work on their own and to develop musical independence in a homogeneous group is extremely valuable. Furthermore, this type of experience has great possibilities for carry-over into out-of-school life.

The individualization of instruction is achieved principally by introducing flexibility into the learning situation: flexibility in classroom activities, in assignments, and in grouping practices. Procedures for attaining individualization are somewhat complex, but the rewards are great and well worth the planning and effort required.

8. *Provide oportunities for exploratory experiences in music.* Since pupils learn not only while undergoing instruction but also from all conditions in the environment, music teachers should provide opportunities and facilities for pupils to explore music outside the framework of the classroom. For example, elementary schools should have a place where children can experiment with rhythm instruments, tone bells, informal instruments, graduated glasses, a piano, and, under supervision, standard instruments. Likewise, pupils should have easy access to books on music, recordings, and instruments for informal reading, singing, playing, and listening.

When pupils feel free to explore music on their own, their real interests come to the fore; and they are uninhibited and enthusiastic. Teachers should encourage participation of this type and be available for guidance when this is desired by the pupils, but they should be careful not to intrude upon or deprecate the efforts of pupils.

9. *Emphasize creativity in all music instruction.* Creativity is much talked about in music education, but little is accomplished except in connection with elementary school music programs. Even there much of what passes for creativity often has a stilted, unspontaneous quality. Spontaneity and originality, essential ingredients of creativity, are often lost because of the increasing compartmentalization of musical instruction, the emphasis on techniques, the striving for quasi-professional standards, and the domination of public performance.

In the second and third decades of this century creativity in music education had the connotation of making instruments and experimenting with them to compose music. Later, creating songs according to formulae became the fashion. Both types of work continue today, but neither has resulted in continued creative work beyond the elementary school. Recently creativity has been more broadly conceived as the personal discovery of one's musical ability and the discovery of a higher level of achievement through musical experience with little or no emphasis on composition itself. This concept represents a sound basic approach to music education but does not necessarily result in creativity.

It seems obvious that all phases of the music education program would profit from real creative work in which composing, performing, and listening are combined into an integrated experience. This can be achieved by emphasis on improvisation or extemporization all along the line, from the elementary school through the secondary school and beyond. Wherever students sing or play instruments, there is an opportunity for creativity. The work of David Barnett, Gladys Moorhead and Donald Pond, and Grace Cushman provides promising leads in this direction, and the practice of jazz musicians demonstrates exactly the kind of direct approach to creativity which can be used successfully in the school music program and in private instruction.

Singing and playing descants to melodies by ear, singing and playing harmonic accompaniments by ear, embellishing a known melody, improvising on a given chord progression, and playing and singing variations on a melody are feasible approaches to creativity which can be used at all levels of the music program. Once this type of work has begun, many students will continue it on their own. If the results are especially pleasing to them, they will want to preserve their work in notation. This will often lead to expansion to a larger form, polishing, and revising.

The results include spontaneous self-expression, more acute listening, freedom with the voice or instrument, functional knowledge and natural use of notation, development of musical understanding, appeal to musical initiative, and enthusiasm for music and music making.

10. *Establish valid and stimulating means of evaluating outcomes.* Evaluation is essential to high levels of motivation in learning and to the improvement of teaching methods. Evaluative procedures should be focused on determining the extent to which pupils are progressing toward the objectives of instruction. This focus can be achieved only when objectives are clear to both teacher and pupils.

Evaluation should be comprehensive and continuous. If objectives are ignored in evaluation, they cease to have potency in giving direction to the learning efforts of pupils. Good teaching methods are characterized by a variety of daily and periodic evaluative procedures which keep the pupil informed of his progress and which develop in him the resources for and the habit of constant evaluation of his own learning efforts. Self-evaluation by pupils and cooperative evaluation by teacher and pupils provide the most meaningful information on pupils' progress toward the objectives of music teaching.

Chapter Eleven treats evaluation specifically and in detail. It suffices here to emphasize that evaluation is an integral part of meaningful learning and successful teaching, and that neither process can be considered complete until the results have been appraised and revealed to the learner.

11. *Establish a favorable social climate in the classroom.* A favorable social climate has a dramatic effect upon the learning situation. Studies of the interpersonal relationships in the classroom have revealed that pupils tend to give high ratings to teachers who develop a high level of personal relationships and acquaintance with their pupils and that the teacher traits most valued by pupils

include, along with knowledge of subject matter, high ideals and fairness to pupils.[9]

In securing a favorable social climate procedures such as the following have tremendous value: (a) cooperative planning, (b) the use of positive incentives, (c) the establishment of an atmosphere conducive to free, friendly discussion among pupils and teacher, and (d) manifestation by the teacher of interest in pupils and of understanding of their problems.

An excellent way to initiate cooperative planning is to begin the year with a discussion of what the pupils would like to get out of the year's experience in music. A typical group will raise numerous questions and problems and offer many suggestions for preferred activities, types of music, class projects, and so on. The teacher may properly help clarify the suggestions and questions, but he should accept all serious suggestions, even though they may not be exactly what he desires to secure. For example, pupils in a secondary-school general music class may express what seems to the teacher an unwarranted interest in popular music. If he disapproves and rejects this interest, any further effort at cooperative planning is useless—the pupils will know that he wants cooperation only on his own terms. The clue for the teacher in this situation is to use this interest in popular music as a means to developing musical understanding and musical skills; he must avoid a simple entertainment situation. Once the serious study of popular music is underway and some musical learning has

[9] See Russell V. Bollinger, "The Social Impact of the Teacher on the Pupil," *Journal of Experimental Education* 13:153-173, June 1945; Wilbur B. Brookover, "Person-Person Interaction between Teachers and Pupils and Teaching Effectiveness," *Journal of Educational Research* 34:272-287, December 1940; and Robert N. Bush, "A Study of Student-Teacher Relationships," *Journal of Educational Research* 35:645-656, May 1942.

taken place, he should organize a discussion of outcomes, again raise the basic question, and lead the pupils
to a broader concept of music and musical achievement.
Once the cooperative climate has been established and
the teacher has demonstrated an attitude of give-and-
take, the pupils are likely to go along with his
suggestions.

The idea of shared responsibility has several advantages. It brings about a close relationship between pupils
and teacher and results in many valuable suggestions
which might not have otherwise been forthcoming. Most
important, it results in cooperative work on problems of
mutual concern and interest—the optimal setting for
effective learning.

The considerable research on the effect of incentives indicates that any recognition of pupils' work,
either positive or negative, is more effective than no
recognition; but positive recognition is more effective
than negative, especially over a period of time. Praise
and pleasant suggestions bring about more effective
learning than blame and scolding. Sarcasm and ridicule
obviously have no place in the music classroom.

Teachers of performance groups and applied music
sometimes tend to use negative recognition preponder-
antly, especially when working under pressure of time.
That is, they emphasize deficiencies and mistakes and
rarely mention strong points in the performance. On the
other hand, teachers of general music sometimes fail to
react in any way when the pupils have sung a song—one
song is finished, the class goes on to another, and that's
all there is to it. Although it would obviously be foolish
to go into raptures over a poor performance which the
pupils probably recognize as deficient, teachers in both
these situations should try to find something to praise in
every performance. The clue to the proper use of incentives lies in giving first attention to praiseworthy aspects

of pupil achievement and maintaining a positive, kindly, and helpful attitude toward mistakes and deficiencies.

To establish an atmosphere conducive to free and friendly discussion the teacher should give concrete evidence of valuing and giving consideration to ideas expressed by pupils and should encourage the free interchange of opinions among pupils without the teacher's always serving as the intermediary. Teachers should also look for and encourage initiative, leadership, and the ability of pupils to think for themselves about music, even though their ideas and opinions do not coincide with those of the teacher.

Music teachers should constantly bear in mind that pupils of every age are, like teachers, only human and that they respond warmly to interest, recognition, and understanding from other people. As a first step the music teacher should learn the pupils' names quickly and habitually use them in class discussion and personal contacts. As the term progresses, he should make a conscious effort to know his pupils well, to become aware of their strengths and weaknesses, and to understand their problems not only in the music class but outside as well. Using interest inventories, consulting the cumulative records kept for each pupil by the central office, and making provision for private consultations with pupils represent valuable ways to understanding. The most important factors, however, are the teacher's warmth and feeling for pupils as persons and his desire to know, understand, and assist them in every way possible.

The establishment of a favorable social climate holds the key to the avoidance of discipline problems. The result is not the rigid submissive discipline attained through force and fear but a far healthier type of inner discipline and self-discipline based on mutual respect and mutual purposes.

SUMMARY

Teaching is defined as the organization and conduct of learning experiences. It serves to arrange the learning evironment for the pupil in such a way as to increase the efficiency of his learning. The procedures used by a teacher to organize the learning experiences of his pupils are called teaching methods. Three factors are held paramount in considering methods of teaching music: (1) pupils do their own learning and must be the center of consideration; (2) pupils learn from all influences in the learning environment; and (3) methods of teaching must be compatible with the objectives sought. Authentic and lasting musical achievement represents the ultimate criterion in judging the success of methods of teaching music.

The bases of teaching methods include the nature of music and the musical experience, the objectives of instruction, the nature of the learning process, the maturational level, past experience and present needs and interests of pupils, and teacher competencies. The teacher must take all these varied and complex factors into account and devise teaching methods in terms of his own unique situation.

The task of music teaching centers on establishing concepts, providing meaningful practice situations in which concepts are clarified and applied to a problem, and analyzing the results of practice. This, in turn, leads to further problem-centered practice to fix correct responses. The psychology of learning and analysis of successful teaching practices provide the basis for the development of principles of method.

QUESTIONS FOR DISCUSSION

1. What is teaching method? How does it relate to the other instructional factors, such as musical materials and

subject matter? In what sense may one's teaching methods extend beyond his actual presence?

2. Identify and describe several basic types or forms of teaching method. What determines the suitability of a particular method?

3. What is meant by "logical versus psychological" organization?

4. What is the measure of successful teaching? Why is it dangerous for one teacher to imitate another's methods? What extraneous factors help determine teaching methods?

5. Describe the general process in teaching performance skills. What dangers are to be avoided?

6. How should one approach the teaching of musical appreciation? Illustrate the value of using contrasting examples of the same music.

7. What is the first step in teaching knowledge and understanding? Why does this imply the value of teaching these in every type of music class?

8. Describe various ways to promote better musical attitudes.

9. How may students be led to define their purposes? Describe how the teacher helps stimulate learning activity of students. What teaching devices are helpful? Why is concrete activity so important?

10. How may new and more useful motives for musical study be established? What kinds of arrangements influence motivation?

11. What are musical standards? Should all students be expected to meet the same standards? Describe methods for achieving individualized instruction.

12. By what means may musical creativity be promoted?

13. Where does the value lie in planning and working with pupils? Why is it important to react openly to the musical efforts of pupils? In what ways can teachers properly demonstrate their interest and concern for the pupils?

SELECTED REFERENCES

Benn, Oleta A. "A Message for New Teachers," *Basic Concepts in Music Education*, National Society for the Study of Education Fifty-seventh Yearbook, Chicago, 1958, Part I, pp. 339-355.

Bruner, Jerome S. *The Process of Education*, Harvard University Press, Cambridge, Mass., 1962.

Callahan, Sterling G. *Successful Teaching in Secondary Schools*, Scott Foresman and Company, Chicago, 1966.

Colwell, Richard. *The Teaching of Instrumental Music*, Appleton-Century-Crofts, New York, 1969.

Diller, Angela. *The Splendor of Music*, G. Schirmer, New York, 1957.

Gage, N. L., ed. *Handbook of Research on Teaching*, Rand McNally & Company, Chicago, 1963.

Gronlund, Norman. *Stating Objectives for Classroom Instruction*, MacMillan Company, Collier-MacMillan Limited, London, 1970.

Hartshorn, William C. "The Role of Listening," *Basic Concepts in Music Education*, National Society for the Study of Education Fifty-seventh Yearbook, Chicago, 1958, Part I, pp. 261-291.

Herndon, James. *The Way It Spozed to Be*, Simon and Schuster, New York, 1968.

Highet, Gilbert. *The Art of Teaching*, Alfred A. Knopf, Inc., New York, 1950.

Hoffer, Charles R. *Teaching Music in the Secondary School*, Wadsworth Publishing Co., Inc., Belmont, Calif., 1964.

Holt, John. *How Children Learn*, Pitman Publishing Company, New York, 1967.

House, Robert W. *Instrumental Music for Today's Schools*, Prentice-Hall, Inc., 1965.

Kozol, Jonathan. *Death at an Early Age*, Houghton Mifflin, Boston, 1967.

Leonard, George B. *Education As Ecstacy*, Delacorte Press, New York, 1968.

Mathis, B. Claude, John W. Colton and Lee Sechrest: *Psychological Foundations of Education—Learning and Teaching*, Academic Press, New York and London, 1970.

Mursell, James L. *Education for Musical Growth*, Ginn & Company, Boston, 1948.

Skinner, B. F. *The Technology of Teaching*, Appleton-Century-Crofts, New York, 1968.

Smith, Louis M. and William Geoffrey. *The Complexities of an Urban Classroom*, Holt, Rinehart and Winston, Inc., New York, 1968.

Smith, Robert B. *Music in the Child's Education*, The Ronald Press Company, New York, 1970.

Swanson, Bessie R. *Music in the Education of Children*, 3d ed., Wadsworth Publishing Co., Inc., Belmont, Calif., 1969.

Weingartner, Charles and Neil Postman. *Teaching as a Subversive Activity*, Delacorte Press, New York, 1969.

Administration
of the Music Program

9 John Simpson has just begun his second job since graduating six years ago from State University; he is a high school band director and supervisor of instrumental music at Centreville. Like all band directors new to a school, Simpson has been pretty well occupied with the task of selecting music, checking out instruments and uniforms, and rehearsing music and show for the first football game. But he had learned from his first position over at Lehigh Junior High School the value of being ahead of the job. He was also aware that this new job carried wider administrative responsibility than his previous one. At Lehigh, he had handled his own band organization and equipment, and worked with his fellow music teachers on certain curricular improvements, but here at Centreville he knew he had to coordinate the efforts of two other instrumental music teachers working in the elementary and junior high schools. So he had gone over current goals, scheduling, and procedures carefully in August with the superintendent, Mr. Thornhill, and with the principals. He had become acquainted with several of the faculty, including the other instrumental teachers. He had also moved his young family to town and had begun to make business and social acquaintances. Even before accepting the school's offer, he had taken a hard look at all the music rehearsal areas and budget figures.

When classes began, therefore, Simpson had some provisional ideas about the strengths and weaknesses of the instrumental music program. He felt that the staff was competent and sincere, and that the school had a fairly adequate plant and equipment. There seemed to be much pride in the performing groups, but a rather small proportion of the students were enrolled in music.

During the first weeks of school, therefore, while he was working with the classes and individuals assigned to him, Simpson also took pains to drop in occasionally on the other instrumental teachers at work. It became apparent to him that the instrumental program was conceived simply as the recruitment, training, and selective admission of players into the senior concert organization. Students were not wanted unless they could be "fed into the pipeline."

Simpson saw that he had a difficult administrative and supervisory task to do. He had to gain the confidence and ears of his associates and cause them to develop a different concept of the music program. He would become involved in bringing the instrumental program gradually around to a more flexible pattern of recruitment and scheduling, new methods and materials of instruction, wider repertoire, and an "expansionist" program involving additional ensembles, more equipment, enlarged rehearsal and storage facilities, additional teachers, and more extensive activity with the community.

Unlike Simpson, most music educators do not recognize their own administrative role. They tend to lump principals, superintendents, counselors, and school board members all together into an unsavory task force called "the Administration." They see themselves operating chiefly in front of students and easily overlook the arrangements that were necessary to put them there. Part of that supportive effort is their own. What proportion of any music educator's concern is devoted to securing and deploying the *means* of instruction, as compared with what he is to do in the classroom? The answer is the measure of his administrative task.

Administration provides the setting for learning; the machinery of organization is administrative. Typical administrative problems include budgeting and financing, purchasing, disbursing supplies, securing the repair of equipment, selecting and promoting teachers, scheduling, instituting program evaluation and reform, keeping student records, providing for student guidance, and public relations. These functions are essential but are not to be considered primary ends in themselves; they represent means to the best possible education for students.

ADMINISTRATIVE PATTERNS

Part of the difficulty in discussing administrative matters lies in the confusion of titles. The onlooker naturally assumes that the music supervisor supervises, the music consultant consults, and the director of music directs. Actually, anyone hired as some form of school music specialist usually discovers the need to supervise and administer as well as to teach. Thus, the music supervisor should not skip to the next chapter; he will doubtless find some of his responsibilities described here.

It is well to recognize the fact of an administrative "chain." Whenever a need arises "at the front," in class session or rehearsal, the instructor turns wherever assistance is most readily at hand. This may be to the music supervisor, the building principal, or simply a fellow teacher who has sufficient know-how and access to solutions. Whatever cannot be handled at that point is likely to be brought to the next level and may continue to the superintendent and school board.

Thus, what one does does not always match his title. Because of the varying degree in which music educators may be charged with administrative responsibility, it is necessary to write in terms of the total administrative concept. This picture should then serve as a point of reference in any specific instance.

TYPES OF ADMINISTRATION

The Autocratic System

The practice of administration varies widely. One of the more common types is, of course, sheerly autocratic. It is the commonly held notion of administration. One person, legally appointed to the position, holds few conferences, makes decisions, gives orders, and sees that these are carried out. Lines and channels of authority are sharply drawn, and each person is accessible to higher authority. Duties and activities are assigned from above and suggestions are referred upward for decision.

This system is clearly based upon the military pattern, its chief characteristic being a kind of line and staff organization. Certain officials—superintendents, principals, heads of departments—carry executive authority; the supervisors, consultants, and specialized experts occupy the position of staff officers, supplying information, advice, and technical assistance.

The administrators themselves are hardly to be blamed for this pattern, since it is so often outlined by school boards and boards of regents and fully supported by the taxpayer in the interest of efficiency. There is ample precedent in the business world for this type of operation.

There are differences, however, between military and commercial pursuits on one hand and the educational enterprise on the other; victory or profit can possibly justify the arbitrary and impersonal deployment of people, but the primary aims of the school are personal development and individuality. The full capabilities of a teaching staff can be released only through individual assumption of responsibility. Direct orders and close checking upon their activities only stultify any creative contributions which music teachers might make. There is also the danger that machinery set up by a central staff will not be fully applicable to the daily task of instruction and these rigid formulae will tend to become ends in themselves. There are instances where roll taking has become surrounded by all sorts of red tape and loss of instructional time, and other cases exist in which extensive test batteries are administered to every student—the results only to be filed away permanently as some sort of "time capsule."

The attempt is usually made to alleviate the more glaring shortcomings of an autocratic administrative pattern through specific provision for cooperation and coordination among the entire teaching staff. This job is usually commenced through the appointment of interlocking committees and subcommittees. The success of the plan depends upon the direct qualifications of the committee members and the actual authority granted them, as well as upon the common educational philosophy which they may be able to establish. Too often the setup is quite artificial, as many teachers can testify. At the least, however, these groups can provide forums for the expression of staff opinion.

Much good can result from a policy of flexible operation, in which the usual line of authority is adjusted to special circumstances. Thus, the band director consults directly with the head of the institution concerning tours and major items of equipment; the elementary teacher requisitions needed materials directly through the music consultant; and news items are not "cleared" but sent directly to the newspapers.

An even more fundamental alteration in the line and staff organization is achieved by the administrators and supervisors who partially maintain their function as teachers. When one is directly concerned with the teaching-learning process, he is more likely to view sympathetically the problems and needs of other teachers. There is no doubt, either, but that the remainder of the staff are not so ready to criticize but tend to view the teaching administrator as a true colleague.

Laissez-faire Administration

Some well-intentioned administrators try to escape the stereotype of autocracy by abdicating their responsibility for leadership. The teacher is left to carry out his duties as he thinks best and is expected to bring his needs to the attention of the administrator. This only results in gross unfairness, since some staff members are more insistent and skilled in presenting their needs; thus, parts of the program will forge ahead while others languish. This type of administrator is eventually relegated to the position of holder of the purse strings and has little or no constructive impact upon the music program itself.

Democratic Administration

The necessity for a democratic concept of administration is inescapable. It is the only way in which efficient management and an imaginative program can be achieved in a truly modern system of education. The basis for this form of administration has been stated in this fashion:

1. To facilitate the continuous growth of personalities by providing all persons with opportunities to participate actively in all enterprises that concern them.
2. To recognize that leadership is a function of every individual and to encourage the exercise of leadership by each person in accordance with his interests, needs, and abilities.
3. To provide means by which persons can plan together, share their experiences, and cooperatively evaluate their achievements.
4. To place the responsibility for making decisions that affect the total enterprise with the group rather than with one or two individuals.

5. To achieve flexibility of organization to the end that necessary adjustments can readily be made.[1]

The democratic concept helps make administration more effective, because, through freedom of action, the abilities and best qualities of everyone are brought to bear upon the problems that need attention. Full right to participate in planning and decision enhances the possibility that the actual work will be carried out thoroughly and completely and in full knowledge of the probable consequences. This process also helps avoid error, since impending problems are fully investigated and intelligent revision of plans is distinctly encouraged.

It must be pointed out that democratic administration eventually depends upon the extent to which the school personnel will accept these responsibilities.

THE ADMINISTRATIVE PROCESS

By whatever means it is conducted, administration has certain functions to fulfill; its relationship to the school has been stated in these terms: "Administration is part of a unified enterprise, which enterprise—school or school system—is somewhat more than the sum of the functions which make it up; . . .the function of administration can have no meaning as a service apart from the other services, unity among the services implying a certain interlocking between administration and each of the other functions."[2]

These other functions include instruction, guidance, research, supervision, and so on; each has a part to play in

[1] G. Robert Koopman, and others, *Democracy in School Administration*, D. Appleton-Century Company, Inc., New York, 1943, pp. 3-4. Reprinted by permission of Appleton-Century-Crofts, Educational Division, Meredith Corporation, New York.

[2] Jesse B. Sears, "The Nature of the Administrative Process in Education: A Partial Analysis of the Factors Involved," *Educational Administration Supervision* 31 (1):4, January 1945.

promoting the educational enterprise. The special part to be played by administration consists in "directing the organized efforts of others toward the accomplishment of chosen objectives."[3]

Sears has accomplished an admirable analysis of the administrative task:

1. In terms of the work to be done, the job:
   a. Formulation and establishment of educational objectives
   b. Preparation of the school program
   c. Grouping of the children
   d. Staffing of the schools and of the program
   e. Provision of shelter and equipment
   f. Giving instruction and care to the children
   g. Financing and keeping of records
   h. Public relations

2. In terms of the process or types of activity required:
   a. Planning—through research activities
   b. Organizing—through a division of labor and written rules
   c. Directing—through regulations or direct orders
   d. Coordinating—through guidance and supervision
   e. Controlling—through authority and knowledge

3. In terms of authority to be applied:
   a. Authority of law
   b. Authority of administration—discretionary power under the law
   c. Knowledge obtained by study of the task[4]

The administrator is not held responsible for accomplishing all these things personally, but for discovering what needs to be done to provide the proper educational setting,

[3] Ibid., p. 3.
[4] Ibid., p. 7.

to place in motion plans to achieve those ends, and to organize and direct the attack. That is, whoever is charged with administration of the music program does not set up the objectives and the problems of instruction; he may not actively engage in teaching; the actual raising of funds and the purchase, installation, and care of equipment may be handled by other people. Yet, all of these matters are his business. The art of administration lies in the skillful use of authority in developing the combined attack upon all these problems, so that the work of the school or department can be carried forward effectively.

Planning

The music program must be based on continuous research and should utilize expertness wherever it is found. Someone must figure out what is to be done, how to do it, and what results should be expected. For example, there is a need to anticipate the size of next year's musical groups and what additional items of equipment will be purchased; concerts and trips must be scheduled, music chosen, and publicity material prepared. New class schedules may need to be set up and teacher work loads adjusted; budget allocations have to be determined.

Organization

Individuals and facilities must be employed in a way which will create the strongest attack upon educational problems. Teachers may need to be organized to deal with poor attendance or discipline. Practical systems must be devised for handling purchases of music and repair of instruments; procedures must be established for the loan of musical equipment.

Direction

People are directed in the accomplishment of tasks by direct written or spoken order or by means of established routines, regulations, and procedures. There is nothing inherently authoritarian in indicating to another what should be done, so long as one is backed by sufficient information. If it is known that a certain teacher is best qualified and free to handle an assignment, it is enough to say so; details of the assignment can be given by simply indicating the facts relating to it.

Coordination

This crucial administrative function depends upon the planning, organization, and direction previously accomplished. As Sears put it, "To coordinate is to see that all participants have the same conception of the purpose and plan of action, to signal them to start their work, and to watch all parts to see that each is played in time, place, intensity, and purpose as planned."[5] There is a great deal of coordination to be done in music education, where individualism is the rule.

Control

An administrator must hold people to their responsibilities. This can only be accomplished by evaluation. That is, in terms of the plans that have been made and the assignments that have been accepted, performance must be checked and reported. The conduct of instruction, staff teamwork, condition of equipment, and every item which affects instruction must come under surveillance.

THE ADMINISTRATOR

Successful accomplishment of the administrative task as it has just been outlined depends upon the manner in which it is approached. Extraneous qualifications, such as personal friendship, seniority, or the possession of advanced academic degrees too often dictate the choice of administrators. It should be noted that administrators must work with and

[5] Ibid., p. 17.

through other people. Failure in this regard causes many fine plans and well-conceived actions to misfire.

Here we are treating the qualifications or attributes of good administrators. An understanding of the factors is important not only in judging applicants or in attempting personal improvement but also in throwing further light upon the actual mechanics of administration.

First of all, an administrator should demonstrate special fitness to lead others. The one who would be prepared to exercise leadership in the music program must be at home within his field of responsibility. In a very real sense he is an authority. For instance, the director of the school instrumental program should have had much experience playing in bands and orchestras, he should be able to conduct instrumental organizations and know their literature; and he should have had experience in teaching beginners as well as advanced students.

At the same time, administrators must suppress any desire to dominate. The power which the administrator holds over the affairs of the music program must not be used to enhance his personal glory nor to advance the cause of a particular musical organization or field of endeavor over another. The cooperative administrator works well with others, analyzing with them the problems which they face and securing the insight of the group. He must be able to recognize and promote leadership in others and encourage them to do things for which they are qualified; he resists the temptation to take care of everything personally.

Intelligence has been defined in several ways, but it most certainly involves quick perception and adjustment to actual circumstances. This quality is plainly necessary in directing the complex affairs connected with a music program.

Personal qualities desirable for an administrator include poise, friendliness, emotional stability, a pleasant demeanor, and interest in and regard for other people, an attribute which will cause them to trust him and react positively to his reasonable advances. The administrator inevitably comes in contact with many people, and he needs to develop skill in meeting them and making them feel at ease.

People can be expected to fail occasionally to measure up to their responsibilities. Since this is true of the administrator himself, he need not expect perfection from his professional colleagues or students.

Good administrators do not vacillate. True, many issues are better left to develop, and no decision should be made without the reasons to back it up. Once the facts are known, however, and due consideration has been given by all concerned, a definite and hopeful course must be chosen.

PRINCIPLES OF ADMINISTRATION

The various elements of administrative practice previously discussed do nothing to restrict its wide latitude of operation. Administration characteristically evolves in each case to meet circumstances. It recognizes few rules but establishes its own precedents; it is intensely practical.

Administration, however, should be more than an effective mechanism. It should be practiced in conformity with sound rules of action, or principles:

1. *Administrative responsibility should cover all factors involved in producing good musical learning.* The administrator secures a place to teach and stocks it with the necessary equipment. He provides for the selection and welfare of the students and teachers. He sees that desirable educational results are defined and proper measures taken to secure them. In accomplishing these matters to the best of his ability he must rely upon higher authority—the board, the community, et al.—and upon the students and teachers gathered around him, thus in fact reassigning portions of his responsibility.
2. *Administrative authority should be exercised to ensure the best operation of the music program, being dele*

gated in part to those held responsible for any aspect of this operation.

The most excellently conceived educative arrangements need constant enforcement and sensible revision. No one person, however, can directly accomplish the work of the school. All personnel must be given the authority to operate as they see fit within the limits of their responsibility. Authority reverts to the administration whenever the essential responsibilities are not being fulfilled.

3. *Administrative policy should be formed and carried out in terms of the objectives of the music program.* All rules and plans should have reference to aims—that is, to the kind of musicianship that is to be produced. This usually implies joint establishment of policy, by those who are most seriously concerned with the objectives. Sometimes the application or enforcement of policy requires arbitrary action by the administrator.

The need for joint policy making has been stated in this way:

> Group formulation of policies merely utilizes the intelligence of more persons. It utilizes the data about learners that teachers are collecting daily as well as data gathered elsewhere. Policies resulting from the application of the group method will be utilized much more intelligently, for the group is motivated to carry out policies it helps to develop. More than that, teachers inevitably grow in power as the result of such experiences. The competency of teachers is thereby increased.[6]

Group policy making is both a means and an outcome of democratic administrative procedure. Staff meetings become situations where unified policy develops *after* the climate of shared authority and responsibility has been created.

---

[6] Koopman and others, op. cit., p. 50. Reprinted by permission of Appleton-Century-Crofts, Educational Division, Meredith Corporation, New York.

4. *Administrative procedure should be adapted to the changing needs of the situation.* Affairs should be handled in the most effective way. For instance, it may be best to communicate individually or in groups or by written memorandum. The method of suggestion will usually work, but some circumstances require direct orders. In certain cases the usual channels and procedures may need to be altered. No established administrative pattern should be considered sacred. In fact, much of the job seems to consist of "trouble-shooting"— finding quick solutions to small problems before they become large. This requires much experience in the field of music education, knowledge of local patterns and procedures and an instinct for pragmatic solutions.

PROGRAM ADMINISTRATION

Administrative activity may be divided into three categories: (1) program administration, having to do with the organization and conduct of instruction; (2) personnel administration, which relates to the welfare of the teachers and the students; and (3) administration of facilities, involving all provision for material goods and services.

Responsibilities in the last two categories are relatively concrete, but the specifics of program administration are more difficult to define. Fortunately, our task here is made easier by the fact that the chief elements of the music program are already treated extensively in this volume.

Establishment of Objectives

It is absolutely prerequisite to effective instruction that the staff shall develop some very specific conceptions about the qualities of musical behavior which it should promote. The process for formulating objectives has been outlined in Chapter Six; the administrative role is to organize and nurture these efforts. This involves setting up evaluative procedures, gathering and promoting the study of various curricular materials, and sponsoring opinion polls and staff discussions. The administration does not dictate the objectives but attempts to keep the staff working effectively to establish them.

Outlining the Program

As the teachers develop their objectives and establish new concepts relating to the conduct of instruction, some administrative readjustment of musical activities usually becomes necessary. Perhaps the staff sees a need to expand the string program; extension of the requirement in general music might be recommended; a practicable method for offering class piano could be sought; possibly steps could be taken toward further development of the small-ensemble program.

At the college level many questions will arise regarding offerings and requirements. What are the basic branches of the music program? Where should courses be divided or combined for best results? What should be expected of students in the way of musical performance and theoretical knowledge? How much time will be needed in each phase of instruction, and thus, how many credits should be required?

Tradition and standardization are great barriers to change in subject offerings, course content, credit allotment, standards, and requirements. Unfortunately, administrators' lack of vision is often a major factor in freezing these arrangements. The administration should take the lead in promoting a flexible attitude toward the music program and must help to effect any practicable changes in its outline.

Evaluation of the Program

Each teacher is responsible for giving marks to the students in his classes; the general basis for these is actually a joint responsibility held by the staff under bond to the administration. If the student is to know upon what standard he is to be judged, it is clearly unfair for one teacher to grade on attendance, another on content mastery, and another on changing skills and attitudes.

But evaluation of the complete music program is a wider effort, transcending the separate classes. Sustained evaluation of the music program should be organized and supported by the administration. There must be a continuing check upon students' progress in relation to the central objectives; simple and adequate procedure must be devised by which the essential facts may be noted, recorded and interpreted. This process, taken up in detail in Chapter Twelve, requires administrative direction.

Scheduling

Various types of schedule are favored by the different school systems. It is generally the building principal's responsibility to establish the basic pattern. But he is susceptible to suggestion by the music personnel in the interests of that program. Careful study is suggested. Local tradition, which is so often the basic determinent of the school schedule, should not be allowed to suppress useful adjustments in favor of the music program. For example, if a change in the schedule would permit more students to enroll in musical organizations, steps should be taken to make the change. By and large, the elective groups—the band, orchestra, and choral organizations—should not be scheduled at the same hours as required subjects; a portion of the school day should be reserved for musical organizations, other elective subjects, and additional sections of required courses. New types of school organization are presenting music educators with new challenges in scheduling the music program. The ungraded classroom, for example, is being adopted in an increasing number of school systems. Children are grouped in each subject according to their level of achievement rather than according to age. Thus, a child does not pass from the first grade to the second and then to the third, but remains on a given level of tasks until he is prepared to move on to the next higher level.

The *open school*, a more radical development, allows students to move to and from the various activities and areas of the school almost at will. This type of organization allows students the utmost in freedom to follow individual interests and needs and stresses individual initiative and responsibility.

Modular scheduling represents a structured yet flexible approach to the organization of the students' day in the secondary school. The school day is divided into modules of about twenty minutes. Different classes and activities are allotted the number of modules that seems appropriate to their time requirements. Thus, the high school band may be assigned three modules, but two modules would be deemed sufficient for a choir, and one, for a small ensemble.

The almost universal adoption of kindergartens, the increasing trend toward nursery schools, and the earlier physical and social maturation of children have resulted in many school systems replacing the junior high school with the middle school. This new organization of the school produces the pattern: elementary school (k—5); middle school (5—8); secondary school (9—12).

It is obvious that traditional concepts of scheduling for the music program are not appropriate for some of the newer forms of school organization. Experimental schedules demand flexibility on the part of music teachers along with a high level of originality in shaping a music program consistent with the situation. For example, elementary school music teachers may be required to provide singing experiences for very large groups of children of different ages in schools committed to the ungraded classroom or team teaching. Likewise, the open school would require the provision of facilities and opportunities for individual and small group work in music.

The organization of a middle school may require offering beginning instrumental instruction in the sixth grade rather than earlier. Furthermore, the exploratory purposes of the middle school imply change in the general music program. It is essential that music educators work within the organizational framework established in the school and that they learn to capitalize upon the opportunities for the music program that are unique to each type of organization.

School administrators should be aware that music teachers must have a lighter class load than teachers of many other subjects. Music teachers need time for special sessions with individuals and small groups as well as for giving attention to business details and public relations, duties not required of teachers of most other subjects.

Coordination of Departmental Activities

Particular concert dates should not "belong" to a particular musical organization. The attempt should be made to adjust the number of public appearances of the musical groups, to spread them throughout the school year, and to avoid any monopoly of the most favored dates. Usually, for example, the final concert date of the year is considered advantageous, in spite of the rush of activity, because of the extended period of rehearsals; likewise, the latest pre-Christmas date is usually sought because of the advantages in programming, publicity, and attendance.

Competition among the orchestra, band, and choir, and other phases of the music program, for equipment and students is also a strong possibility. Friction most often arises in the period just prior to an important concert or contest, when there are conflicts in the use of the auditorium, and for musicians wanted simultaneously at two rehearsals. The solutions to such problems require reference to stable policy on the use of personnel and equipment, setting up and clearing away stage properties, and so on; combined concerts will also help alleviate these difficulties.

Printed Materials

Concert programs, news copy, brochures, printed regulations, bulletins, and catalogues are all definitely related to the music program. In fact, they constitute a very concrete manifestation of the work of the school. The administrator often assumes the role of managing editor, outlining the content and format, setting deadlines, collecting and editing the copy, and arranging for printing and distribution. Teacher participation in these tasks will help build a united and realistic school policy.

Forms and Records

In some schools the overmeticulous handling of forms and records interferes with instruction, while in others this service is so antiquated that all value is lost. It must always be remembered that records and forms are valuable only to the degree that they help summarize and systematize the gathering of information. This information must then be made available for the people who need it.

Among the items ordinarily kept are records of tests given, subjects taken, attendance, and marks; records of teachers' qualifications, experience, and teaching loads; inventories of equipment; records of purchases; and requests for equipment. All of these are necessary in making intelligent plans and recommendations. The whole system must be periodically checked to avoid obsolescence.

Promotion of Enrollment and Expanded Activity

No matter how smoothly a school music program may be operating, its benefits can and should be extended to include a greater number of students. General music instruction should be provided every student at the elementary, secondary, and college levels, and an expanding series of special musical activities should accompany that program.

Increased enrollment is largely a matter of successful instruction and advisement in the secondary school, while, in the case of the college, the message must be carried to all schools and communities within its orbit. Music tours, clinics, personal visits, scholarship offers, and general publicity are all serviceable in this regard. Such promotion, however, must never encroach upon the legitimate interests of other subject fields or schools, nor should any student or musical group be sacrificed on the altar of showmanship.

PERSONNEL ADMINISTRATION

Selection and Assignment of Teachers

Probably the most vital administrative task lies in securing good replacements or additions to the teaching staff. Teachers who are really qualified for their particular posts produce a better music program and make the work of administration much easier and more effective. Teacher selection merits the greatest attention and care.

For any vacancy, it is imperative that the selection process be thorough. A concise job description should be prepared and disseminated widely, until a good list of candidates is secured. Their qualifications should be examined until it is reasonably clear which provides the nearest match to the needs of the vacant position. All this speaks against hurried, impulsive judgment.

In short, it is helpful to rely on the judgment of several, including those who have the most experience and those who must work most closely with the new teacher. These people should be involved in examining credentials, interviewing, and in the final judgment. This will result in a finer music staff and more musically qualified classroom teachers. By thus causing earnest consideration of the objectives and needs of the school, morale and understanding of the faculty should also be improved.

Parallel with the responsibility for teacher selection goes that of assignment to handle specific courses or areas of endeavor. This involves an intimate knowledge of the needs of the school and the strengths and weaknesses of each teacher. It is not enough to assign one to the choral program, one to handle bands, and another to strings and General Music. What will each teacher's schedule be? What specific choral groups are to be offered? Is a musical to be produced regularly each spring? How important is the marching band and how much instructional time and money should it consume? Is beginning instrumental instruction to be basically in the form of class lessons or individual lessons? Are the elementary classroom teachers expected to carry on the music program between visits of the music specialist? These sorts of questions relate to the administrative realm because they affect the direction of the school.

It is essential, therefore, that administrative personnel be well acquainted with the music program and its directions, as well as with the teaching personnel, in order to assign responsibilities fairly and effectively. It is also necessary to modify these assignments from time to time as conditions change and as the need for contraction or expansion in certain directions is foreseen. Part of the administrative job is to look ahead and anticipate change.

Of course, the need for change is often initiated by the individual instructor who decides it would be well to organize a stage band, or to set a lower number of beginning students to be accepted, or to insert an additional concert into the yearly calendar. Even though done with approval from above, such a move is clearly administrative and will tend to alter the equilibrium of the music program.

One of the most critical problems in assignment concerns who shall be assigned to handle music instruction in the elementary school. Is it a job for the classroom teachers or for a corps of music specialists? This matter has been a recurrent topic for debate within the profession.

It is obvious by now that most classroom teachers do not possess, nor is it practical to give them, enough musicianship to handle the job properly. It is equally true that it has not been possible to interest and prepare enough music specialists to accomplish the needed instruction. If there are to be one hundred minutes of useful music instruction per week in each elementary classroom in America—which is the common standard to be sought—then stronger efforts are needed in both directions. The profession must do everything possible to encourage prospective music teachers to specialize in general music for the elementary schools, and to see that these people get the necessary training. There must be a parallel effort to find those future classroom teachers who are musically apt, and give them as much musical background as possible. The third aspect of this job is to organize all these people into an effective corps for music instruction; that is a local administrative responsibility. It then remains, finally, to continue the development of the teachers' musical and teaching competence through a vigorous and sustained program of in-service education. Only major effort along all these fronts provides much hope of material improvement in the national level of musicianship.

Orientation of New Teachers

The administration must provide the new teacher with an adequate notion of the situation he will face. These are some of the matters to be treated:

1. review of contract and tenure provisions
2. the pattern of teaching responsibilities and purposes for which he is being hired
3. indication of predecessor's record and problems
4. starting salary, method of payment, system of raises, and leaves
5. provisions and options for insurance, medical care, retirement, etc.
6. introduction to other members of the immediate staff and the general faculty
7. tour of departmental area and classroom and office space to be assigned him
8. inspection of equipment and facilities pertaining to the particular job
9. explanation of school procedures and special services
10. indication of usual pattern of relationship among faculty and school officials
11. indication of any special local customs, traditions, or expectations
12. indication of any out-of-school responsibilities or limitation which may apply (religious, civic, or professional affiliations; policies with regard to private lessons, summer school attendance, etc.)

These and similar items can be cared for in any fashion that seems wise. Informality is usually a good rule. As a matter of fact, much of the orientation is covered in explanation of the job and prior to the offer and acceptance of it; most of these are questions which the wise candidate will ask in determining his liking for the job. Some of the material will obviously be more comprehensible in printed form.

Advisement on New Procedures and Policies

Those who are teaching in a school need to know how the situation is developing in order to do their most effective work. The administration should be in the best position to interpret any information on proposed salary increases, future enrollment figures, building or staff expansion, arrival and use of new equipment, budget requests, and similar matters.

Release of such information at the proper time and in the right way brings helpful counsel from the teachers and promotes wider acceptance and better execution of plans. News letters, bulletin boards, memorandums, staff meetings, and ordinary conversation are among the means which may be used to accomplish this task.

Provision for Teacher Growth and Extended Influence

Teachers will react well to arrangements which afford them the opportunity to do their job more effectively and to make their full contribution within the faculty, the community, and the profession. The teacher should be given:

1. full participation in solving problems of the school
2. an effective program of supervision
3. committee assignments based on true interest and expertness
4. access to a truly professional library
5. encouragement and recognition of efforts in research
6. opportunities for public performance

7. encouragement of original musical composition and its performance
8. opportunities to attend rehearsals and concerts of other musical groups
9. schedule adjustment to allow participation in music clinics and festivals and attendance at professional meetings
10. encouragement of wise cooperation with religious, civic, and cultural groups of the community
11. leave and credit for summer school or extension study
12. assistance in personal evaluation

The Student Body

Although the students are not school personnel in the strict sense of the word, they do come under administrative control; and the relationship is most conveniently discussed as part of the human factor in administration. The best interests of the student remain the prime purpose of the music program and must be protected and promoted by the administration.

Recent and widespread conflict between students and school administrations, particularly at the college level, highlights the necessity for greater attention to students as *people* as well as *learners*. Changing social and economic conditions, evolving customs and morés, and new ideas will produce stress and strain in normal school-pupil relationships. But the pace of change has become more and more explosive, causing a severe "generation gap." Some students, therefore, seem unreasonably determined to attack the very fabric of society and to attempt the overthrow of its most cherished institutions. Student extremists are apparently few in number and few of these have turned out to be habitues of the school music programs. Nevertheless, the entire life of a school can become intolerable unless there are wise administrative moves to produce respect and trust among all the people who work there.

The role of the school remains paramount; it is a laboratory for the young to be inducted into their role as useful adults in society. They must become involved there in the kinds of experiences which will helpfully influence their behavior. This process is usually assisted by considerable flexibility to meet student desires and needs, yet essential direction must be maintained by the teacher.

So the administration must work to establish a good climate for learning. In essence, it is like a good home environment. There must not be a formalistic, unreal approach. Motives must be sincere and actions taken openly. There must be tolerance of dissent and unexpected reactions. Deliberate antisocial behavior must be firmly curbed.

Student advisement.   Advisement has two facets: (1) discovery of the student's needs and capacities and (2) guidance or counseling. Advisement is too often mechanical and completely paternalistic; the student is "advised" only on registration day. Real advisement, however, is continuous and largely informal. The best adviser is the teacher who is most closely associated with the pupil and who commands his admiration and trust. Most often, this will be the teacher whose musical specialty most closely corresponds to the student's and who is thus a natural counselor in terms of the student's development.

The important thing is to find out what the student really wants to do and can possibly do in relation to his current schooling and future musical accomplishment and then to lay the possibilities for action before him. Some of this information may be had through testing, questionnaires, and auditions, but the greater part must come from ordinary observation; then, influence should be exerted to widen the student's opportunities along the indicated line of endeavor. That is, if a student wants to be a fine clarinetist and *does* show promise in that line, college catalogues and pep talks may not be as good a form of counseling as simply arranging the opportunity for some solo performances.

Fair and impartial treatment of students. Certain rules, regulations, and precedents must be set up to govern the conduct and activity of students within the school. Privileges and prohibitions must be clear.

There is also a definite administrative responsibility to determine whether any students are being discriminated against or held to regulations which do not serve their legitimate interests. For example, there are instances in which the standard prerequisites and sequences should be waived and in which a student's change to a different instructor or class section may be advisable.

It is vitally necessary that students be given opportunities commensurate with their demonstrated aptitude and effort. Administration can be of great service in arranging for special projects and incentives which encourage freedom of choice for the students.

Sponsorship of worthwhile student activities. Student musical societies, stage bands, variety shows, and similar activities, while called extracurricular, have a definite part in shaping student experiences. Cooperation with and guidance of such activities is extremely important. It must be recognized that these represent attempts by the students to develop the leadership and initiative which are important objectives of the music program.

Effective communication among students and teachers. Most educational policies are of direct concern to students. For instance, they are affected by contemplated disciplinary regulations, changes in courses and schedules, projected musical tours, and purchases of uniforms or instruments. Informal student opinion can be sought on such matters. If nothing else, open decisions tend to lessen their unpopularity.

Students and teachers should have normal social contact in any case. Such a condition will result in greater understanding and a more effective program of instruction. Means to this end include easy conversational attitudes, cooperative school enterprises, and social gatherings of parents, students, and teachers.

A warning must be sounded, however, against any attempt to break down natural status barriers. A teacher can never successfully be "one of the boys." Certain distinctions always go with differences in age, sex, and professional expertness. A teacher, therefore, is addressed differently, maintains accepted standards of language and dress, and avoids special attachments with students. These things are necessary in the role of teacher.

ADMINISTRATION OF FACILITIES

Educational facilities include the buildings, equipment, and supplies supporting instruction. Problems center around purchase, distribution, and maintenance. Because these matters are relatively clear-cut and plainly pertain to administration, even the more well-meaning administrators tend to act arbitrarily in this realm. This should not be the case, for school personnel are capable and willing to do much of the work. Successful facilities for the music program are achieved through cooperative endeavor by the entire music staff.

Financial Operation

Educational finance involves (1) fund raising, (2) budgeting, (3) ordering, and (4) paying for the goods and materials which are necessary in the educational enterprise. Different methods and procedures for accomplishing these matters are used in various institutions.

Funds may come from concert receipts, special drives, tuition, or contributions; private schools and colleges are financed entirely on this basis. In general, however, funds for the operation of the music program are not raised directly by the department but are part of the total school budget from tax revenues. Fund raising, therefore, becomes a matter not of promotion but of justification of need. Certain funds will be allocated to the music program as a matter of course and based upon past needs; but if these funds are actually insufficient, a very thorough account will have to be given of the program and its costs.

In a sense, then, budgeting is often accomplished before funds are allocated. Whether or not this is the case, some plan for spending should be drawn up. A budget is simply a systematized statement forecasting expenditures and balancing them with revenues. Sometimes the breakdown is carried out in great detail, with a definite amount being reserved for each musical activity and each class of equipment. But it is usually more practical to divide the music budget into a few main categories to guide in controlling purchases.

Purchasing is accomplished as the need arises, although the administration should control the "tempo" so that funds neither pile up nor become exhausted. Major items are usually advertised for bids while incidental and emergency supplies are procured by special order or direct purchase. Payment is made by the school when bills are signed by the person ordering and receiving the goods.

Plant Construction and Utilization

A new building program seems a rare enough occasion, but when the time arrives the music staff must have some very definite contributions to make. It is the nature of music instruction to require considerable extra space and extra construction cost per pupil. Rehearsal space, individual practice facilities, complex storage arrangements, humidity control, and acoustical problems all contribute to this expense. Partial sound isolation between rooms is even more difficult to arrange than internal acoustics; at this point architects must begin to include in their estimate the extra cost of individual ventilation systems, special flooring and doors, double ceilings, and multiple-slab walls. Music teachers cannot be expected to draw the specifications, but they must understand the general requirements and be sure that school officials and architects are aware of them in the early stages of planning.

In buildings not originally designed to handle music instruction it is usually desirable to reserve an isolated wing or section for the music program. Regular classrooms and offices are of an awkward size for music purposes and may require that partitions be added or removed to establish group rehearsal and individual practice areas. Acoustical treatment and storage facilities can be added.

Acquisition of Basic Items of Equipment

The necessity for additional musical instruments is nearly always immediate to the music teacher. Once he gets the authorization, however, he is often torn between quality and quantity. Should he get those fine tympani, or should he order the cheaper model and also pick up that reconditioned tuba? Clearly, the administration must promote stability of thought toward long-term goals.

In orchestral instruments, for example, a reasonable estimate must first be made of the instruments which the school must own in reaching a balanced instrumentation. The desired models (sousaphone or recording tuba), finishes (silver or lacquer), and brands of instruments should be determined. It must then be decided which of the present instruments must be traded off and which may be wisely kept and reconditioned. Finally, the necessary expenditures must be apportioned over a period of years. Only in this way can wise decisions be made regarding the quality of instruments to purchase.

Band uniforms represent another serious purchasing problem. The uniform companies must be trusted to help in selecting the style and specifications which will give a unique effect and yet will retain serviceability for a long time. It is important that uniforms be selected to suit the basic function for which the band is used—marching, concert, or a rather equal combination of the two. The uniform style chosen depends somewhat upon the age level of the group. The long-term problem of fitting can sometimes be improved by ordering a standard selection of sizes for the age level rather than by tailoring the uniforms for the current band members.

Instruments and uniforms are given as examples of the purchasing problem. Many other types of equipment may be specially acquired for the music program, among them, chairs, racks, choir robes, record players, music cabinets, duplicating machines, and typewriters. In purchasing school equipment, it is generally wise to observe these rules:

1. The standard of value is educational need.
2. Purchase nothing for which a use cannot be demonstrated.
3. Purchase in large, consolidated amounts when feasible.
4. Try to purchase the latest, most improved model.
5. Look for simple, rugged construction.

Provision of Instructional Materials, General Supplies, and Services

Progress in the music program requires steady improvement and expansion of materials. Textbooks must be provided; the music libraries of the major organizations and small ensembles must be regularly supplemented; a basic music library of authoritative references and source material must be maintained; and regular acquisitions must be made for the library of recordings. Budgeting and selection of these items should be systematic.

Irregular needs for expendable supplies must be anticipated. A teacher should not have to requisition a few sheets of score paper, neither should he be forced to make a flying trip to the music store to replace a split bassoon reed. A supply of these incidental articles—reeds, strings, clarinet pads, and so on—should be kept on hand.

General supplies—typing paper, filing cards, thumbtacks, examination booklets, stamps—should be made available on some regular basis from the central office. Similarly, there must be standard arrangements for use of office services—typing, duplicating, and mailing.

Usage and Maintenance of Equipment

For protection and ease of handling, instrumental and choral libraries should be arranged in large steel filing cabinets. Labeled racks or pigeonholes are sometimes provided in the rehearsal rooms for music lent to the students. Long cedar-lined cabinets should be built in which to hang uniforms and robes.

School instruments should be under lock and key, and individual lockers should be provided for *privately* owned instruments. The difficulty is, of course, that lockers must be built in tailored fashion for the different sizes of instruments and installed in some compact space under temperature and humidity control.

A card-filing system or running list must be devised for conveniently checking in and checking out musical equipment. Many school instruments, uniforms, recordings, and copies of music are lost each year because the identity of the borrower has been forgotten. Furthermore, it is often necessary suddenly to exchange equipment between students.

Though there is a general school inventory, a separate inventory of musical equipment should be maintained for convenience in inspection and in planning purchases. In order to be of real value, the listing should include the item, make, model, serial number, accessories, year purchased, purchase price, and estimate of present condition and value.

There must be stable arrangements for routine moving jobs such as setting up for rehearsals and concerts. This may be done by the regular school work force, by paid student help, or by appointees from the musical groups themselves. Transportation of large or unusual units, such as pianos, must be specially arranged for.

One side of maintenance is that of prevention. That is, one tends to avoid excessive wear and tear, obsolescence, accident and theft of equipment by (1) enlightened purchasing, (2) regular inventory and inspection, (3) convenient storage, (4) systematic lending procedures, (5) instruction in care and use, and (6) enforcement of rules and penalties for misuse.

The other aspect of maintenance consists in repair (or replacement). Many incidental repairs can be accomplished by the music teachers themselves, but the individual should be compensated when any special tools or skills are required. A repair bench or shop is a valuable facility and is particularly useful in promoting student experience in the care and repair of instruments.

As a general rule, however, the administrative role becomes that of finding and diagnosing the need for repair, securing the estimate of cost, and arranging for the repairs to be made. This requires some understanding of the functioning of musical instruments and the other types of equipment pertaining to the music program. An excellent plan for accomplishing the major share of this task is to make, with the people who will do the repairing, a general inspection of equipment in the summer or other period of slack operation. At this time the basic estimates can also be made. Repairs can then be arranged immediately or on a schedule.

THE TEACHER AND THE ADMINISTRATOR

Throughout this account of the administrative task the fundamental tie between instruction and administration should be increasingly apparent: instruction is an effort to produce specific changes in students' behavior, while administration provides for and directs those efforts. Therefore, a prime duty of the teacher is to see that the administration is kept informed of his needs in carrying out the task of music teaching.

These needs should not be narrowly conceived. They include not only the necessary material things—music, instruments, and so on—but also items pertaining to the outline of the program, procedural details, student problems, and the teacher's welfare. In short, the various administrative problems are also the teacher's problems.

This duty of providing information or intelligence on

now the battle is going involves constant evaluation by the teacher; he must objectively assess his teaching situation in order to discover what elements need strengthening. Then he must present his conclusions to the administrator. Of course, the administrator tries to help both in the process of evaluation and in the reporting, by providing all sorts of blanks and forms and opportunities for discussion. Nevertheless, it is the teacher's responsibility to give more than a perfunctory report; anything but a factual and well-supported explanation is nothing more than a complaint.

The second half of the teacher's responsibility lies in a wholehearted response to the suggestions of the administrator in his job of directing the music program. The success of democratic administration is a two-way responsibility. The teacher must show the qualities of friendliness and purpose and must give evidence of the ability to plan cooperatively and with initiative. He must subscribe wholeheartedly to the objectives of the program which he has helped to form, and he must drive vigorously in his sector of the operation. To the extent that this is not so, the administrator must become autocratic.

The key to successful administration often lies in the development of the necessary attitudes on both sides. The failure of many administrators is due to almost incorrigible attitudes on the part of some teachers. And of course, the process of changing attitudes is quite slow. It is because of the latter that successful changes in administration often take years to complete.

On his part, the administrator must handle all of his responsibilities without interfering in any essential way with instruction. He must remember that a great deal of activity and bustle may accomplish little or no change in the substance of the program. More than anything else, the teacher resents the imposition of extra "study" and detail which do no more than obstruct education; hence one of the hallmarks of good administration is simplicity of design and operation. The administrator must always remember that his purpose is to *facilitate* instruction.

SUMMARY

Educational administration works to provide the setting for musical learning. Since all music educators are connected in some respect with that task, they must understand administrative operation and their part in it.

Administrative conduct has often been autocratic, but democratic procedure is equally possible. In reality, there is no inherent mode of administration; it is essentially practical. The process is one of planning, organization, direction, coordination, and control. In other words, administration does not actually *execute* the work of the school, but, rather, it makes provision for the job and sees that it is done.

The job must be undertaken in a spirit of cooperative endeavor and enlightened leadership. The administrator must demonstrate his understanding of people and capability for decision; his actions must be governed by principles outlining his field of responsibility and the exercise of authority.

One category of administrative problems concerns arrangements for instructional activity. The administration must help establish objectives for the music program and an accompanying system of evaluation. Educational arrangements must be outlined and constantly adjusted. Musical activities must be coordinated and expanded.

There are vital administrative tasks in connection with teachers, beginning with their careful selection and orientation. Teachers must be kept well advised of developments in the school's music program, and they should be given every chance to participate and grow professionally.

In working with the students in the music program it is necessary to create the proper kind of advisement and to establish the climate of fair play and freedom of opportunity. The administration should back student musical activities and promote the proper social atmosphere.

It is also an administrative responsibility to provide and maintain the necessary facilities for instruction. Needed musical equipment and supplies must be budgeted, purchased, and distributed. All these musical items require special handling and storage and rather systematic control of their use.

All administrative operations are in the interest of instruction, so that the music teacher has a fundamental obligation to state his needs. In turn, the administration is committed to give him the means and the freedom to instruct.

QUESTIONS FOR DISCUSSION

1. What is the essential relationship between administration and the music program? How are music educators involved? Is administrative responsibility necessarily confined to top-echelon personnel?
2. Is administrative conduct inherently autocratic? In what respects can autocratic administration be modified? What is required in order to operate democratically?
3. What are the essential facets of the administrative process? Why has it been termed a vicarious function? What qualities are essential to its performance?
4. Illustrate how administrative responsibility may be delegated, along with the equivalent field of authority. What is administrative policy and how should it be formed?
5. How may the administration assist in developing the pattern of musical instruction? Why is sustained evaluation so effective in this regard?
6. Why do music class schedules and special events require careful coordination? In what other ways may the interests of the music program be managed and promoted?
7. Why is the process of teacher selection so important? What factors should be considered in securing new music teachers?
8. What types of information should be supplied the new teacher? In what other ways may teachers be assisted?
9. What attitude should administration hold toward students? Describe measures which can be taken in the interest of student welfare.
10. What types of expenditure are related to musical instruction? How are these items purchased?

11. What special factors need to be considered in fitting buildings for musical instruction?
12. Upon what bases does one select musical equipment? How are instruments and music protected?
13. Describe the essential relationship between teacher and administrator. What does each have a right to expect?
14. Study the schools in your area to determine recent changes in scheduling and other administrative factors. What effect have the changes had on the school music program?

SELECTED REFERENCES

Baranek, Leo J. *Music, Acoustics and Architecture*, John Wiley and Sons, Inc., New York, 1962.

Bewley, S., C. E. Brow, and J. S. Martin. "Music to My Ears; Three Superintendents State Their Views," *Music Educators Journal* 54, February 1968, pp. 92-96.

Chamberlain, Leo M., and Leslie W. Kindred. *The Teacher in the School Organization*, Prentice-Hall, Inc., Englewood Cliffs, N.J., 1966.

Committee on Music Buildings, Rooms and Equipment. *Music Buildings, Rooms and Equipment*, Music Educators National Conference, Washington, 1966.

Hovey, Nilo. *Administration of School Instrumental Music*, Belwin, Inc., Rockville Centre, L. I., New York, 1952.

Klotmann, Robert H. *Scheduling Music Classes*, National Education Association, Washington, 1968.

Miller, Van, and Willard B. Spalding. *The Public Administration of American Schools*, The Macmillan Company, New York, 1965.

Sachs, Benjamin M. *Educational Administration*, Houghton Mifflin Company, Boston, 1966.

Supervision
in Music Education

10 The job of music supervision means many things to many people. The task usually calls for direct assistance to others who are teaching music in their classes, but in some schools the supervisor actually does all or most of the music teaching; in other instances the term has grown to mean a special administrative assistant or liaison officer. These different functions are reflected in the various titles applied to the position; besides being called a supervisor (which title we will regard as generic) one may be referred to as a director, consultant, chairman, or specialist. In Chapter Nine, the reader has already seen many normal duties of the music supervisor classed as administrative.

This chapter, therefore, does not attempt to describe the total activity which may be expected of a music supervisor but only that part which is actually supervisory in nature. It discusses the function of supervision in the schools, common patterns of responsibility, and the general process of supervision. Finally, it points out the essential problems to be faced and the supervisory techniques which may be employed in solving them.

THE CONDUCT OF MUSIC SUPERVISION

Few words are so glibly used in educational circles as "super-vision." One might think that the supervisory role is as cleanly defined and executed as the other school services. Nothing could be further from the truth. The fact is that many supervisors really have little constructive influence up-on music instruction in their schools. They merely occupy posts mapped out by some more vigorous predecessor, and the students and their teachers come to accept this. The supervisor is conceived as a supernumerary or itinerant educa-tor working loosely in their interests. One of the blackest marks against music supervision is this apparent *lack of purpose*.

Second, much supervision is unplanned. It is easy to see why; the typical day of the music supervisor is crowded with issues to be met and details to be handled. Gradually, deci-sions are based on expedience. There is a *lack of continuity*.

Actual operations are too often superficial. The supervi-sor visits classes, speaks pleasantly with the teachers, and offers a few opinions. He does not dig into real problems at all. This *lack of depth* is usually accompanied by *lack of inspiration*; the supervisor slips into a dull routine of prescrib-ing each week's classwork and holding regular conferences and staff meetings to explain how the material should be taught.

Then, there are supervisors who possess an understand-ing of the game and some excellent ideas to put into practice; but they encounter opposition, and the problems seem too severe to be met. Their difficulties stem from *lack of vigor*.

There are also "strong" supervisors who have a plan and the ability to put it across, but in the process they infringe upon the teachers' prerogatives. They are too blunt in their methods and actively interfere with the normal progress of learning. Theirs is a *lack of understanding*. Finally we come to the *lack of investigation*. Supervision cannot live without intelligence on the daily activity of students and their teach-ers. Too many supervisors have good ideas which would work very well at another time and place. They do not follow and observe the results of their own work but assume that much activity means the job is being done.

Music supervisors are not entirely to blame for these conditions. The school officials, teachers, and citizens of any community can ruin the work of the most qualified supervisor. By understanding the task, they can create better conditions for its fulfillment.

THE FUNCTION OF SUPERVISION

Music supervision is defined as the effort to improve the learning environment of music students; its purpose is to improve the design and process of music instruction. This is accomplished by very direct means. The supervisor is an expert musician and educator who is able to work effectively with other teachers in providing a better musical education for children.

The previous chapter has shown that the music supervisor may also help administer the music program. The school principal likewise occupies this dual role. This does not mean that the two tasks are not fundamentally distinct, however; while administration is a directing and organizing force, supervision works at the firing line, so to speak. For example, *orientation* of new teachers is essentially an administrative task, while it is a supervisory responsibility to *induct* the new teacher into the job—seeing that the necessary equipment is in the classroom, discussing the pupils and the first day's work, and actually observing or being on call to assist in any way that is needed at this crucial period.

Again, supervision in itself does not include the direct function of instruction, although the appointed supervisor may often be called upon to teach. In his special role the supervisor works with both teachers and students.

The task has been outlined in this way:
The improvement of the learning situation for children cannot be provided by centering attention on teaching

techniques. . . . To improve instruction, supervision must provide: leadership that develops a unified school program and enriches the environment for all teachers; the type of emotional atmosphere in which all are accepted and feel that they belong; opportunities to think and work together effectively as a faculty group; personnel procedures that give the teacher confidence in the school system; and program change based on honest evaluation.[1]

This concept of the supervisory function has not always been followed. In earlier days music supervision was generally quite restrictive, since the instructors themselves were supposed to know little or nothing about music. The general plan was for the supervisor to construct the course of study, outlining the work for each music period, the music to be used, the facts to be presented, the outcomes to be sought, and the methods to be employed. With only slight variations in the plan it was a simple matter to test the students and thus to determine the relative efficiency of the instructors. The supervisor himself would appear at stated intervals in order to conduct the music lesson and thus help correct any deviations that might occur.

More recently, the supervisor was placed in charge of the in-service education of teachers. Laudable as this may be, it has not focused attention on the students and the educational program itself but upon the teachers and their teaching methods. The effort is made to supplement the learning activities of the teachers themselves; in this case, the supervisor is a teacher of teachers.

In-service education is still considered a part of the supervisory function, but the concept has become broad enough to include all means for studying and improving the actual learning environment of students. The point of view is expressed in these terms.

[1] Kimball Wiles, *Supervision for Better Schools*, Prentice-Hall, Inc., Englewood Cliffs, N.J., 1950, p. 10.

Traditional supervision consisted largely of inspection of the teacher by means of visitation and conference, carried on in random manner, with directions imposed on the teacher by authority and usually by one person. Modern supervision, by contrast, involves the systematic study and analysis of the entire teaching-learning situation, utilizing a carefully planned program that has been cooperatively derived from the situation and which is adapted to the needs of those involved in it.[2]

Supervision of music is essentially a task for a specially trained music educator. The most typical supervisory job is that of the elementary school music supervisor or consultant. The need is most apparent here, because there are seldom enough music specialists to handle the job alone and the classroom teachers, while they may be accounted good educators, are too often ill-prepared to teach music. Hence, there is a very real need for the person who can work continually with the classroom teachers to develop the best possible music program; a number of these teachers will be found who, with proper support, can carry a significant share of the task in their own classrooms. This holds music in the core of the curriculum, rather than laying it before the child in the guise of a specialized feat.

Where the supervisor is dealing more with music specialists, as in the secondary schools and some elementary schools, his duties are likely to be largely administrative, owing to the more specialized nature of the teachers' preparation and instructional duties. The supervisor may double as director of the choral groups, the band, or the orchestra and yet maintain the responsibility for the coordination and development of the music program in the one or more high schools of the city. The responsibilities in such a position are very similar to those of the head of the college music department. In either case, the individual must assume not only the

[2] William H. Burton and Leo J. Brueckner, *Supervision: A Social Process*, Appleton-Century-Crofts, Educational Division, Meredith Corporation, New York, 1955, p. 13

administrative duties delegated by the head of the school system but also whatever supervisory work seems needed in producing better musical learning.

Another plan for supervision is accomplished by separate supervisors for the vocal and the instrumental programs throughout the school system. In a large city system this may entail a close connection on the part of the supervisor with the directors of the various musical organizations in several high schools and junior high schools, with the classroom teachers in the elementary schools, and with a corps of special assistants and private instructors in music. In smaller school systems it is common for the high school choral director to be termed vocal supervisor, maintaining direct and daily contact with the elementary music program, while the instrumental supervisor, i.e., the high school band and orchestra director, assumes the actual instruction of beginning instrumental classes in the upper grades. The small school must entrust its music program to one person.

The disadvantages of the vertical pattern for supervision, with its separation of choral and instrumental phases of music, center upon the possibility of competition for students, funds, and prestige. It also tends to take instrumental instruction out of the elementary classroom. But it is usually more successful than the horizontal structure which jeopardizes continuity of policy and procedure as the students move on from grade school to junior high to high school. The horizontal organization often leaves a promising group of young band or string players without a high school band or orchestra to play in. In other localities, it may force the delay of beginning instrumental instruction until the seventh or even the the ninth grade.

THE PROCESS OF SUPERVISION

What happens in music supervision is a general involvement with the work surrounding instruction. This may be divided into several characteristic types of activity.

Analyzing the Program

The supervisor must study the various facets of the music program in operation. By this is meant continual observation of students and teachers at their tasks, gathering and interpretation of data, and formulation of well-grounded conclusions regarding what is actually happening and should happen in the music program. The supervisor attempts to determine the needs of students and teachers, the value of the experiences being undergone, and the strengths and weaknesses in program organization, materials, and facilities. Only in this way can the constructive task of building supervisory plans be undertaken.

For example, the supervisor may observe that children in a certain class are generally restive during the periods of musical activity. Contact with the teacher of this group may establish the fact that he feels insecure in the subject and is fundamentally going through the motions, because it is expected, until he can relax in the more compatible realms of language or social studies. Nevertheless, the supervisor notes that this teacher actually possesses adequate musicianship and technical ability. Assuming that the difficulty stems from past teaching experiences or from present fear of the supervisor, he seeks to assure this teacher that his ability is unquestioned; he asks his opinions, emphasizes his successes, and gives him a leading part in planning and producing the annual Christmas pageant. Continued study reveals the outcomes of these efforts and what further steps might be taken.

Enlisting Aid and Support

Another element in the supervisory process is enlisting the efforts of others in improving the music program. Rapport must be secured within the school and community. This calls for an understanding of the situation, of the needs and goals of the music program, and demonstration of some progress.

Stimulation of Teachers and Students

The heart of the supervisor's job lies in developing the enthusiasm of school personnel toward their work. This is done by a variety of means—research, planning, demonstration, guidance—indeed, every supervisory technique can have a stimulating effect. This will not be so, however, unless the supervisor takes care that an inspirational tone attends his efforts. For instance, when several music teachers are called together to make plans for an all-school concert, or for threshing out some problems in school discipline, the teachers must leave the room with new insights and determination to do the task

Advising School Personnel

It must not be forgotten that the music supervisor is an expert, a specialist, and a consultant. His special capabilities, plus the careful analysis of the music program which is one of his primary responsibilities, should cause him to be an authority to whom school officials, students, and teachers may turn. He must at all times have an answer or some adequate suggestions for getting answers to legitimate questions which are brought to him. If a school principal needs recommendations concerning better scheduling or if a teacher asks advice on songs to use or instruments to buy, the supervisor should be able to help. Students should be able to turn to him for informal counseling. The supervisor is a resource person in every sense of the word.

Expediting Instruction

Much of the job of supervision consists in smoothing the path of instruction. This service is a natural result of the knowledge of the needs of students and teachers, coupled with a vision of the operation and final goals of the program. The music supervisor is thus able to anticipate requests from teachers for special items of equipment or for rearrangements in the outline of the program itself. He carries requests to higher officials of the school, and fills in for teachers when emergencies arise.

THE COMPETENT MUSIC SUPERVISOR

In order to carry out the sort of task which has been outlined it is apparent that one must have a good measure of the qualifications deemed desirable in any field of music education—namely, an adequate personality, the ability to work with others, an understanding of human growth, skill in teaching, and musicianship. These need not be reviewed here in detail.

At least two additional qualifications should be sought in the music supervisor. One of these is the quality of a master teacher. If the supervisor is to command the full confidence of his associates and work effectively in the school, he needs successful experience in teaching the area which he is supervising.

The second special qualification for successful supervision is executive ability. To execute something is to carry it into effect, which is exactly what music supervision means; to carry out any supervisory task means to see that the job is done. This is an ability that teaching experience in itself will not guarantee, but it can be developed by teachers on the job who take advantage of special opportunities. This ability must be a goal of every program which purports to prepare music supervisors. The essential factor in acquiring it is practice in problem solving in the area of music education.

PRINCIPLES OF SUPERVISION

Certain principles are implicit in the conduct of supervision as it has been outlined; they are designed to avoid the pitfalls suggested at the opening of this chapter.

1. *Music supervision should be planned and operated in the interests of the objectives of the music program.* The purpose of supervision—to improve instruction—can

have meaning only in respect to the increasing competence of students.

2. *Music supervision should maintain continual evaluation of the music program.* Study of the program in operation is the means by which weaknesses may be discovered and measures taken for their correction.

3. *Music supervision should seek to create and use objective methods of improving instruction.* Techniques should be orderly and systematic; the operation should be as precise and scientific as possible.

4. *Music supervision should seek to develop the utmost capacities of both students and teachers.* Supervision works *within* the staff, promoting individual leadership and responsibility; there must be respect for human personality and the needs and interests of all.

5. *Music supervision should be conducted informally and flexibly.* The problems with which supervision must deal are so complex that no rigid pattern can be established. Methods must be devised to meet the situation, just as the relations between the individuals working together on these problems must be kept on a free, working basis.

6. *Music supervision should move gradually to produce a united effort for more effective instruction.* Supervision deals directly with the moving machinery of instruction, and hence can never be imposed as an abrupt and permanent system.

THE WORK OF SUPERVISION

Planning the Program of Supervision

The new *teacher* has relatively concrete problems to deal with; he knows in advance what subjects he will teach and should be able to plan his work to a considerable degree before instruction begins. The new *supervisor*, however, has less clearly defined duties which will crystallize largely upon the basis of professional relationships and developing problems. In a very real sense, each supervisor must carve his own niche within the local educational scene.

His efforts must be directed along these lines:

1. consulting local circumstances and expectations regarding the school and its music program
2. studying all the factors which affect the learning of students, including human nature and needs, the school and community environment, personnel, and administrative structure
3. developing provisional objectives and selecting areas of primary importance for first efforts
4. selecting the most appropriate supervisory techniques for effective solution of problems
5. formulating plans to evaluate progress continuously in specific areas

These points should be attacked simultaneously and take precedence just prior to and following the assumption of a new supervisory position.

Before classes begin.   The new supervisor should accomplish much before classes begin. It would be unsound to initiate sweeping moves at this time, but considerable groundwork can be laid. He should try to become acquainted with the school officials and staff and ascertain their conceptions of the music program. He should learn something of the expectations of those who hired him and of the work of his predecessor. He should examine student records and become familiar with the buildings, rooms, and equipment he must deal with, noting any items which are entirely inadequate or in serious need of repair. He should study established business and procedural routines of the school. He should take steps to identify himself with appropriate community groups and activities.

One problem often encountered at this stage by elementary supervisors is the exemption from music teaching that certain of the teachers may have established. The supervisor must determine whether there is any possibility that the situation can be rectified. Meanwhile, he must make temporary arrangements for other teachers to handle the assignment or to accomplish it himself.

In short, the new supervisor must orient himself so that he is ready to take constructive action as soon as possible. He must be ready for opening day with an understanding of the operation of the school and some tentative judgments about weaknesses in the music program and remedies to be applied.

After school opens.   Preliminary judgments have little reliability until confirmed and expanded in the light of actual school operations. The supervisor now has the opportunity to observe musical instruction firsthand throughout the school system, using every chance to show that he is a normal, likable human being who understands and can handle problems of musical instruction. He initiates planning for cooperative evaluation of the music program, including self-evaluation by teachers and pupils.

The supervisor should now be ready to indicate the problems which he believes are most important and can be solved. He should not be too glib about this, however, or about proclaiming remedies; the instructional staff must believe likewise that these matters can and should be improved.

In order to focus attention on these particular problems, the supervisor may initiate a testing program or group discussions or set up a demonstration class. The reader is referred to the section on the Sequence of Program Development (p. 246) for further ideas. The supervisor does, in fact, whatever the nature of the case and the personnel seem to indicate. He must capture the imagination of the teaching staff. Once sufficient momentum is created, the supervisor is ready to plan on a more exact basis.

The staff should be organized by individual assignment or committees or should work as a whole. Objectives should be drawn up to cover any weak elements of the program. A system of evaluation should be established for determining future progress in those directions. Through frank discussion of each area of the program a helpful and effective working pattern should be established for the supervisor.

In other words, the supervisor begins his full-scale program of research and experimentation; he starts to find and make available music better suited to the musical results desired; he commences intensive work with this class for more accurate music reading—and with that class for a more relaxed feeling toward music. He formulates plans and assignments for the approaching Christmas pageant.

The music supervisor has now outlined his task (although the plans will be steadily revised and extended). In the meantime he has pitched in whenever possible to help the teachers, as all supervisors do. Such activity will now become more and more consistent and purposeful.

Areas of Special Responsibility

Introduction to better materials and classroom aids.   Both teachers and supervisors tend to rely upon the easiest way, which is to follow the familiar path. Such teaching is lacking in imagination and actually tends to lose vigor with each repetition. One of the primary responsibilities of the supervisor is to bring all the human resources in the school to bear on the problem of discovering and using good musical films, new recordings, books, and other instructional materials. He should, for example, make provision for cooperative evaluation of materials by committees composed of principals, classroom teachers, and music specialists. He should encourage all persons concerned with the music program to experiment with new materials and bring them to the attention of the entire music staff. In selecting instructional materials, as in all supervisory functions, the supervisor serves not as "the authority" but rather as the coordinator of widespread efforts to improve instruction.

Promotion of better teaching plans and techniques. Improvement in the order and pattern of relationship among experiences undergone by pupils will greatly alter the learning outcomes. By means of observation, joint planning, and experimentation more favorable combinations of activity are discovered. It may be found that syllables might profitably be learned much earlier, for instance, or that notation is being introduced too formally and abruptly. These are problems in program organization which the supervisor must help to solve.

Teachers will usually be eager to try new ideas in the way of program organization or materials, but their actual method of teaching is part of themselves. There can be no direct attack on this matter, therefore. Indeed, the greatest improvement in musicianship will sometimes be achieved by the group of students who are taught by the most unlikely methods. This is the very reason why a constant program of evaluation is required.

Any shortcomings in their present style of teaching must be discovered by the teachers themselves, and to accomplish this is, of course, a major undertaking. Teachers must be led to careful observation of other teachers, to considerable professional reading, and to personal experimentation. In short, changing the behavior of teachers—like changing that of their pupils—requires a well-planned program of educative experiences rather than sharp pronouncements.

Preparation of curriculum guides.   Music program development is the primary function of music supervision. An excellent means to program development lies in the preparation of a curriculum guide.

A curriculum guide usually consists of: (1) a statement of the philosophical orientation of the educational organization for which it is being prepared, (2) a statement of program objectives, (3) suggestions of learning experiences, instructional materials, and teaching methods useful in attaining the objectives, and (4) suggestions for evaluating the results of the program.

Preparing a curriculum guide is properly a group effort. Ideally, all music teachers who will use the guide should participate in its development. In large school systems and in state-wide program development projects, however, it is necessary to select representative teachers for active work on the guide.

The preparation of a curriculum guide represents a worthwhile educational project for a number of reasons. In the first place, the process of exchanging ideas, reconciling different philosophical orientations and arriving at consensus on objectives is beneficial to participants. Secondly, the very act of writing a philosophy and specifying objectives in writing inevitably results in a higher level of clarity in thinking. Third, developing a guide brings the resources and competencies of the group to bear on the identification and solution of curricular problems. Finally, the final product serves as a unifying force in the music education program, useful to all music teachers, but of most value to teachers joining the music faculty for the first time.

Induction of new teachers.   Teachers new to a system, and especially those new to the profession, require added attention and help during their period of induction. The help required will naturally depend upon the individual and upon the type of teaching position. The supervisor must stand ready to advise and assist when asked or when the need is obvious. A great deal can be determined by the attitudes of the new appointees; those needing the most guidance may cover up either by silence or by brash confidence. It is the supervisor's job to see that the necessary aids and materials are available and that the teacher has a chance to discuss the individual students and the work of the class, and aid should be offered in planning the opening phases of instruction. Observation can be direct or oblique, as suits the occasion. In any case, the music supervisor cannot rest until a new member of the staff has actually become a full-fledged working partner.

Production of staff unity.   United effort is of major importance at the college and high school levels; it is even a more complicated matter at the elementary level, where teachers are not specialized in the field of music and may not regard themselves as part of a group attacking joint problems in music education. The answer is not necessarily found in providing occasions for group discussion and social contact. Unity comes with the discovery of common interests and problems.

The task of the supervisor is to see that these common interests and problems are highlighted and that each individual contributes to and profits from their solution. In other words, the supervisor does not handle each point as a separate matter between himself and an individual teacher. One teacher, for example, may be having difficulty with pupil concentration. The supervisor, upon inquiry, discovers that most of the other teachers are having similar difficulty. Different lines of procedure are suggested by several teachers. These are discussed, tried, and evaluated by all concerned with the problem, and the supervisor informs all the teachers of the results achieved. In this way problems are solved and greater staff unity emerges.

One result of consensus upon instructional problems may be the development of a common course of study. This helps to standardize basic sequence and materials and provides a "track to run on" for new or uncertain teachers. In Chapter Seven, however, where the construction of courses of study was discussed, it was pointed out that the truly useful course of study will be modified and embellished by the individual teacher.

In-service education.   In-service education is a broad effort; it is at once the basis for an improved program and a result of the entire supervisory effort. When properly done, the supervisor practically works himself out of his job.

Some large school systems, indeed, assume complete responsibility for on-the-job training of their new classroom teachers in music and certain other subjects. Their attendance is required at workshops, held once or twice per month during school hours under the direction of the music supervisor and his assistants. Other systems prefer to have concentrated sessions directly preceding the opening of school in fall, with extra pay for attendance.

In-service education is not an end in itself, however, and it is not to be pursued in the fashion associated with programs of teacher preparation. In-service education is of practical value to teachers because *all educative activities* are related to the actual problems which the teachers find in their own classrooms. What makes these activities deliberately educational—the workshops, planning conferences, research projects, and so on—is that they are guided by the supervisor in the manner of any worthy educational program, that is, toward specific objectives.

In other words, true in-service education is neither a sort of formal night school nor a series of random activities. The very reason why music supervisors have often been so unpopular with teachers is that they have instituted much activity that seemed to be busy work, unrelated to the daily tasks of the teachers.

Spokesmanship. The music supervisor speaks for the music program to the school officials, the parents, and the public at large; at the same time, he is in a position to help interpret for the teachers the means of carrying out school policies and legitimate public desires. There are two main requirements here: (1) effective participation at all levels in discussion and planning and (2) honest, authentic interpretation of the results. In other words, the music supervisor must take pains to find out what the teachers need and believe in order that he may represent them.

On the other hand, new professional directions, local criticisms of the music program, and administrative plans should be reported to the music staff as part of the general information from many sources that may affect their work. Failure in this task drives a wedge between the supervisor and the staff, and he finds himself in a precarious position when serious difficulties arise.

Part of the job amounts to a consistent campaign to

inform the school administration and public about the nature and purpose of music instruction. The object is to build favorable attitudes toward the values of school music which will support later requests for assistance. It is too late to bring up the topic of aesthetic sensitivity when the music budget has just been cut. The supervisor is also exercising spokesmanship when he arranges concerts, exhibits, and guest performances of students. He must make sure that programs are well planned, representative of the best work of students, adequately publicized, and well presented. The supervisor must always proceed with the thought in mind that the purpose of these enterprises is not to entertain the public nor to bring credit to himself or even to the teachers but to provide both an opportunity for enriching the educative experiences of students and a chance for others to evaluate the work of the music program.

Major Supervisory Techniques

The general type of work identified with music supervision has just been outlined. No attempt, however, has been made to describe fully the ways in which such duties may be handled. The methods to be used will vary with the circumstances. The techniques themselves can be indicated, however, and related to their possible use in the work of supervision.

Everyone does not work in the same way. Some people seem to lead by inspiration, making mistakes but never failing to command the best efforts of their associates; others are tireless workers and thinkers, and their enterprises move like well-oiled machines. In accomplishing supervision, this first type of individual will improvise much of the detail, but he should also give preliminary thought to these questions:

1. How may I find out what needs to be done?
2. How may I proceed to do these things?
3. How may I discover and correct my errors?

These are all engineering questions, dealing with techniques for accomplishing a specified task. The answers are
found in the proper use and combination of the basic supervisory tools.

Observation.   Observation, in the broad sense, is perhaps the
primary tool of the music supervisor. One can see and hear
and take testimony in many situations: class visitation, talk '
ing with students, talking with teachers, talking with parents
and friends, attending musical performances, examining stu
dent work and records, and examining teachers' plans.

Observation is one excellent way of gathering evidence
required to decide what needs to be done and to determine
whether the measures taken are working. It may also have the
desirable active result of producing in other individuals an
awareness of the supervisor's interest and concern. In other
words, people who are being observed tend to perform better
and with greater purposiveness, unless they perceive the observer as critical or hostile.

Part of this information is objective enough to be recorded, and making records is one method of adding to the
usefulness of observation. Whenever a specific answer is
sought, all pertinent evidence should be recorded for more
accurate interpretation in answering the question.

Testing.   Testing is a means of gathering precise data. Tests
are often valuable for purposes of selecting students, motivating them, and determining the extent of their progress.
Results may be used in the guidance of pupils and in revising
classroom practices.

It is important that standardized tests be selected and
self-made tests be constructed which bear relation to the
information sought. The extent of a person's musical knowledge, for example, is comparatively simple to test; one's
attitudes and appreciation for music, however, can hardly be
determined by a few direct and objective questions. Even

musical capacity can not be judged solely on the measurable ability to detect small differences in pitch, loudness, and so on.

Research.   Much effort on the part of supervisors and teachers might be classified as research. Such efforts would include any deliberate investigation aimed at discovery of a solid basis for the music program. It is valuable, for instance, to study and experiment with various psychological principles relating to musical growth of children. The sequence of musical activity should not be based upon rule of thumb but upon active experimentation.

The practices of other schools, expert opinion, and experimental research reports may be useful, but these findings must be evaluated in terms of local application. Many teachers feel that true research is conducted only in laboratories and fail to see that their own classrooms are the most practical laboratories. If one wants to know when and how to start instrumental instruction, let him experiment with different age groups and methods. When conditions are carefully controlled and results are sensibly gathered and interpreted, this constitutes legitimate action research. [3]

Individual consultation.   Here are some of the things music supervisors accomplish through individual contact with students and colleagues:

1. arranging details; passing information
2. receiving assistance and counsel
3. ascertaining the extent of problems
4. explaining procedures
5. giving encouragement and recognition
6. providing answers to questions

---

[3] See Stephen M. Corey, *Action Research to Improve School Practices*, Bureau of Publications, Teachers College, Columbia University, New York, 1953; and Association for Supervision and Curriculum Development, *Research for Curriculum Development*, National Education Association, Washington, 1957.

7. arriving at joint decisions
8. discovering areas of mutual agreement and disagreement
9. giving direct aid; coaching
10. outlining plans and assignments

To consult or confer it is not necessary to face one another across a desk by appointment. These are simply ordinary business conversations, to be carried on in the normal surroundings of the day's work. It is a most natural means of communication between co-workers, and its very commonness can make it effective in avoiding the formalistic and limiting tone of the staff meeting or office memorandum.

Group sessions. Two considerations are basic in group deliberations: (1) that conditions be such that each individual brings his special knowledge and abilities to the matter at hand, and (2) that one's position be overruled only when clearly unacceptable to the group and after he has had full opportunity to promote his point of view.

In spite of the often unwieldy character of group sessions they can be used more advantageously than individual consultation in several respects: (1) gaining open and official sanction to act, (2) discovering new points of view, (3) direct and efficient distributing of information, and (4) achieving a unified philosophy or esprit de corps.

If group sessions are to have this effect, however, music supervisors should consider certain points in addition to the basic principle of democratic procedure. First, meetings should include only those individuals directly concerned with the matters at hand. For instance, vocal instructors should not be asked to sit through a meeting concerned only with problems pertaining to the instrumental program. Second, it is seldom wise to schedule regular sessions, because problems do not arise on schedule. Third, problems should be outlined for presentation to the group, so that there is no unnecessary misunderstanding. Sometimes the essential facts need to be written up and distributed with the call to the meeting for prior consideration. Fourth, the music supervisor should refrain from "preparing" individuals to present certain points of view or to propose certain actions; this is only autocracy in disguise. Last, it is often a valuable practice to distribute a short written summary of the viewpoints discussed and decisions made, in order that the members of the group may review and confirm their understanding.

Demonstration.   Demonstration is a favorite method of instructing others through illustration of facts or principles related to their actual usage. For instance, a music supervisor may find it practical to demonstrate how a song may be taught, how an opaque projector is operated, how to devise plans for teaching performance skills, or how a student's music-reading difficulties may be diagnosed. It is important that the teachers know what to look for in the demonstration.

Demonstration conditions should be as realistic as possible, because the application is more readily apparent. Thus it is better to demonstrate methods of teaching a song through using students, rather than their teachers, as subjects. For the same reason it is often better for one of the regular teachers, rather than the supervisor, to do the demonstrating. Not only will conditions more nearly approach normality, but the observers are also more likely to credit the possibility that they can do the same thing.

Occasions arise, however, when the music supervisor must assume responsibility for demonstrating new techniques and materials. He should not shirk the responsibility on the theory that it is "showing off," for that quality of behavior can only be deduced from the manner in which the demonstrator proceeds. It must never be forgotten that a prime requisite for the supervisory task is that one can do himself whatever is asked of the teachers.

Experimental classes.   Experimental classes constitute a form of research combined with extended demonstration. In effect, certain conclusions are reached which seem excellent in theory but must be tried, confirmed, and revised before being introduced as aspects of the regular program. Whether the trial can really be termed effective depends upon two matters: (1) the extent to which the group of students resembles other groups to which the change may later be applied, and (2) the extent to which the alteration can be limited to a single factor.

In other words, a truly experimental class should contain students of the same age, intelligence, socioeconomic background, and measurable musical competence as another group. So far as is humanly possible, the teaching is the same for both groups, except for one thing. For example, one group may have a regular twenty-minute listening session per week, while members of the other class may listen individually with earphones to the same material. After a period of time, achievement is measured, and any significant differences in knowledge and appreciation should be traceable to the method of instruction.

This stringent application of research procedure is seldom possible or needful in schools. The more feasible approach is for the supervisor or a teacher with new ideas regarding the way music theory, music history, or some other area of music should be taught to form a class and teach it. Other teachers observe the teaching and evaluate the learning achieved. In this way a climate favorable to general reformation of instruction may be secured.

Workshops.   Long-range, persistent problems pertaining to the music program may require the use of workshops. These projects really constitute a form of the group process, combined with aspects of research and demonstration which have already been discussed. They can be an excellent means to the in-service education of teachers, the promotion of better methods and materials, and the basic study of human growth and the learning process.

The term workshop carries bad connotations to some teachers and supervisors. They have attended too many poorly conceived sessions devoted to lecturing and busy work—

without pay and on their own time. Real workshops arise spontaneously, the teachers are self-motivated in their work, and results are concrete. Real workshops are rare but wonderful occasions.

Several conditions have been found to favor "successful group activity leading to program improvement":

A first and basic condition for enlistment and for keeping the members of a staff interested is that the jobs on which they work should truly seem to them to be their jobs, tasks the accomplishment of which seems both appropriate and important. . . .

A second condition is that individuals should work on jobs where they can make a positive contribution. . . .

A third condition . . . is that a high degree of flexibility should be maintained with reference to all group activity and all related individual activity . . . considerable freedom to shift emphasis as a result of experience is an essential condition to progress. . . .

A fourth condition . . . is that people should work as friends and equals; equals in the sense of assurance of mutual acceptance without regard to title or position. . . .

A fifth condition . . . is that the means of converting thought into action should be such as to permit a reasonably easy and continuous flow. . . .[4]

Briefly put, successful workshops are practical, flexible, relaxed, and aimed at real changes in the educational program; when these conditions are not present, interest and purpose are soon lost.

Specially prepared materials. The music supervisor may find it helpful to make up special bulletins, bibliographies, lists of musical materials, and other compilations for the teachers. Although there is an impersonality about written

---

[4]Charles E. Prall and C. Leslie Cushman, *Teacher Education in Service,* American Council on Education, Washington, 1944, pp. 442-445.

material, many ideas are not so well transmitted by word of mouth. Many things once discussed, as a matter of fact, need to be organized and set down in concrete fashion in order to help produce action.

Here are some of the kinds of special communications which the music supervisor may need to distribute:

1. outline of decisions reached by the staff
2. procedural detail in securing instructional supplies, printed music, teaching aids and services, etc.
3. notice and confirmation of meetings, plans, deadlines, etc.
4. graded lists of new musical materials, with comments
5. lists of recommended books and magazine articles
6. check lists or other questionnaires asking for information affecting the music program
7. tables, graphs, and summaries of evaluative data which have been gathered
8. brief digests of important research affecting instruction

Material must be presented in a way that readers will understand. Furthermore, the effect will be in direct proportion to the quality of the supervisor's preparation and follow-up. That is, if the staff decisions are not implemented, if recommended musical materials are never discussed or tried, if procedures are constantly bypassed and deadlines postponed, the teachers will learn to ignore the bulletins and lists that are prepared for them.

Joint musical projects.   Opportunities afforded by combined musical events should be fully exploited. Not only do such enterprises create the means to enrich student experiences, but they can also greatly step up the processes of observation and exchange of ideas among the music staff. In a sense, the regular classroom patterns are temporarily suspended or supplemented by fresh, new influences; a new frame of reference is introduced. In preparing for a Christmas concert, for example, teachers have to decide upon the music to be presented; many jobs in connection with the concert itself become special responsibilities of particular teachers; students and teachers judge their work in comparison with that of other groups; combined groups offer a test of the effectiveness of teachers; new insights are formed. Joint concerts, all-school operettas and pageants, visiting-day exhibits, clinics, and festivals are affairs of this type.

Such projects should not consume an inordinate amount of school time nor upset school schedules. When teachers have prepared their students and when the timing is figured, the music in the folders and on the racks, the stage arrangements set, and the necessary announcements planned, the rehearsal time can be very short. Schools can profit from the example of professional organizations, which operate of necessity in this way.

The supervisor must take an important part in the planning but needs to allow much rein to the initiative of individual teachers. At all costs, the supervisor must not dominate the performance itself.

Outside assistance.   When the teachers and the supervisor do not possess the abilities or insights necessary to solve certain problems in instruction, it is time to call upon someone else for assistance. Special consultants are sometimes valuable in setting desirable change in motion; visiting clinicians can often reinforce and open up new avenues to musical experience for both students and teachers; commercial display of musical materials and equipment can often be arranged to assist in promoting understanding and use of these items.

SUMMARY

The conduct of supervison often reflects vague understanding on the part of supervisors and their colleagues. It is an extremely important function and should be designed to improve the teaching-learning process. One works with and within the staff in solving problems directly affecting instruction.

The job is typically confined to the elementary, secondary, or college level or assigned in terms of instrumental and vocal fields. Each of these plans has certain strengths and weaknesses.

The process of supervision is one of analyzing, advising, enlisting, stimulating, and expediting. It requires the services of a musical expert—one who has the qualities necessary to the music teacher plus successful teaching experience and executive ability. His activity should be purposeful, scientific, and democratic.

The new supervisor must plan his work, determining its goals, first problems to attack, and procedures he can best use. He promotes the use of better materials and teaching methods. In-service education is one part of the job, along with the induction of new teachers. Other areas of service include the development of a more unified staff, more professional activity, and spokesmanship for the staff.

The music supervisor has many tools with which to accomplish his job. He observes and measures, conducts research, consults with individuals and groups, provides demonstrations and experimental classes, organizes workshops, keeps necessary and useful information before the staff, develops joint musical projects, and engages outside assistance when needed.

QUESTIONS FOR DISCUSSION

1. What duties besides supervision commonly fall to the music supervisor? Would you call him more of a teacher or an administrator? How greatly do the responsibilities vary from school to school? What are some of the causes of this variation?

2. What is the essential task of supervision, as distinct from administration? Have you observed weaknesses in its performance?

3. To what degree do teachers need supervision? What forms has this assistance taken?

4. Why do we usually think first of the elementary school

in connection with supervision? Would it be better on the whole to have specialists to teach elementary school music? Do you consider it more effective to organize supervision separately in the vocal and instrumental fields?

5. Describe the general supervisory process. What special qualifications does this kind of job require?

6. What steps may be taken by the new music supervisor in planning his operation? By what means does he discover what is needed and how his efforts are succeeding?

7. In what direct ways can the music supervisor be of help to the teachers? Why does he do these things?

8. Describe the various tools or techniques which may be applied by the music supervisor. Is any one of these an end in itself? How does one know which technique to use at a given time?

SELECTED REFERENCES

Benjamin, D. "Take Inventory of Your Supervisory Program: A Psychological Approach," *National Elementary Principals* 47, Fall 1968, pp. 33-35.

Brown, E. J. "Do It By Suggestion: Improvement of Supervising and Teaching Practices By Indirection," *Clearing House* 42, October 1967, pp. 110-115.

Committee on Public Relations in Music Education. *The Music Teacher and Public Relations*, Music Educators National Conference, Washington, 1958.

Eye, Glen G., and Lenore A. Netzer. *Supervision of Instruction: A Phase of Administration*, Harper & Row, New York, 1965.

Franseth, Jane. *Supervision as Leadership*, Harper & Row, New York, 1961.

Hanson, E. L. "Responsibilities of Supervision," *School Musician* 38, March 1967, pp. 70-71.

Harris, Ben M. *Supervisory Behavior in Education*, Prentice-Hall, Inc., Englewood Cliffs, N.J., 1963.

Herman, Edward J. *Supervising Music in the Elementary School*, Prentice-Hall, Inc., Englewood Cliffs, N.J., 1965.

Marcus, C. M. "Supervising Is Learning," *Michigan Educators Journal* 45, Fall 1968, pp. 20-21.

McKean, Robert C., and H. H. Mills. *The Supervisor*, Center for Applied Research in Education, Washington, 1964.

Snider, Keith D. *School Music Administration and Supervision*, 2d ed., Allyn & Bacon, Inc., Boston, 1965.

Sybouts, W. "Supervision and Team Teaching," *Education Leadership* 25, November 1967, pp. 158-159.

Weyland, Rudolph H. *A Guide to Effective Music Supervision*, William C. Brown Co., Dubuque, Iowa, 1968.

Evaluation in
Music Education

11 Testing of some kind has always been an integral
part of the educative process. Oral tests, essay examinations, and objective tests of achievement and
aptitude represent approaches to testing widely used
in schools over the years.

Early American schools relied largely on oral tests conducted by school committees and by teachers, but the difficulty of administering such tests to the growing school population and the criticism of the tests by educators on the
grounds of their lack of uniformity and accuracy led to the
wide use of essay examinations.

The first decade of the twentieth century saw the beginning of a large group of studies which revealed a shocking
lack of reliability in the scoring of written school examinations. Studies involving examinations in mathematics, English, and other subjects showed that not only did different
scorers assign widely varying marks to the same examination
paper, but teachers also assigned different marks when they
regraded papers of their own pupils without knowledge of
the marks they had previously given. The revelation of the
deplorable state of existing examinations, the influence of
such men as J. M. Rice and Edward L. Thorndike, and the

school-survey movement gave impetus to the educational-measurement movement.[1]

In February, 1918, Thorndike published what has proved to be probably the most influential paper that has ever appeared on educational measurement. In the "Seventeenth Yearbook of the National Society for the Study of Education: Part Two" (1918) he began with the dictum, "Whatever exists exists in some amount and can be measured," and called for understanding of quantitative thinking in education and for active experimental work to improve educational measurement.

Since 1918 educational measurement has undergone startling development, and tremendous strides have been made in the development and application of tests of many types. More recently educators have realized that adequate pupil appraisal involves more than the construction, administration, and scoring of valid and reliable measurement tools and that attention must be given to the formulation of instructional objectives, the definition of objectives in terms of pupil behavior, and the development of techniques to evaluate the behavioral outcomes. As a result, the term evaluation has come into wide use. Thus, three successive phases in the development of techniques for pupil appraisal can be identified: testing, measuring, and evaluating.

EVALUATION DEFINED

Evaluation is the process of determining the extent to which the objectives of an educational enterprise have been attained. It involves three steps: (1) the identification, formulation, and validation of objectives; (2) the collection of data relevant to status in relation to those objectives; and (3) the interpretation of the data collected.

Measurement refers to the use of evaluative tools the results of which are precise, objective, and quantitative. The

---

[1] For an excellent and concise survey of the historical development of educational measurement, see Julian C. Stanley, *Measurement in Today's Schools*, Prentice-Hall, Inc., Englewood Cliffs, N.J., 1964.

data from measurement tools are stated in terms of amount, number, and so on, and lend themselves to statistical treatment. Thus measurement represents a means of gathering data and is frequently used in accomplishing the second step in the evaluative process. If measurement tools relevant to the objectives of the music program are available, they should by all means be employed. Owing, however, to the comprehensive nature of the objectives of music education and the lack of tools to measure many of them, music educators must frequently employ less precise and less objective observation al techniques to gather data.

Previous chapters of this book have emphas zed the importance of valid and clearly stated objectives in program planning and instruction. In evaluation the role of objectives is even more clear-cut because of the fact that no status, however precisely measured, has meaning except in relation to an objective. Thus, the music teacher must begin with clearly stated objectives of instruction in order to know what data to collect.

Data should be collected only to determine status in relation to objectives. Routine testing which gives no information on pupil status in relation to a specific objective has no place in the music program.

The interpretation of data involves logical-philosophical thinking by which the teacher arrives at sound conclusions on the basis of the data collected. Results of the interpretation are used to guide the musical development of pupils and to appraise the effectiveness of the music program and the teaching methods used and to make indicated modifications in them.

Evaluative tools include tests, score cards, achievement scales, rating scales, observations, logs, interviews, case histories, anecdotal records, check lists, and other procedures by which observations are made and judgments recorded.

THE USES OF EVALUATION

Evaluation has a number of important uses in the music education program. They include the appraisal of pupil progress, pupil guidance, motivation, the improvement of instruction, the maintenance of standards, and research.

Appraisal of pupil progresss.   We have taken the position that the purpose of the music education program is to promote musical learning. A teacher who accepts this proposition must take steps to determine to what extent musical learning takes place in his pupils. Only through evaluation can he gain insight into the success of musical experiences provided in the music program and of teaching techniques he uses.

Guidance.   Like all teachers the music teacher has the responsibility for guiding pupils. The guidance problems he encounters include assisting pupils in choosing musical activities in school, electing specialized musical opportunities in and out of school, and deciding whether to pursue a professional career in music. In order to provide intelligent guidance the music teacher must have the fullest possible information on the capacities, interests, and accomplishments of pupils. Only continuous and comprehensive evaluation can provide the teacher and the pupil with the needed information.

Motivation.   Chapter Five, "Foundations of Musical Learning," and Chapter Seven, "Methods of Teaching Music," have emphasized that the pupil, in order to be highly motivated, must be aware of and accept the objectives of instruction and must know his status in relation to the objectives. To the latter end constant evaluation by the pupil himself and by the teacher is essential.

Evaluative procedures affect directly the amount and direction of effort expended by pupils. If there is a lack of consistency between the avowed objectives of instruction and the evaluative procedures used, pupils are likely to accept as the real objectives those implied by the evaluative procedures. For example, if a music teacher proclaims broad objectives for elementary school music but tests only knowledge of sol-fa syllables, the pupils are likely to view passing the tests as their real objective and pass over the other objectives even as the teacher does in evaluating pupil progress. Thus, in order to secure high levels of motivation the teacher must ascertain that there is consistency between objectives and evaluation and that all objectives are included in the evaluative procedures used.

Improvement of instruction. The authors have repeatedly stated their conviction that the measure of successful teaching is pupil progress toward the objectives of instruction. Evaluation provides the principal means for the teacher to determine the worth of the musical experiences he organizes for his pupils and the validity of his teaching methods. Furthermore, it enables him to identify strengths and weaknesses in his methods of teaching and his instructional materials.

Evaluation on a broad scale provides a means for determining the worth of the entire program of music education. It involves determining the validity of program objectives and the extent to which the musical competencies implied by the objectives are being established in pupils.

Maintenance of standards. The term standards has many different connotations and is frequently bandied about carelessly and without precise definition. Standards in music education are properly considered as attainment goals. They can only be set logically through agreement on values, since, for the most part, they have not yet been objectively determined nor can they be set in terms of test scores with currently available tests.

Music education requires flexible standards adaptable to individual differences in ability and goals. Although the maintenance of standards represents a legitimate function of evaluation in music education, music educators should exercise great care in applying standards. When applied without regard to individual differences, standards may actually hinder musical development.

Music educators should work together to establish standards for music literature used in the music program, performance difficulty of compositions, tone quality, music-reading ability, and other musical behaviors. The individual teacher should make every effort to uphold legitimate standards and, especially, to reveal to pupils standards expected in the different phases of musical endeavor.

Research.   Music education is urgently in need of well-conceived research at every level of the program. Evaluation represents a crucial item in all research, since the soundness of the conclusions reached depends directly upon the validity of the evaluative procedures used.

The importance of evaluation in the music education program should be clearly established. It is essential that all music teachers develop a clear understanding of the evaluative process, that they be well informed about available evaluative procedures, and that they evaluate thoroughly and systematically all phases of the music education program.

Factors in selecting evaluative tools.   In selecting evaluative tools several factors must be considered. These include the relevance of the tools to the objectives of the music program, validity, reliability, objectivity, administrative economy, and cost.

Relevance.   It is essential that the objectives of the music program be clearly established before evaluative procedures are selected. Without objectives, evaluation and measurement are worse than useless, since the data can have significance only as they reveal status in relation to objectives. Thus the first criterion for a test or other type of evaluative tool is the *relevance* of the resulting data to one or more of the objectives of the music program. That is, does the test reveal significant information on the status of pupils in relation to the objectives of the program? For example, a given test of musical information may have real value in an advanced class in music literature, because it is relevant to the objectives of that particular course, but have no place in a secondary school general music class or a performing activity.

Each objective implies the type of evaluative procedure which is relevant to its evaluation. Succeeding sections on each area of musical learning will consider specifically the choice of evaluative tools. It suffices here to establish the necessity for determining the relevance of the information revealed by an evaluative procedure to the objectives of the program.

Validity.   An evaluative tool is valid to the extent that it measures what it purports to measure. Two types of validity must be considered, *statistical validity* and *curricular validity*. Statistical validity is determined by comparing test scores with criteria such as school marks, teacher ratings, differences in scores obtained by two or more groups known to vary greatly in ability, and scores on similar tests. The greater the correlation between test scores and the criterion measure, the greater the validity of a test. For example, scores on tests of musical aptitude have been compared with such criteria as teachers' estimates of musical aptitude and grades in music courses to establish the validity of the tests. Statistical validity is described in terms of a coefficient of correlation which may range from −1.00 through zero to +1.00.

Curricular validity, a concept frequently used in connection with standardized achievement tests, depends upon the content of the test rather than test scores. To establish curricular validity, test content is compared with courses of study, statements of objectives, analyses of the content of textbooks, pooled judgment of qualified persons, and other significant criteria. The extent of curricular validity determines how accurately and comprehensively a test measures achievement in accomplishing the objectives of a course of instruction.

Reliability.   *Reliability* refers to the consistency with which a test measures whatever it measures. Any test measures something, and if it does so consistently, it is reliable, even though it may not measure what it purports to measure. Thus a test may be reliable without being valid, but to be valid it must of necessity have some degree of reliability. The concept of validity includes reliability, but reliability does not necessarily include validity.

The reliability of a test is established by securing at least two measures of the same group of pupils using the same instrument, by administering two parallel forms of the test to the same group, or by the split-test method. In the last method the items of a single test are divided into halves, and two scores are obtained for each person taking the test. The agreement between the two sets of scores provides the basis for estimating the reliability of the test. Reliability is stated in terms of a coefficient of correlation.

Other factors.   Relevance, validity, and reliability are closely interrelated and represent the most important factors in the selection of an evaluative procedure. Several other factors, however, must be considered before a decision is made to use a test or other evaluative tool. These include objectivity, time requirement, cost, and the availability of equivalent forms.

Objectivity refers to the degree of uniformity with which different teachers may score the same tests. The less the chance for variations in scoring, the greater the reliability of a test. Some excellent tests require so much time to administer and score that they intrude seriously on the time available for instruction. Financial cost involved in securing equipment, materials, and personnel to administer and score the test must also be considered. All other things being equal, the choice of the least expensive test is indicated, but validity should never be sacrificed for financial reasons.

Since it is frequently desirable to make provision for retesting after a lapse of time, the availability of equivalent forms of a test is also highly desirable. This is especially true in testing pupil achievement and in evaluating methods of teaching and materials of instruction.

Procedure for selecting an evaluative tool.   The first step in selecting an evaluative tool is to determine precisely the purpose of the evaluation. These may include appraising musical aptitude, musical achievement, the worth of teaching materials, the success of teaching methods, the value of the music program, and so on. Once the purpose is clear the teacher should seek out all available tools which suit his purpose. The *Mental Measurements Yearbooks*[2] provide critical evaluations by competent experts of many standardized tests in the field of music. Other sources of information include reports in professional journals such as *Journal of Research in Music Education, Educational and Psychological Measurement, Journal of Educational Research, Review of Educational Research*, and publications of the American Educational Research Association. Perusing publications of this type gives the teacher the kind of preliminary information required in intelligent test selection. On the basis of this information he should secure and examine personally the tests which seem to meet his requirements.

He should inquire carefully into the relevance, validity, and reliability of the test. After personally taking the test, he can judge whether it is material to his purposes. Information on the validity of a test should be included in the manual accompanying the test. This should include how the test items were selected, what criteria were used in validating the test, and the degree of validity established between the test content and test scores and the criteria employed. The degree of reliability required for a test depends somewhat on the way in which the data are to be used. If a test is being used for individual measurement, the reliability coefficient obviously must be higher than if it is being used for group measurement. Although testing authorities are reluctant to

---

[2] Oscar K. Buros, ed., *Second, Third, Fourth, Fifth, and Sixth Mental Measurements Yearbooks*, Gryphon Press, Highland Park, N.J., 1941, 1949, 1953, 1959, 1965, respectively, and subsequent editions.

give specific guides to reliability coefficients, there seems to be consensus on the soundness of the following prescription:

.85 - .99 high to very high; of value for individual measurement and diagnosis

.80 - .84 fairly high; of some value in individual measurement and highly satisfactory for group measurement

.70 - .79 rather low; adequate for group measurement but of doubtful value in individual measurement

.50 - .69 low; inadequate for individual measurement but of some value in group measurement

below .50 very low; inadequate for use

There is a tendency on the part of some test makers and test users to overemphasize the importance of reliability and to give insufficient attention to validity. Teachers should bear in mind that the reliability of a test makes little difference unless the test is valid and relevant to his purposes. Some manuals accompanying tests of musical aptitude and musical achievement give impressive and detailed statistics on reliability and rarely mention validity. When this is the case and when test authors fail to give specific information on validity and reliability, one is usually justified in assuming that the unmentioned quality has not been established and that the test is of doubtful value.

Once the teacher has satisfied himself concerning the relevance, validity, and reliability of one or more tests, he can make his final selection on the basis of cost, time required, availability of duplicate forms, and any other administrative considerations.

THE EVALUATION OF STUDENTS

The evaluation of students includes evaluating musical capacity and musical learning. The former has received an intensive research effort, and tests of musical capacity are widely used, principally to select students for specialized musical opportunities. The development of tests of musical learning has been, on the whole, sporadic, but encouraging achievements have been made in the area.

Evaluating Musical Capacity

The testing of musical capacity has been marked by controversy on three issues: (1) the nature of musical capacity, (2) the ways in which such tests should be validated, and (3) the use of the tests in the music program.

Seashore constructed his tests on the basis of a theory that musical talent consists of a number of separate capacities, including the ability to make fine discriminations of differences in pitch, loudness, timbre, and so on. He hypothesized that a person who can make such discriminations should also be a fine musician. Schoen takes a similar view of the nature of musical capacity but identifies the specific talents differently. Mursell, with his consistent field-theory orientation, did not agree with this theory of specific capacities. He held that "musicality depends on and consists of an awareness of tonal-rhythmic configurations or tonal patterns and an emotional responsiveness thereto."[3] Lundin more recently has stated his conviction that musical ability consists of "a number of acquired interrelated behaviors built up through a process of interaction of individual organisms with musical stimuli throughout the life history."[4]

These positions imply disagreement over whether musical capacity is composed of several specific abilities or is a unified coordinated phenomenon and whether musical capacity results principally from native endowment or musical experience. Neither question can be settled definitively with presently available knowledge.

[3] James L. Mursell, *The Psychology of Music*, W. W. Norton & Company, Inc., New York, 1937, p. 49.

[4] Robert W. Lundin, *An Objective Psychology of Music*, The Ronald Press Company, New York, 1953, p. 176.

Vigorous controversy has likewise grown out of differing conceptions of the validity of tests of musical capacity and of ways of establishing it. Mursell holds that the tests should be validated in relation to external criteria such as the ability to sing at sight, piano-playing facility, and other musical competencies.[5] Seashore maintains that measures of such external criteria may be less reliable than the tests themselves and that the real criterion of the validity of his tests lies in their internal consistency.[6] The weight of professional opinion seems to support Mursell's position on this issue.

A third issue centers around the question of what use tests of musical capacity have in the music education program. Some music educators believe that the tests should be used as a basis for the selection of pupils for specialized musical opportunities. For example, the Rochester, New York, public schools have for many years used the *Seashore Measures of Musical Talent*, teachers' estimates of musical excellence, average grades, and other factors to identify pupils with musical talent. Larson believes that the program has resulted in a high level of performance achievement for gifted pupils and a saving in time and energy of pupils, teachers, and parents.[7]

Other music educators reject tests of musical capacity, either because of doubts concerning their validity or because of a conviction that all pupils should be permitted to begin specialized instruction on the basis of their interest, regardless of their scores on tests of musical capacity. According to the latter view no pupil should be deprived of special musical opportunities, even though he cannot meet an arbitrary standard. The point is frequently made that all kinds of musical

[5] James L. Mursell, "What about Music Tests?" *Music Educators Journal* 24:16-18, November 1937.

[6] Carl E. Seashore, "The Psychology of Music: XI" *Music Educators Journal* 24:25-26, December 1937

[7] Ruth C. Larson, "Finding and Guiding Musical Talent," *Music Educators Journal* 42:22-25, September 1955.

experience have value for all pupils and that each pupil should have the opportunity to pursue his musical interests, even though he may never develop into a superior musician.

It seems reasonable to emphasize the fact that many factors besides capacity operate in determining success in musical performance and other special musical activities. A pupil with a moderate level of musical capacity and high levels of motivation and interest frequently accomplishes more than the most talented pupil lacking in interest and motivation.

Another point to consider is whether limiting the opportunities of pupils with moderate or even low levels of musical capacity is consistent with the purposes of general education and music education in our American democracy.

The decision to use or not to use tests of musical capacity requires careful consideration of all the factors involved and should not be taken lightly. The conclusion of the present authors is that such tests should never be used as a sole factor in screening pupils for specialized musical opportunities. Using test results as one source of evidence, along with all other available information about the pupil which bears on his potential for successful and rewarding experience with music, may be advisable under one condition: The test used should have demonstrated validity in relation to significant external criteria, and the reliability coefficient should meet the standards required for significance in individual and group guidance. It is, furthermore, urgent that teachers use extreme caution in interpreting and using test results.

A carefully compiled cumulative record of pupil achievement in music can provide a high level of insight into both musical capacity and other factors important in success with music. Such a record is especially valuable if the elementary school music program includes varied exploratory experience in all phases of music, including keyboard, instrumental, and creative experiences.

A relatively recent development in musical aptitude testing requires comment at this point. Several commercial tests have appeared on the market designed specifically for use in recruiting pupils for the instrumental music program. Some of these tests have been published without an effort to establish their validity or reliability. While it is not germane to our purpose to discuss the ethics of recruiting practices, it appears obvious that tests of musical capacity constructed and published without rigorous effort to establish validity and reliability have no place in the music education program. Their use for any purpose whatsoever cannot be rationally justified.

Selected tests of musical aptitude are listed at the end of the chapter.

Evaluating Musical Learning

It is essential that teachers evaluate all kinds of learning implied by instructional objectives. These may include appreciation, musical knowledge, musical understanding, skills of listening, skills of performance, attitudes, and initiative. The breadth of objectives for a given musical activity governs the scope of evaluation. For example, a general music class should probably include objectives in all the areas of musical learning mentioned, and a comprehensive evaluation program would need to appraise pupil status and pupil progress in all of them. From time to time primary emphasis might properly be given to a single type—for example, skills of listening—and during that period evaluation would logically be focused primarily on that type of learning. On a long-range basis, however, both objectives and evaluation should be comprehensive in scope.

In more highly specialized musical activities evaluative procedures are properly directed primarily toward appraising the specialized learning desired, but related types of learning should not be ignored either in the development of objectives or in the appraisal of pupil progress. For example, the teacher of an instrumental class has as his basic objective the development of performance skill, but this does not mean that he can rightly neglect musical understanding, appreciation, or skills of listening either in instruction or in evaluation. The point is that all musical instruction, whether general or specialized in nature, should be focused on the development of broad musicianship, even though the principal focus of a given activity is on one specialized aspect of musicianship. Fine musicianship is an integrated behavior, and musical instruction should result in integrated learning. That is, every phase of musical instruction, whether general or specialized, should assist the learner in pulling together and refining *all* his musical learning and in applying it to the musical problems he encounters. For example, a voice teacher is primarily concerned with the development of skill in singing, but if he discovers that a pupil is deficient in his ability to read music or has a low level of musical understanding, he should do more than censure the theory teacher; he should point the instruction partly toward removing these deficiencies. Obviously he cannot turn the vocal lesson into a theory class, but he should work toward improving the pupil's general musicianship as well as his performance skill. Thus, as his objectives are broadened, his evaluative procedures should likewise include evaluation of the pupil's progress in music reading and musical understanding.

It is essential that evaluative procedures be consistent with the avowed objectives of instruction and that the teacher discover means for evaluating status and progress in relation to all the objectives. Excellent published evaluative tools are available in appraising some aspects of musical learning, but serious gaps in the evaluation of musical learning remain. As a result, the music teacher must frequently supplement published tools by constructing his own tests and other evaluative tools and by employing informal observation as a means to evaluation.

The following sections consider the evaluation of each type of musical learning and present suggestions for techniques of evaluation. Selected published tests and scales are listed at the end of the chapter.

Evaluating musical knowledge.   Musical knowledge represents an important aspect of musical learning and is essential in the development of musicianship. Some teachers, however, tend to limit evaluation to testing knowledge and to overemphasize its importance. If the objectives of a given course of musical instruction include the accumulation of knowledge, and most will to some extent, results in that direction should by all means be evaluated, but knowledge testing should not dominate the evaluation program.

Several tests of musical knowledge have been published and standardized and may be useful in the music education program if the teacher selects a test clearly relevant to the objectives of instruction. The proper sequence is to determine the objectives and then seek a test that measures status in relation to them, rather than to select a test first and derive objectives from the test content.

Teachers should probably rely largely on tests of their own making, which can have unique levels of curricular validity and relevance to their instructional objectives.[8]

Evaluating appreciation. Appreciation of the expressive import of music is revealed by the quality of performance, by the ability to make valid value judgments of performance and compositions, and to an extent by the degree of absorption a person exhibits during a musical experience. The evaluation of appreciation involves identifying overt behaviors and knowledge and understanding which can logically be associated with appreciation.

The following criteria for evaluating appreciation seem reasonable: Is the pupil deeply moved and closely attentive during musical experience? Does his performance reveal the consistent movement of the line? Can he develop arrangements and accompaniments for performance on his own level that increase the expressive appeal? Can he make judgments of musical compositions and musical performances which approximate the judgments of connoisseurs of music?

Hevner's tests of aesthetic appreciation[9] represent an

---

[8] For excellent instructions on test construction see Norman E. Gronlund, *Constructing Achievement Tests*, Prentice-Hall, Inc., Englewood Cliffs, N.J., 1968.

[9] Kate Hevner (Mueller), "Tests of Aesthetic Appreciation in Music," *Journal of Applied Psychology* 14:470-477, 1930.

excellent approach to measuring some aspects of appreciation. At the present time, however, teachers must rely largely on setting up their own testing situations. This can be accomplished by playing several compositions of the same type, judged by connoisseurs to vary in quality, and asking pupils to state their own preferences. The same technique can be applied to recordings of the same compositions which vary in quality.

Informal appraisal of appreciation can be accomplished in performance-group and applied-music instruction by varying the interpretation of a composition and asking pupils to select the most expressive one. Significant inferences concerning appreciation may be drawn through observing the attitude, the level of concentration, and the intensity of the affective response of pupils during performance and listening experience.

Informality must characterize the evaluation of appreciation. Otherwise, the response of pupils is more likely to represent what they think it ought to be rather than what it really is. Morrison's statement on this point is still well taken:

> In most cases in the appreciation type, it is almost impossible to utilize the written test even for securing the evidence. The reason is to be found in the fact that we can never tell whether the pupil is recording what he knows his preferences or standards ought to be or is disclosing what they really are. . . . In general, the examination attitude and atmosphere must be entirely avoided. There must be no question of "passing" in literature or conduct, the appreciation of music or the fine arts. The penalty for failure at this point is to convert the teaching staff into an organization of snoopers and the pupil body into a crowd of more or less willing time servers.[10]

The use of informal direct observation, pupil logs, case histories, and activity inventories is indicated in appraising

[10]Henry C Morrison, *The Practice of Teaching in the Secondary School*, University of Chicago Press, 1931, p. 358. Copyright 1931 by the University of Chicago. Reprinted by permission of the publisher.

appreciation. The logic behind their use lies in the principle that appreciations can be inferred from such records of unsupervised behavior.

Evaluating attitudes.   Attitudes are revealed by the opinions people hold, by their behavior, and by their interests. Attitudes must be inferred, since they are not directly observable.

Attitudes are inferred bases for observed consistencies in behavior of individuals. Inferences may be based on observations of either verbal or non-verbal behavior. Attitudes express themselves in what people do or abstain from doing and in the manner in which they do things as well as in what people say. In ordinary social intercourse how an individual feels, what he is attempting to do for what purpose may be surmised by other people involved in the same situation from his facial expression, his tone of voice, his bodily stance and movements and his verbal statements.[11]

The evaluation of attitudes takes much the same direction as the evaluation of appreciation. It involves the discovery of attitudes, determining their direction and appraising their intensity. The most common instrument for measuring attitudes is the opinion scale. Forms of the opinion-scale technique have been developed by Thurstone and Remmers. No scales have been published for appraising attitudes toward music, but teachers can adapt opinion scales and interest inventories for this purpose.[12]

Opinion scales and questionnaires to be filled out by students provide an indication of attitudes, especially if they feel free to express their actual opinions rather than what they think the teacher wants. Logs and anecdotal records of

[11]Eugene L. Hartley and Ruth E. Hartley, *Fundamentals of Social Psychology*, Alfred A. Knopf, Inc., New York, 1952, p. 686

[12]For descriptions of instruments for measuring musical interests and attitudes toward music, see John H. Mueller and others, *Studies in Appreciation of Art* 4(6): 1938-1942, University of Oregon Publications, February 1934; and Paul R. Farnsworth, "Rating Scales for Musical Interests," *Journal of Psychology* 28:245-253, 1949.

pupil behavior in class can be used to advantage in inferring attitudes. Records of verbal statements, tone of voice, facial expressions, examples of attention and inattention, and cooperation or resistance during musical activities all give a pattern of information which can be interpreted to determine 'attitudes.

Personal interviews may be used to advantage to supplement other techniques of evaluating attitudes. They are especially useful in the case of pupils who show extremely negative attitudes in that they enable the teacher to get at the causes of negative behavior and, when skillfully handled, they provide a means of securing rapport with the pupil.

The evaluation of appreciation and attitudes is essential to successful music teaching. It not only enables the teacher to appraise results in important areas of musical learning but also provides him with valuable insights into the nature and needs of his pupils, both as a group and as individuals. The evaluation admittedly lacks precision and is open to errors in observation and judgment. It should be recognized, however, that teachers inevitably make value judgments of attitudes and appreciation and that the effort to systematize and objectify the evaluative process can only result in more valid and reliable judgments.

Evaluating musical understanding.   The presence or absence of musical understanding is revealed by the way a pupil tackles a musical problem confronting him. This provides the clue to evaluation of musical understanding. Is he aware of the problem? Does he approach it systematically? Does he apply his knowledge and skill to it systematically? If questions such as these can be answered affirmatively, he is evidencing some measure of musical understanding.

The principal means to the evaluation of understanding lies in direct, systematic, and continuous observation of the musical behavior of pupils when confronted with musical problems. The following procedures are suggested to reveal the extent of musical understanding and can be adapted for use at various levels of the music program:

1. After pupils have heard or performed a composition several times, ask them to discuss verbally or in writing the style and structure of the composition and to compare it with other compositions with which they are familiar.
2. Ask students to improvise parts and accompaniments to a song and evaluate them on consistency with the style and expressive intent of the song.
3. Play an unfamiliar composition for pupils and ask them to identify its style and structure, to name possible composers or sources, and to give reasons for their decisions.
4. Ask the pupil to prepare a performance on his own and tell why he performs it as he does.
5. Play two or more performances of a composition and ask pupils to state which performance they prefer and why.

Available tests measure only limited and highly specific aspects of musical understanding, and many facets of understanding are not subject to paper-and-pencil testing. Essay examinations and objective tests can be used to advantage, however, in appraising stylistic understanding.[13]

Evaluating skills of performance.   Rating scales represent the principal means to the evaluation of performance skills. The scales may produce either qualitative or quantitative results. For example, the results of scales for measuring music reading skill are usually stated in terms of the number of correct notes read, while the results of scales intended for more general aspects of performance skill are often stated in qualitative terms. The latter, however, can also have quantitative values assigned. The crucial point in the selection and construction of rating scales is the clarity and preciseness with which the qualities to be evaluated are defined.

[13]For a valuable discussion and description of tests of musical discrimination and musical concepts, see John H. Mueller and others, op. cit., pp. 115-138.

Several rating scales designed for evaluating performances in contests are available. For example, the Adjudicators' Comment Sheet prepared by the National Interscholastic Music Activities Commission defines with some precision the qualities under appraisal in performance. There remains a need, however, for more precise definition of some of the less tangible qualities of musical performance. Phrasing, for example, is a term with different connotations for different people, and concepts of good phrasing may vary greatly among evaluators. Clarification and definition of the concept of phrasing and of the relationship of phrasing to musical structure and to words in vocal music would be useful to evaluators of musical performance.

In order to increase the precision and objectivity of observation, the teacher should habitually employ a rating scale in evaluating performance in musical classes and in private instruction. The use of a systematic scale is especially urgent in periodic and final examinations and in auditions for entrance to performing groups and music schools.

Evaluating skills of listening.   In evaluating skills of listening the teacher must first specify the types of awareness and discrimination in listening which represent his objectives and then select or develop evaluative procedures which appraise the extent to which the desired behaviors have been developed.

Kate Hevner Mueller, in a quite comprehensive proposal for a program of testing in music appreciation, lists the following basic listening skills:

1. merely to hold a sustained attention to music for a shorter or longer interval
2. to hear the basic rhythm and deviations from it
3. to identify the choirs of instruments and notice their use in the total structure
4. to orient himself correctly in the basic tonality and follow the fluctuations and contrasts from it
5. to hear the repetitions of both small and large patterns

and perceive the relation of the separate units to the structure as a whole

6. to identify a group of related music elements as a subject, figure, or theme
7. to perceive the changes in musical subjects which constitute their growth or evolution toward a preconceived and satisfying goal.
8. to catch the traditional affective tone associated with certain elements, for example, the more depressive effects of slow tempos, low pitch, minor mode, etc.[14]

She has devised a procedure for testing music appreciation in terms of the intellectual process of perceiving its formal structure. She presented one complete musical composition and repeated it three or four times. The subjects were provided with a list of twenty-nine statements about the music derived from study of the score and the recorded performances of it. The statements dealt with the general outline of the form, and detail of the themes and their manipulations, tonality and harmonic structure, meter and rhythm, and instrumentation. They were arranged in chronological order, with items about the introduction listed first and those concerning the total structure at the end. Some statements were true and others false.

The subjects checked each statement on a five-point scale, indicating their opinion as follows: "strongly agree," "probably agree," "no opinion," "probably disagree," and "strongly disagree."

Examples of the type of statement she used follow:

1. There are many repetions of sections of the piece.
2. There are three parts and the third repeats the first.
3. The main theme has two melodic fragments.
4. The piece uses 3/4 time (meter).

[14]Kate Hevner Mueller, "Studies in Musical Appreciation," *Journal of Research in Music Education* 4:3-25, 1956.

She reported an odd-even item reliability coefficient of .80 and a significant relationship (r = .70) between test scores and interest and listening experience as measured by John H. Mueller's scale.[15]

Mueller's approach has excellent possibilities for measuring listening skills, and teachers are urged to adapt it to their own situations. In addition, less formal means of evaluation can be used with good effect. For example, apprehension of a melody of a composition may be revealed by having pupils sing or play at least a phrase of each theme in a composition they have heard. Advanced pupils may be asked to write themes they have heard, but it should be remembered that this requires a high development of skill other than listening. A simple test of harmonic perception is to have pupils sing the bass line while the melody is being played.

Evaluating musical initiative.   The ultimate criterion for judging the success of musical learning lies in its effect upon the living of a pupil and the extent to which he uses what he has learned. Does he pursue musical learning further on his own? Does he share his musical ability with family and friends? Does he seek to refine and extend his musical competencies? Does he seek opportunities to play and sing with others? Does he put into use an intelligent approach to the solution of musical problems? Does he have a record collection—go to concerts regularly—support community and school music activities—listen selectively to musical radio and television programs? Answers to such questions as these reveal the extent to which the music education program is affecting the lives of those who participate in it.

Observational techniques and self-evaluation are indicated in the appraisal of musical initiative. These should include close observation of behavior in the classroom to ascertain whether knowledge, understanding, skills, and appreciation are operating in day-to-day musical behavior. Co-

---

[15]John H. Mueller and others, op. cit., p. 150.

operative evaluation with parents, private teachers, and persons in charge of church and community musical activities is essential in the evaluation of initiative. These efforts can range all the way from informal conferences to systematic follow-up studies. For example, queries to parents of young children on the extent of carry-over of school music activities to the home reveal at least partially the effectiveness of school music experiences and learning.

THE EVALUATION OF THE MUSIC PROGRAM

The final criterion for judging the effectiveness of a program of music education is its effect on the musical behavior of students. It follows that, when possible, the best means of evaluating the program is to ascertain the progress of students toward the objectives sought. Earlier sections of this chapter have dealt with the evaluation of students.

Present conditions of evaluative techniques, however, make it difficult or impossible to appraise accurately some of the direct results and many of the indirect results of music education. Some evade precise evaluation and others are so remote that they must be appraised indirectly for the most part. For example, the carry-over value of music education is often immeasurable until years have passed. Furthermore, it is sometimes difficult to determine whether the presence or absence of carry-over is due to the experiences provided in the school music program or to influences outside the school. Therefore, an evaluation of factors that may logically be expected to produce the desired outcomes is essential as a supplement to the evaluation of students.

The steps in program evaluation are (1) to indicate the objectives of the program and ascertain their worth, (2) to collect data about all factors related to the objectives, and (3) to interpret the data collected and then take steps to improve the program.

Preparation and Validation of Objectives

The task of preparing and validating music education objectives involves interpreting the best theory and practice in the light of the demands of the immediate situation. This process has received systematic attention in Chapter Six. The validation of objectives must depend primarily on the judgment of expert professional personnel, parents, and pupils, since objectives represent value judgments about what the music program should accomplish.

Collection of Data

In evaluating the total program of music education, data should be collected concerning the status of the following factors:

1. the scope of the program, including the extent and types of experiences offered in music classes and performance activities for the general pupil and for pupils with a special interest and aptitude in music
2. the extent of pupil participation in the music program
3. administrative policies and procedures, including scheduling, class size, teaching load, time requirement, marking, and so on
4. qualifications of teaching personnel
5. facilities for the music program
6. equipment and teaching materials available
7. relationship of music education to other parts of the curriculum
8. quality of instruction
9. relationship of the music program to the community

A variety of procedures may be used in gathering data, including program score cards, check lists, analyses of administrative policies and procedures, analyses of attitudes and opinions of those concerned with the music program, analyses of school records, existing program standards, evaluative criteria, and general survey techniques.

Published tools for evaluating the music education program are scanty, but some worthwhile sources of assistance are available. These include *The Evaluation of Music Education*, prepared by the Commission on Accreditation and Certification in Music Education of the Music Educators National Conference. This publication suggests standards for the evaluation of the college curriculum for training school music teachers. Other publications useful in evaluating specific portions of the music program are *Minimum Standards for Stringed Instruments in the Schools, Music Rooms and Equipment*, and *Outline of a Program of Music Education*, all published by the Music Educators Conference.

Evaluative Criteria[16] contains both items pertaining to the music program and others of a more general nature which can be adapted to the evaluation of instructional, administrative, and supervisory aspects of the music program.

CRITERIA FOR EVALUATING MUSIC PROGRAMS

The following criteria are suggested for the guidance of persons interested in evaluating a program of music education. They represent an objectification of the authors' philosophical orientation and have proved useful in several general surveys of school music programs. They are presented for illustrative purposes and to provide a basis for individuals and groups to develop criteria consistent with their own philosophical orientation and applicable to a specific situation:

1. The controlling idea underlying the entire program is the development of musicianship and musical responsiveness.

[16] *Evaluative Criteria* National Study of Secondary School Evaluation, Washington, 1960.
Evaluative Criteria for Junior High Schools, National Study of Secondary School Evaluation, Washington, 1963.

2. The program operates on the basis of a well-formulated statement of objectives which are consistent with and contribute to the objectives of the school and which have been developed cooperatively by the music education staff.
3. The program is organized and operated to contribute to the stated objectives.
4. The program exhibits continuity from the elementary school through secondary school.
5. General Music provides the core of the music program with specialization growing out of it.
6. The program provides musical experiences that reach all pupils in the school.
7. The musical experiences provided meet the diversified interests of pupils,
8. The program makes provision for individual differences in musical capacity, background, and aspiration.
9. The program results in the development of musical leadership on the part of able pupils.
10. The program develops musical interests and competencies which carry over into out-of-school life.
11. The program serves to make music a vital factor in the life of the school.
12. There are adequate opportunities for public performance growing out of the program and serving as a means of promoting musical growth.
13. The program utilizes the musical resources and traditions of the community.
14. The program promotes constructive relationships with private music teachers in the community.
15. The program has a desirable impact upon and promotes constructive relationships with community agencies such as churches and adult music groups.
16. The program operates within a framework of long-range plans.
17. The music education staff exemplifies organic unity, community of purpose, and coordination in planning and working.

18. The musical resources of teachers other than music specialists are utilized in the program.
19. All participants in the program, including staff and pupils, participate in planning on appropriate levels.
20. There is a provision for systematic procurement of facilities, equipment and instructional materials.
21. Equipment and instructional materials are adequate, varied, up-to-date, in good repair and easily available for use.
22. The quality and extent of facilities for music contribute to the attainment of the objectives of the program.
23. The program has the support and approval of the school administration and faculty.
24. The program has the support and approval of an informed public.
25. Provision is made for continuing and constructive evaluation of all facets of the program

SUMMARY

Evaluation is the process of determining the extent to which the objectives of education have been attained. It involves three steps, the formulation of objectives, the collection of data, and the interpretation of data. Measurement attempts to secure improved precision and objectivity of observation. The uses of evaluation in music education include appraisal of pupil progress, guidance, motivation, improvement of instruction, maintenance of standards, and research.

There are two aspects to the evaluation of students in music education, evaluating musical capacity and evaluating musical learning. The former has attracted considerable research attention, and numerous tests have been standardized and published. The decision to use tests of musical capacity requires close examination of one's philosophical orientation toward music education and of many other complex factors. Using tests which have established validity in relation to significant external criteria and a high level of reliability may be advisable if the results are interpreted cautiously and if other indications of musical capacity are taken into account.

It is essential that music teachers evaluate all kinds of learning implied by their instructional objectives. These may include appreciation, musical knowledge, musical under-standing, skills of listening, skills of performance, attitudes, and habits in varying combinations. Evaluation should always be consistent with objectives, and the scope of evaluation for a given course of musical instruction depends upon the breadth of the objectives for the course. Although numerous tests and other evaluative tools valuable in the music program have been published, the music teacher must rely to a great extent on tests and other evaluative tools which he designs and constructs. Observational techniques and cooperative evaluation by teachers and pupils are essential in most phases of musical learning.

Since the present status of evaluative techniques makes it impossible to evaluate accurately many of the results of the music education program, evaluation of the program itself is essential as a supplement to the evaluation of students. This is accomplished by the cooperative formulation of criteria for evaluation pertaining to all facets of the program and the application of the criteria to the program.

QUESTIONS FOR DISCUSSION

1. What is the difference between "measurement" and "evaluation"? In what way is evaluation the more com-prehensive term?
2. What steps are involved in the process of evaluation? How are these related to the objectives of the music program?
3. Describe the uses or applications of evaluation. How does evaluation affect the work of the teacher and that of the student?
4. When is an evaluative tool judged valid? How does this

relate to its reliability? What is the procedure in selecting an evaluative instrument?

5. How would you define musical capacity? Do you think it can be measured? What purpose might such measurement serve?

6. Why should evaluation of musical instruction be comprehensive? Why does the nature of the particular musical behavior dictate the evaluative procedure?

7. Why is it difficult to find relevant tests of musical knowledge? What can the teacher do in this case?

8. Why must musical appreciation be measured indirectly? In what ways does one reveal his appreciation? Why is it important to avoid formal evaluative situations in this instance?

9. Describe the ways in which musical attitudes are revealed. What techniques may be used in gathering such data?

10. What is the key to evaluating musical understanding?

11. Why are rating scales most useful in evaluating skills of performance? Describe methods by which listening skills may be evaluated.

12. How may musical initiative be appraised?

13. Why is program evaluation actually a survey of the educational environment rather than its product?

14. Describe the general factors to be explored in securing data on the music program. How may such data be interpreted?

SELECTED TESTS OF MUSICAL CAPACITY

Drake, R. M. *Drake Musical Aptitude Tests*, Science Research Associates, Chicago, 1954. Two tests, one of musical memory and one to forecast rhythmic ability. The former uses especially composed melodies; the latter, the device of counting to the sound of a metronome. Reported reliability coefficients: .85 to .95.

Gaston, E. Thayer. *A Test of Musicality*, Odells Instrumental

Service, Lawrence, Kansas, 1956. This test is designed to
measure ability to apprehend configurations of tone and
rhythm. It is based on the notion that musicality consists in perceptive responsiveness to actual musical structures. Reported reliability coefficients: .88 to .90.

Gordon, Edwin. *Musical Aptitude Profile*, Houghton Mifflin
Company, Boston, 1965. An eclectic test containing
preference and nonpreference subtests. The musical dimensions measured by the battery are classified into
three divisions: tonal imagery, rhythm imagery, and
musical sensitivity. Subtests include melody, harmony,
tempo, rhythm, phrasing, balance, and style. The content of the test items consists of especially composed
music performed by professional musicians. Reported
reliability coefficients for composite scores: .90 to .96.

Seashore, Carl E., and others. *Manual: Seashore Measures of
Musical Talents*, The Psychological Corporation, New
York, 1956. Includes six tests of pitch, loudness,
rhythm, timbre, time, and tonal memory. Reported
reliability coefficients: .62 to .79.

Whistler, Harvey S., and Louis P. Thorpe. *Whistler-Thorpe
Music Aptitude Test: Series A.*, California Test Bureau,
Los Angeles, 1950. Based on the presentation of musical
rather than tonal stimuli. Reported reliability coefficient: .91.

SELECTED   TOOLS   FOR   MEASURING   MUSICAL
ACHIEVEMENT

Aliferis, James. *Aliferis Music Achievement Test*, University
of Minnesota Press, Minneapolis, 1954. Consists of three
sections: harmonic, melodic, and rhythmic. Designed
for use at college-entrance level to measure auditory-
visual discrimination of musical elements.

Colwell, Richard. *Music Achievement Tests I, II, III, and IV*,
Follett Educational Corporation, Chicago, 1967 and
1970. Designed to measure achievement in relation to

commonly accepted objectives of the general music program in elementary and secondary school.

Farnum, Stephen E. *Farnum Music Notation Test*, The Psychological Corporation, New York, 1953. Designed to select students for serious instrumental instruction at the junior high school level.

Knuth, William E. *Knuth Achievement Tests in Music*, Educational Test Bureau, Inc., Philadelphia, 1936. Designed to measure pupil achievement in recognition of musical form from its notation.

Kwalwasser, Jacob, and G. M. Ruch. *Kwalwasser-Ruch Test of Musical Accomplishment*, Bureau of Educational Research and Service, State University of Iowa, Iowa City, 1927. Actually a test of musical knowledge. Includes knowledge of such items as time and key signatures, musical symbols, recognition of syllable names, and detection of errors in a melody.

Watkins, John G., and Stephen E. Farnum. *Watkins-Farnum Performance Scale for All Band Instruments*, Hal Leonard Music, Inc., Winona, Minn., 1954. Consists of a series of fourteen sight-reading exercises in order of increasing difficulty.

SELECTED REFERENCES

Ahmann, J. Stanley and Marvin D. Glock. *Evaluating Pupil Growth: Principles of Tests and Measurements*, 3d ed., Allyn and Bacon, Boston, 1967.

Anatasi, Anne. *Psychological Testing*, 3d ed., The Macmillan Company, New York, 1968.

Barnes, Fred P. *Research for the Practitioner of Education*, Department of Elementary School Principals, National Education Association, Washington, 1964.

Bentley, Arnold. *Musical Ability in Children and its Measurement*, October House, New York, 1966.

Bloom, Benjamin. *Stability and Change in Human Characteristics*, John Wiley and Sons, Inc., New York, 1964.

Buros, Oscar K., ed. *Tests in Print; A Comprehensive Bibliography of Tests for Use in Education, Psychology and Industry*, Gryphon Press, Highland Park, N.J., 1961.

Colwell, Richard. *The Evaluation of Music Teaching and Learning*, Prentice-Hall, Inc., Englewood Cliffs, N.J., 1970.

Colwell, Richard. "An Investigation of Musical Achievement Among Public School Students," *Journal of Educational Research* 57: 355-359, 1964.

Farnsworth, Paul. *The Social Psychology of Music*, The Iowa State University Press, Ames, 1969.

Gage, N. L., ed. *Hand Book of Research on Teaching*, Rand, McNally and Company, Chicago, 1963.

Gerberich, J. Raymond, Harry A. Greene, and Albert N. Jorgesen. *Educational Measurement and Evaluation*, David McKay Company, New York, 1962.

Gronlund, Norman E. *Constructing Achievement Tests*, Prentice-Hall, Inc., Englewood Cliffs, N.J., 1968.

Kwalwasser, Jacob. *Exploring the Musical Mind*, Coleman-Ross Company, Inc., New York, 1955.

Lehman, Paul. *Tests and Measurements in Music*, Prentice-Hall, Inc., Englewood Cliffs, N.J., 1968.

Lindesmith, Alfred Ray, and Anselm L. Strauss. *Social Psychology*, 3d ed., Holt, Rinehart and Winston, New York, 1968.

Lindvall, Carl M. *Measuring Pupil Achievement and Aptitude,* Harcourt, Brace & World, New York, 1967.

Lundin, Robert. *An Objective Psychology of Music*, 2d ed., The Ronald Press Company, New York, 1967.

Seashore, Carl E. *The Psychology of Music*, McGraw-Hill Book Company, 1938.

Stanton, Hazel M. *The Measurement of Musical Talent*, vol II, *Studies in the Psychology of Music*, University of Iowa, Iowa City, 1935.

Thorndike, Robert, and Elizabeth Hagen. *Measurement and Evaluation in Psychology and Education*, John Wiley and Sons, Inc., New York, 1969.

Wing, Herbert D. "Some Applications of Test Results to

Education in Music," *British Journal of Educational Psychology* 24: 161-170, November 1954.

Whitla, Dean Kay, ed. *Handbook of Measurement and Assessment in Behavioral Sciences*, Addison-Wesley Publishing Company, Reading, Mass., 1968.

Index